T0211825

Digital Media, Friendship and Cultures of Care

This book explores how digital media can extend care practices among friends and peers, researching young people's negotiations of sexual health, mental health, gender/sexuality, and dating apps, and highlighting the need for a multifocal approach that centres young people's expertise.

Taking an "everyday practice" approach to digital and social media, *Digital Media, Friendship and Cultures of Care* emphasises that digital media are not novel but integrated into daily life. The book introduces the concept of "digital cultures of care" as a new framework through which to consider digital practices of friendship and peer support, and how these play out across a range of platforms and networks. Challenging common public and academic concerns about peer and friendship influences on young people, these terms are unpacked and reconsidered through attention to digital media, drawing on qualitative research findings to argue that digital and social media have created important new opportunities for emotional support, particularly for young people and LGBTQ+ people who are often excluded from formal healthcare and social support.

This book and its comprehensive focus on friendship will be of interest to a range of readers, including academics, students, health promoters, educators, policymakers, and advocacy groups for either young people, LGBTQ+ communities, or digital citizenship. Academics most interested in this book will be working in digital media studies, health sociology, critical public health, health communication, sexualities, cultural studies, sex education, and gender studies.

Paul Byron is Postdoctoral Research Fellow at the University of Technology Sydney, based in the School of Communication. As a digital and social media researcher, his current research focuses on LGBTQ+ young people's digital peer support, and how this can inform Australian mental health policy.

Routledge Research in Gender, Sexuality, and Media
Edited by Mary Celeste Kearney, University of Notre Dame, USA

The *Routledge Research in Gender, Sexuality, and Media* series aims to publish original research in the areas of feminist and queer media studies, with a particular but not exclusive focus on gender and sexuality. In doing so, this series brings to the market cutting-edge critical work that refreshes, reshapes, and redirects scholarship in these related fields while contributing to a better global understanding of how gender and sexual politics operate within historical and current mediascapes.

Queercore
Queer Punk Media Subculture
Curran Nault

Lifestyle Media in American Culture
Gender, Class, and the Politics of Ordinariness
Maureen E. Ryan

Emergent Feminisms
Complicating a Postfeminist Media Culture
Edited by Jessalynn Keller and Maureen E. Ryan

Producing Queer Youth
The Paradox of Digital Media Empowerment
Lauren S. Berliner

Girls, Moral Panic, and News Media
Troublesome Bodies
Sharon R. Mazzarella

Digital Media, Friendship and Cultures of Care
Paul Byron

Digital Media, Friendship and Cultures of Care

Paul Byron

Routledge
Taylor & Francis Group

LONDON AND NEW YORK

First published 2021
by Routledge
2 Park Square, Milton Park, Abingdon, Oxon OX14 4RN

and by Routledge
52 Vanderbilt Avenue, New York, NY 10017

Routledge is an imprint of the Taylor & Francis Group, an informa business

© 2021 Paul Byron

British Library Cataloguing-in-Publication Data
A catalogue record for this book is available from the British Library

Library of Congress Cataloging-in-Publication Data
Names: Byron, Paul, author.
Title: Digital media, friendship and cultures of care/Paul Byron.
Description: Abingdon, Oxon; New York, NY: Routledge, 2021.
| Series: Routledge research in gender, sexuality, and media |
Includes bibliographical references and index. |
Identifiers: LCCN 2020026722 (print) | LCCN 2020026723 (ebook) |
ISBN 9780367183462 (hardback) | ISBN 9780367625412 (paperback)
| ISBN 9780429060953 (ebook) | ISBN 9780429592430 (adobe pdf) |
ISBN 9780429590498 (epub) | ISBN 9780429588556 (mobi)
Subjects: LCSH: Internet and youth. | Online social networks. |
Digital media–Social aspects. | Friendship. | Interpersonal relations.
Classification: LCC HQ799.9.I58 B97 2021 (print) | LCC HQ799.9.I58
(ebook) | DDC 302.23/1–dc23
LC record available at https://lccn.loc.gov/2020026722
LC ebook record available at https://lccn.loc.gov/2020026723

ISBN: 978-0-367-18346-2 (hbk)
ISBN: 978-0-429-06095-3 (ebk)

Typeset in Sabon
by Deanta Global Publishing Services, Chennai, India

For my friends

Contents

Acknowledgements   x

Introduction: who cares?   1

Young people are not going online   2
Young people in this book   4
A public discourse of care   5
Digital intimacy as everyday practice   6
Beyond risk approaches   10
Cultures of care   12
The research   16
The chapters   18
Notes   19
References   19

1   **More than just friends**   23

Knowing friendship   25
Friendship and popular culture   30
Friendships and social media   32
Changing modes of friendship   39
Friendship as affective practice   42
Notes   44
References   45

2   **What do we know about peers?**   49

Peer influence   50
Peers and friends: sexual health disruptors   51
Peer education   53

Redefining peers 57
Peer support 60
Is digital support friendship? 62
Tumblr care 65
Digital peer support cultures 68
Notes 71
References 71

3 Young people's social media expertise   75

Social media use 77
Thinking beyond "health information seeking" 78
Sexual health promotion and social media 80
Friendship and social media use 83
A crisis of authority and the changing nature of expertise 87
Partnering with experts 89
Notes 91
References 91

4 Friendship and sexual intimacy   96

Intimacy, bodies, and feeling 98
Friendship and sex 101
Safe intimacies 102
The distance of sexual health promotion 103
Sexual information sharing 106
Sex with friends 108
Friendship as health promoting 110
Attending to intimacy 111
Notes 115
References 115

5 LGBTQ+ peer support for mental health   118

Digital information and support 119
Digital care structures 122
Community reports: friends and peers 123
Digital mental health support 127
Mental health on Tumblr 131
Beyond "help-seeking" 135
Notes 139
References 139

6   Friends with dating apps   144

Approaching dating/hook-up apps as friend spaces 146
Making friends on dating/hook-up apps 151
The safety of mutual friends 155
Friendship support for app use 156
Friends with apps   163
Notes   166
References   166

Conclusion: everyday care   170

Social media, safety, and being online   171
Returning to everyday practice   172
Formal care   173
Digital cultures of care   174
Friends and peers   176
Friends, sex, dating, intimacy   177
The Tumblr affect   178
Mental health care   179
Digital health promotion   180
Some final words   181
References   181

Index   183

Acknowledgements

Firstly, I acknowledge the Gadigal people of the Eora Nation, on whose land this book was written. I pay my respects to Elders past and present, and to young Indigenous people whose leadership will guide us. I recognise that sovereignty was never ceded and that this country we call Australia is Aboriginal land. Always was, always will be.

Writing a book is quite an effort. I have newfound respect for anyone who ever wrote one and I'm endlessly grateful to those who helped me get through this. It's a tiring and taxing journey with many detours into self-doubt. But it wasn't all terrible. It was great to finally clarify some things I've been grappling with for many years now.

A book like this is written by hundreds of people. In this case, thousands of people gave their time and stories to the research projects involved. First and foremost, thank you to everyone I interviewed in this last decade. I hope you got something out of that, and if you see yourself in this book, I hope I've adequately presented your experiences. The same applies to everyone who took part in a survey or focus group for any of these studies. Thank you for your generosity, and for helping me and my co-researchers think through the issues covered in this book. I've been lucky to work with, and learn from, some of the finest qualitative researchers who I thank below. My single name on the cover of this book feels nice but it also feels misleading. This writing and thinking wouldn't exist without the research teams and networks I've been part of, nor the young people I've engaged with.

Nicholas. Thanks for putting up with me throughout the writing process and for making it seem like that was easy. Thanks for your love and affection and for being a necessary source of down time. Sleeping next to you, sharing meals, taking walks, your storytelling, and more has sustained me and this writing. These things also kept me attuned to the everyday intimacies at the heart of this book.

Kath Albury. Thanks for being there throughout my academic journey and all the stages that comprise this book's research. I couldn't imagine a better PhD supervisor and mentor and Taurean role model. Love your work, and your queer and feminist approach to scholarship. I've learnt a lot, including how to navigate academic systems while staying focused on what matters. Thanks too for initiating many of the projects within, and I look forward to more collaboration. Pray hands emoji. Bull emoji.

Thanks to my many other mentors, particularly Anna Poletti, Justine Lloyd, and Alan McKee. Anna, thanks for two decades of conversation and friendship that has stretched my thinking and being. It's good to grow old with you and to continue learning from your critical perspectives and feminist praxis (though I still need you to write a film review of *Cats*). Thanks for your spare room and all the tea and chocolate. Justine, thanks for being my first academic mentor, for early inductions into teaching and research, and for your friendship and politics. I wouldn't have stayed in academia without you. Alan, thanks for your recent mentorship and many opportunities to learn new ropes and to cross-discipline (or not). Thanks for pushing me to write this book proposal, for keeping it queer, and for your charisma, uniqueness, nerve, and talent.

Thanks, also, to my "peer mentors", particularly Crystal Abidin, Brady Robards, and James Meese. Crystal, I remember looking at the 2013 QUT Winter School line-up and zooming in on you (but I was confused about the penguins). Thanks for being my conference buddy and co-conspirer of many antics. I look forward to future adventures, selfies, dreams, and your wisdom. May the power of Maiuspala continue to guide us. Brady, I matched your Twitter face with your real face in Daegu in 2014 and I've been enjoying your friendship ever since. Thanks for being such a wonderful collaborator, co-author, schemer, thinker, and human. Looking forward to more scholarshipping with you. James, our UTS time was brief, but I'll forever be impressed by your mentorship, energy, and the endless support you gave while I wrote this book and applied for the fellowship. You probably should move back to Sydney!

Writing a book on friendship and peer support seems too fitting, since this is what holds this book up. Much of my academic time has been precarious, and at one point I learnt that this could be a hostile environment. I continue to be reminded of this from the experiences of my friends. Many of my friends are dealing with precarious academic employment and it's shit. Like any broken system, it necessitates peer support. The support I received meant everything, though fixing broken systems would be nicer still. I'm sorry to everyone who struggles.

This book is dedicated to my wonderful friends. Some special mentions follow, but this is not an exhaustive list. Jessie Lymn, we've travelled far since our postgrad days in Enmore, and it's nice to continue that journey and be part of your family. Thanks for the writing retreats and many adventures. Jess Neath, I'm glad you moved to Newcastle way back when and became an instant fave. Thanks for teaching me how to collaborate and how to manage projects with care, and thanks for my Melbourne home and family. Thanks also to Ash Baker, Vanessa Bowden, Joal Bryant, Emily Cachia, Ana Celestino, Ye Chen, Niki Cheong, Gareth Commins, Anwen Crawford, Nour Dados, Emma Davidson, Fernando Ariel Gallardo, Renaud Goyette,

Miguel Heras, Mitch Hibbens, Jet Hunt, Tamara Joksimovic, Amanda Kerley, Dominique Lett, Ryan Ling, Louis Sanders Lymn, Máire MacCana, Gayatri Nair, Cass Pomroy, Jonno Revanche, Jackie Ruddock, Christoph Sawyer, Paul Sinkovich, Malcolm Smith, Warren Summers, Kathleen Williamson, Yiorgos Zafiriou, Mark Zaki, and other friends mentioned above and below. Some of you have been more involved in this book than others, but all of you have influenced my writing on friendship and care.

Big thanks to the *Scrolling Beyond Binaries* team (and sorry for stealing so much data for this book). Thanks Brady Robards, for initiating this project, and thanks Son Vivienne, Benjamin Hanckel, and Brendan Churchill for being awesome and smart and lovely. I'm pretty sure SBB is the best DIY research team that ever happened.

Thanks Team Hook-Up Apps. I've had a great time working with you Kath Albury, Tinonee Pym, Anthony McCosker, and Kane Race. We did a lot of great research in a short amount of time, and I'm thankful to have experienced that. I loved our Melbourne intensive research days with whiteboards and coffee that usually ended in blurry Instagram photos. Thanks also to Daniel Reeders and Chris Dietzel for swooping in towards the end. And further thanks to the ACON folk who kept me honest on Elizabeth St, particularly Félix Delhomme, Harrison Sarasola, Viv McGregor, and Teddy Cook.

I've had enormous support from brilliant scholars who have been generous with feedback, pep talks, and mutual academic sighing. Special thanks to Kristian Møller for all the hospitality, writing adventures, conference adventures, and "cross-cultural exchange". Thanks also to Tom Apperley, Amy Dobson, Jamie Hakim, Nat Hendry, Amelia Johns, Shaka McGlotten, Lucy Nicholas, Gabriel Pereira, Terri Senft, Francis Shaw, Clarissa Smith, Jackie Ullman, Katie Warfield, and others previously mentioned. Many fine scholars have also engaged with my work and/or informed my thinking over the years, including Feona Attwood, Jean Burgess, Bronwyn Carlson, Rob Cover, Stefanie Duguay, Tim Highfield, Akane Kanai, Jenny Kennedy, Amparo Lasén, Ben Light, John Mercer, Sharif Mowlabocus, Susanna Paasonen, Jenny Súnden, Matilda Tudor, Katrin Tiidenberg, and Florian Vörös. Thank you all, and thanks to the Association of Internet Researchers (AoIR) conference and the Digital Intimacies symposium where our paths often cross.

I'm grateful for being around many younger, impressive researchers engaging with digital media, peer support, and wellbeing, including Tommaso Armstrong, Sab D'Souza, Sujith Kumar, Giselle Newton, Samantha Mannix, and Lexi Smith. Thanks for the many chats and I look forward to more.

Thanks to the Digital & Social Media team within the UTS School of Communication: Ben Abraham, Francesco Bailo, Tisha Dejmanee, Heather Ford, Suneel Jethani, Amelia Johns, and Natalie Krikowa. I appreciate your support, generosity, and all-round loveliness, and I feel very lucky to have landed here.

Thanks to Twenty10 for the formative experience of doing community-based research in such a strong, queer, and gentle environment. Thanks to my research team there: Kerry Robinson, Roanna Lobo, Dani Wright Touissant, Sophia Rasmussen, and Brett Paradise. Thanks to staff and volunteers at the time, particularly Susan Farrar, Rebecca Howe, Dan Kaplan, Jagur McEwan, and Fi Paskulich for welcoming me into that space and teaching me many things.

Thanks to many other colleagues and collaborators, including Harry Blatterer, Nicola Boydell, Cristyn Davies, Emma Jane, Roger Ingham, Melissa Kang, Kyungja Kung, Judy Lattas, Katerina Litsou, Nicole Matthews, Lisa McDaid, and Ash Watson.

Thanks to the team at Routledge – to Mary Kearney for commissioning this book, and to Alex McGregor and Eleanor Catchpole Simmons whose support and patience were very much appreciated. Thanks also to anonymous reviewers of this manuscript and book proposal for their generous engagement.

And finally, thanks to my niblings – my new informants on digital cultures of care. Cleo, Stella, Dana, Penny, Isaac, and Jade, I look forward to being schooled by you.

Introduction
Who cares?

This book introduces the concept of *digital cultures of care* through an exploration of young people's friendship and digital peer support practices. Throughout, I argue that *care* contours everyday digital and social media use. My attention to digital cultures of care brings media studies into dialogue with health research – encompassing public health, health sociology, and health promotion – to broaden current understandings of how health and wellbeing are understood and practised. In doing so, this book is guided by Michel de Certeau's *The Practice of Everyday Life* (1988), as a text that foregrounds our *ways of operating* and our everyday *use of space* – aspects often overlooked in top-down accounts of social and digital life. Focusing on how space is used, including our tactical negotiation of digital spaces, reveals a common orientation to care.

My central focus on informal care practices is not only useful for understanding how health and wellbeing are practised and supported through digital media but encourages us to think about the diversification of care practices. Through digital media, informal and lateral practices of care have become more pervasive and more visible and are embedded in social media platform cultures and infrastructures. Historically, care has been framed as a private practice administered in the home, by the family or outside the home through medical, health, therapeutic, and educational institutions and settings. In the latter case, professionals are tasked with improving and facilitating the health of individuals and populations. But this book's focus is on the everyday practices of care that circulate beyond professional and familial spaces and are particularly common to friendships and communities of shared interest. Informal care is often overlooked by health policy which tends to take a top-down approach to health, being guided by the provision of services and programmes for grouped populations. But because digital cultures of care increasingly influence our health and wellbeing, these demand attention. I do not argue that we need to monitor and regulate these cultures, but that researchers, health professionals, and policymakers must better recognise, support, and learn from them.

The concept of "digital cultures of care" offers a productive model through which to consider young people's experiences and practices of giving and receiving support, as well as how friendships and other intimacies are shaped by, and give shape to, digital media practices. Through friendship and peer support, care has become a staple element of media life. The concept of care is useful in its broad application, as it accommodates support seeking, giving, and receiving, while also accommodating care's practice and its affective force. A tendency to focus on care as practice but not feeling overlooks its affective aspects and therefore lacks a fuller understanding of how care orients our everyday media practices. In other words, care is not simply a side-effect of digital media cultures, but it can also be what keeps us there, scrolling, sharing content, responding to each other, and more. Despite a tendency to locate care in actions, such as actively helping or supporting somebody through a health issue or difficult time, care is also mundane. That is, when we read, scroll, and drift through our social media feeds, we are seeing and remembering the people, practices, and things we care about. We scroll because we care. A simple "like" of a friend's post can be felt and understood as an act of care – by that friend, by the liker, and by others who witness this gesture.

This book presents research findings from various studies to demonstrate the wider social and political significance of digital care and support. Drawing from a decade of qualitative research with young people in Australia, this book connects different themes of social and digital media practice through digital orientations of care. These research projects consider young people's digital intimacies through exploring practices of friendship, sexual health, mental health, peer support, and dating/hook-up app use. While young people are the centre of these discussions, this book will resonate for older readers too, since intimate practices of care, friendship, and peer support exceed a strict age category.

Worries about digital media negatively impacting young people's health and wellbeing are as abundant in academia as they are in mass media. Far less is said about how these media offer everyday emotional support and health guidance (Third et al., 2019). While digital and social media are not always supportive and nourishing, I focus on their positive aspects of care and support because this has been under-researched and because endless volumes of literature centring the harms, risks, and dangers of young people's digital media use already exist. Risk-focused research on young people has limited our attention to young people's skills and expertise in negotiating health and digital media (Michaud, 2006; Third et al., 2019). Taking an *assets-based* approach (Brooks & Kendall, 2013) to young people's health and media practices, this book centres young people's skills and practices of wellbeing.

Young people are not going online

We often say or hear that young people are "going online" for health information and support. But what does it mean to "go online" if they (like most of us) are always already online thanks to mobile devices, data plans, and wireless connections? When our phones beep or vibrate, we are reminded of where we are and who we are with, and this typically exceeds our material settings (Lasén, 2004). Despite the common use of the term "new media", digital communications are never entirely new but are steeped in historical communication practices. And while current digital life differs to pre-digital life, it makes no sense to split our histories between pre- and post-internet. As part of everyday practice, we often engage digital media without noticing the digital aspects of those engagements. We quickly adapt to digital change. As Horst and Miller observe, "perhaps the most astonishing feature of digital culture is not the speed of technical innovations, but rather the speed at which society takes all of them for granted and creates normative conditions for their use" (2012, p. 107). Indeed, we use digital media differently to how we did a couple of years ago, given the shifting ecology of digital spaces, networks, platforms, and devices. These things are contoured by the broader shapes and rhythms of our lives – lives that change when we move to a new city, take up a new job, or become a parent, for example. Digital media accommodates our changes as much as we accommodate theirs. They are part of the fabric of everyday life, and while their use is habitual, it is also dynamic. My point is that we should avoid repeating well-worn sentiments and frameworks that imagine "online" as a place young people go to for support, because this is a place where they live.

We do not leave our regular worlds, nor remove ourselves from the pace of everyday life, in order to find digital information, support, or chat. These actions are embedded in everyday rhythms and often we have many channels, apps, browsers, tabs, and devices open, or notifying us. Our attention shifts and moves as we engage with numerous people, often in a short span of time. These and other temporal dimensions of digital culture need to be taken into consideration when we think about young people's cultures of care and support, operating in spaces that do not resemble clinics, schools, or any other physical venue.

Not believing that young people are "going online" for support and information is the first rule of this book and its approach to digital cultures of care. More rules will unfold – each attending to the complexity of young people's digital media practices. Much adult commentary on young people's digital lives argues that social media are more isolating than social, depleting rather than fostering young people's communication skills. These arguments tend to trivialise the social/friendship aspects of these media, arguing that online interactions are less authentic, where young people are more motivated by "likes" than "real intimacy". These arguments depend on simplistic accounts of digital media that fail to engage with their embodied, emotional, and everyday use. Because digital media practices are ubiquitous (for the young people in my research), these cannot be considered in isolation from young people's other communication, friendship, and media practices. They comprise communicative tools and practices embedded in most people's lives to the point that we forget they exist, like oxygen. As Mark Deuze reminds us, "there is no external to mediated life" (2012, *x*), and a life is not *lived with* media so much as it is *lived in* media (2012, p. 2). To scientifically measure the *effects* of digital media on our lives would therefore require an impossible extraction from mediated life, but there is no elsewhere.

Young people in this book

Qualitative research presented throughout this book involves young people, aged 16–35 years, yet my discussion and analysis of these data can be applied to wider populations. My research responds to intensive public interest in what young people are doing online, and what this means for their health and wellbeing. I am reluctant to claim that young people's digital media practices are unique to them, or that young people are less focused on health and wellbeing than adults.

Much of the empirical research in this book engages with queer and gender diverse young people, herein referred to LGBTQ+[1] That the digital media experiences of LGBTQ+ young people significantly inform this book's arguments should not be read as a limitation of this book. Rather, it offers an important intervention to the space of research on young people.[2] Firstly, I do not promise nor offer generalised discussion of young people. Throughout, I include research participants' self-nominated identities, highlighting connections between identity and experience, as well as presenting the diversity of participant identities alongside diversities of media practice. Statements throughout the book (including my own) are situated and reflect the experiences of each speaker. I use discourse analysis (Foucault, 1978; 1991) to consider these data, for its attention to how language and practice, together, foster understandings of care. Foucault describes discourse as "practices that systematically form the objects of which they speak" (2010, p. 49). Accordingly, young people's statements throughout this book, considered alongside statements from research, health promotion, and popular culture, underscore cultural knowledges (and coherent understandings) of digital media and their orientation to care. As much as I can, I adopt the language and framings of research participants.

The language and terms young people give to their experiences suggest something about those experiences, and the media cultures they are part of. These also speak to differences – sometimes between younger and older people, but also among young people. As Gill Jones argues, "To talk about young people as though they were a social unit, with common interests, strengths and weaknesses at a biologically defined age, is itself an obvious manipulation" (2009, pp. 3–4). While I refer to "young people" throughout, this should be read as a diverse grouping of subjects who relate to each other through shared cultural practice and discourse, not a population with the same experiences, needs, or worldview.

Some readers may flick through this book for a take-home message about how digital media influence the lives of young people, but they will be disappointed. They may decide that the focus on "some young people" is too specific and not evidence enough for them. But this book is definitely for them. General accounts of young people's lives have limited value and tend to obfuscate much detail of their everyday lives. Perhaps the take-home message is that digital cultures of care are significant to many young people (and other people) and this concept is useful for diversifying current attempts to understand digital media and their health impacts on an entire generation. It is also a useful concept for thinking through our own practices of engaging with young people, whether as health practitioners, educators, policymakers, health promoters, community service workers, peers, or friends.

A public discourse of care

In June 2018, Melania Trump boarded an aircraft that would fly to Texas where she would visit a facility for detained immigrant children. She was photographed boarding the flight wearing a coat with the words "I REALLY DON'T CARE, DO U?" printed on the back. Photos of this event circulated widely and the inappropriateness of wearing this jacket to visit imprisoned children generated fiery public discussion. She also wore the coat when disembarking from the aeroplane upon her return. In the *Washington Post*, Lauren Wright called it "The jacket that launched a thousand tweets" (2018). While Trump and her stylist insisted that it was "just a jacket", many wondered why this was her choice, noting that such a move was unlikely to be accidental. That she was doing media appearances with children in detention and seeking to demonstrate a level of care and concern was undermined by this choice. In trying to make sense of the event, Arwa Mahdawi wrote,

> There is, understandably, a strong desire amongst many liberals to believe that Melania Trump does genuinely care; that she is a force for good. It would be comforting, after all, to think that there is a moral compass of sorts within the White House.
>
> (2018)

Twitter indeed fired up with commentary, as well as jacket memes. In an interview several months later, Trump admitted that she intentionally wore the jacket, but its message had been for "the media" whom she felt bullied by. To this day, people are still tweeting images of Melania wearing this jacket in response to her occasional gestures toward care.

While I was writing this book, New Zealand experienced their worst massacre in history, where 51 people were killed by a White man with a gun in two Christchurch mosques on 15 March 2019. In the days and weeks that followed, Prime Minister Jacinda Ardern was heralded by many as a true leader for her demonstration of empathy, compassion, and care. Her public expressions of grief were described as authentic and the stuff of a "true leader" – a common phrase used in Twitter commentary. In *The Guardian*, Nesrine Malik wrote: "This is the distressing dimension of Ardern's compassionate poise, that it is so unfamiliar, so rare" (2019). Ardern's response, depicted through mainstream news coverage, generated broader social media discussions of leadership that is compassionate and caring. Susanna Moore wrote: "Martin Luther King said genuine leaders did not search for consensus but moulded it. Ardern has moulded a different consensus, demonstrating action, care, unity" (2019). A strong narrative of international commentary was that Ardern's response was atypical, but desirable, of a political leader. In Australia, tweets calling for Jacinda Ardern to become *our* Prime Minister were common to the point of cliché. Central to commentary on Ardern's response to the event – including her meetings with grieving families and Muslim communities and changing gun laws within days – was a discourse of strength. This was strength founded on emotional response, listening, and care.

These are just two examples of how a discourse of care emerges and circulates through social media discussion of public events. They also speak to the gendered aspects of care, though arguably this is asked of male political figures too (see Australian Prime Minister Scott Morrison's *uncaring* response to bushfires in late 2019, for example). What might have once been considered peripheral to political action (i.e. visible emotions or a lack thereof), is now often centred and amplified through critical discussion that dominates our social media feeds. Reading the actions of public figures as caring or otherwise references current socio-political tensions enmeshed with our interpersonal discussions of qualities that make people good or decent. A mediated circulation of emotions – including public grief, anger, and a range of "wtf moments" – is part of a broader cultural discourse of care as something we need to witness and feel.

I offer these anecdotes to situate this book in its historical and geo-political frame – a setting in which *digital cultures of care* are visible, affective, and increasingly contour our lives. We seem to be very concerned with care practices and care politics – globally, socially, and in our interpersonal relationships. This may include our concerns for the situation of incarcerated refugees, climate change and its effects, a woman's right not to be sexually harassed, trans rights, Bla(c)k people dying in police custody or from police bullets, and a host of other concerns that often come with hashtags citing cultural moods and *a politics of feeling*. Often there is an unclear distinction between a global, national, local, or personal mood as we engage discussions of care. While this book is not global in its focus, its data and discussions reference a broader, transnational politics of care.

Digital intimacy as everyday practice

This book is part of a wider scholarship of *digital intimacies* – a sub-field of media studies that focuses on the everyday and intimate uses of digital and social media. Digital intimacies scholarship attends to how digital media support and influence our intimacies, but also how media themselves – platforms, tools, interfaces, and their affordances – are intimate. The sound or sight of an app notification, for example, can generate warm feelings, or sometimes anxious feelings, depending on the app, the sender, the time of day, and more. As described by Jenny Sundén, the three dancing dots of someone composing a message can trigger embodied anticipation (2018, p. 74). Susanna Paasonen also argues that we must pay attention to *infrastructures of intimacy*, where intimacy does not solely involve human agents (2018). She argues that "Network connectivity functions as an infrastructure of intimacy that plays a key role in the creation and maintenance of friendships, sexual arrangements and affairs of the heart, as well as in forging their shapes and intensities" (2018, p. 118).

As per the opening line of Nancy Baym's *Personal Connection in the Digital Age*, "There have never been more ways to communicate with one another than there are right now" (2015, p. 1). Like many digital media scholars, Baym warns against a technological determinist understanding of digital media – that is, an understanding that media tools, channels, or platforms have directly changed our communication and intimacy practices. She also recognises that users of digital media are constrained by these media in some ways, and therefore a social construction of technology perspective is not useful either (2015). Rather, a *social shaping* perspective "sees technology and society as continually influencing one another" (2015, p. 26). Similarly, José van Dijck considers social media platforms as technocultural constructs on the basis that the technical and cultural aspects of these media are co-constructive (2013).

At the time of finishing this book, Netflix released its programme, *The Circle*. Like all reality TV, the reality of this is questionable, yet it reminds us of what we have come to know and expect of digital interactions and the intimacies they offer. Participants are isolated in their own apartments and can only communicate through "the Circle", a fabricated social media platform. Here, they chat privately or in groups, read each other's profiles, update their profiles, and like each other's "status" posts. Aside from obvious questions about the programme in terms of editing (accelerated time), choice of participants (all extroverted), and constructed drama, participants seem to quickly build intimacy with each other. While often hesitant and careful (they know catfish are among them), alliances, tears, and strong feelings emerge in early episodes. Like all of us who are literate in social media, participants quickly develop a sense of each other; who is trustworthy, who is a friend, and why those friendships make sense. Among viewers too, the programme quickly makes sense because digital infrastructures of intimacy are familiar.

Social media have made our experiences of intimacy more public (Baym, 2015; Pascoe, 2010), and the ways we engage with digital and social media continue to blur and disrupt understandings of public/private (Baym & boyd,

2012; Chun, 2016; Papacharissi, 2015). While intimacy has long been public practice (Illouz, 2007), social media have extended its *publicness* (Baym & boyd, 2012). The affective dimensions of digital media are well-discussed and this book draws on extensive scholarship of this (Dobson et al., 2018; Karatzogianni & Kuntsman, 2012; McGlotten, 2013; Papacharissi, 2015). Much of this work elaborates on Lauren Berlant's theorisation of intimacy (1998) and intimate publics (2008) and Sara Ahmed's queer theorisation of affective and emotional cultures (2004), which also inform this book.

Not only do digital media offer us space to practice and forge intimate relationships, they also allow us "to trace the words of care and support that people share with each other" (Dobson et al., 2018, p. 7). These two movements – practising and witnessing care – are integrated, as we learn about care from participation and watching, from proximity and distance, from caring and also not caring. This prefaces the need for a cultural analysis of digital care, and the need to move beyond conceptualising care as unidirectional, transactional, and hierarchical – as guided by formal approaches to health care.

Dobson and colleagues note that social media make intimacies more public, but also suggest that digital intimate publics fostered through social media use are perhaps not public enough (2018). They highlight the political importance of researchers "paying attention to the public, digital inscription of unpredictable relations, attachments, feelings, and expressions of care that 'don't fit' the mould of heteronormative social reproduction" (2018, p. 22). Their argument draws upon Berlant and Warner's theorisation of intimate publics and queer world-making (1998), and highlights the normative approaches we unwittingly take, as researchers, when we engage with digital publics.

Bringing affect theory into digital media studies, Adi Kuntsman discusses the "affective fabrics of digital cultures" (2012, p. 3), citing Ahmed's argument that texts have emotionality. Kuntsman states, "feelings and affective states can reverberate in and out of cyberspace, intensified (or muffled) and transformed through digital circulation and repetition" (2012, p. 1). This concept of reverberation suggests our need, as researchers, "to follow the circulation of texts and feelings" (2012, p. 2). This relates to Shaka McGlotten's argument that intimacy is not simply a practice, but a feeling and a force (2013). Citing Berlant's argument that "Intimacy builds worlds", McGlotten highlights the potentiality of intimacy, where its force collides and integrates with digital media space and practice.

This book's focus on digital care as everyday is informed by Michel de Certeau (1988). Certeau makes a case for inverting top-down approaches to the study of culture, beginning at the level of *everyday practice*. In foregrounding practice, his work offers political value to the site of "the everyday" where social activity is not simply contained by structural arrangements but is negotiated through social relations, use of space, and negotiations of power. Certeau's approach broadens the sociological emphasis on *structure and agency*, instead focusing on *strategies and tactics* – terms committed to complex layers of everyday interactions. As he suggests, humans can challenge, undermine, or subvert everyday norms and systems (strategies), through their creative use of these same systems (tactics). For example, while digital media infrastructures and platform regulations (strategies) may seem to restrict and define permissible interactions, these can also be exploited or circumvented through tactical use of these media. Such tactics, Certeau would argue, do not necessarily oppose these strategies (we should not think of this as a simple power/resistance dichotomy), but can re-convene them through practices that were not intended or foreseen by media developers/ corporations and their platform policies and regulations. A simple example is the use of Instagram for political organising and protest – a practice that the platform developers were unlikely to have had in mind, but one that co-opts its affordances of reach, visual marketing, intimate engagement, and affective resonance. Another example would be the use of dating/hook-up apps for making friends or strengthening existing friendships (as discussed in Chapter 6).

An *everyday practice* approach does not only consider human agents, although human relationships are the central focus of this book. Digital media objects and infrastructures play a vital role in the shapes, meanings, and enactments of intimate relationships, as Paasonen highlights (2018). This includes our access to media devices, telecommunication signals, and data; the platforms we use (and don't use); the affordances of such platforms; the different levels of privacy and freedom we negotiate and expect; the places we live, how we live, and how digital media integrates with our living spaces and mobilities; and finally, how we find and position ourselves through digital media use and how this relates to negotiations of our identities, personal networks, and cultural affiliations. These points demonstrate how digital life vs. non-digital life is an artificial binary (Deuze, 2012) and an insufficient approach to contemporary cultures of care.

Certeau's approach can illuminate sites of everyday practice where culture thrives, operating within (but also beyond) institutional and corporate agendas. In a similar vein, this book foregrounds young people's accounts of their everyday practices of care and considers their digital expertise against current public health research and policy. I am not arguing that public health is not valuable, nor that this knowledge should be replaced with young people's experiential knowledge, but I am highlighting the need to explore the gaps and intersections between traditional public health frameworks and young people's everyday (and digitally mediated) understandings of health and wellbeing – where "personal experience" carries much weight and influence. If informal circuits of information are more accessible and constant, and the price of healthcare (especially mental health care) prevents many young people from accessing those systems of support, then formal healthcare becomes less relevant. Meanwhile, freely available peer support offers more expansive and reliable forms of care. This suggests a critical need to rethink care, including the public provision of health care. While I propose that peer and friend-based care is significant and valuable, I do not argue that this can replace or forfeit the need for formal health care, nor government responsibilities for providing this in accessible, responsible, and culturally sensitive ways.

Beyond risk approaches

Unfortunately, a key framework for discussing young people's use of digital media has been a risk framework, extending from a longer social history of positioning young people as always "at-risk" (Kelly, 2001). This has limited our research, education, and health policy approaches to young people, as will become evident throughout this book. Accordingly, this book foregrounds young people's digital media skills and expertise to offer a more useful and productive approach to the question of care, and how this can inform further health policy and practice and its engagement with digital media.

As Gill Jones has outlined, there is ongoing tension between seeing young people as being "corrupted by society" and so needing to be saved, or young people being "a corrupting influence upon society" and thus needing to be controlled (2009, p. 16). This dynamic continues today, but I would add that it is also raced, classed, and gendered, and in Australia (as with many other places), young men of colour are understood as a greater threat (Grewal, 2007), while young White women are more frequently discussed as needing protection, including from "unsafe" digital media use, as per discussions of teen sexting (Albury et al., 2013; Dobson & Ringrose, 2015). This also carries into popular discussions of "selfie culture", where selfies have been unfairly discussed as outcomes of young women's narcissism and low self-esteem (Senft & Baym, 2015).

This tension – youth as risking/at-risk – is not useful for engaging with young people's lived experiences of health and wellbeing, nor their digital media practices. An everyday practice approach helps to centre young people's experiences and concerns, and how they negotiate and practice health and wellbeing, including through digital media. No doubt some young people feel "at risk" sometimes, but my research has found little evidence of young people framing their health or media practices as risky. This makes sense because centring yourself as vulnerable and "at risk" is neither a useful nor healthy perspective for any of us. Yet, many adults continue to try and engage with young people by insisting that they are vulnerable and at-risk. Evidently, commitment to a social hierarchy in which adults have power and control over young people is a default position for many adults and their institutional agendas, but this worldview fails to actively engage young people. A key part of that failure is inadequate and piecemeal consultation with young people.

Recent work by Amanda Third and colleagues (2019) seeks to shift this "control paradigm" of young people and digital media research that pervades education and health policy responses to "online risks" and offers important discussion on how to do so. As Livingstone and Görzig argue, risk differs to harm (2014), and while many digital media practices include a level of risk-taking, this does not always result in harm. In risk-focused research, however, risk and harm are typically conflated to produce a sense that all risks must be avoided and eradicated, where possible. But communication (digital or otherwise) always carries risk.

In our social imaginary, young people are "at-risk" (Michaud, 2006) and the frequent reiteration of risk has made this seem like an immutable fact through which we continue to research, evaluate, and question young people. This excuses our need to involve young people in these discussions. A risk paradigm ensures that those of us wishing to foreground and involve young people's experiences and understandings of their health and wellbeing, will find it difficult to be heard and understood by many health researchers and other "concerned adults".

Research on the impacts of social and digital media also often adopt a risk-approach by centring the dangers that media may present to children and young people (Livingstone, 2008). The worry that screen cultures affect youth learning is as old as television, and the anxiety about screen-based media enjoyed by young people is resuscitated with every "new" media event – from video games to personal computers to the internet, from early mobile phones to smartphones, from MySpace to Facebook to Snapchat to TikTok, and so on. Perhaps it is less of a resuscitation than an ever-present worry that encircles our understanding of who young people are and what they need. Perhaps we imagine young people's minds and bodies as soft, malleable, and sticky for information; and therefore, at risk of receiving and imbibing bad information if we cannot properly supervise and intervene.

Within these anxieties we can trace legitimate concerns for young people, and the hope that they can access the information and support they need for optimal health, connection, and wellbeing. This book, and its central concept of *digital cultures of care*, emerges from that space and hopes to offer useful insight and discussion regarding young people's digital media practices of friendship, peer support, and care. As we cannot return to a pre-digital media era, or separate digital from non-digital life, we must adjust our thinking to accommodate how digital media are used by, and are useful to, young people. So long as "concerned adults" are determining the risks of digital media to young people without listening to young people's concerns about these matters, adult fears and assumptions will continue to be centred in these debates. As adults, worrying about young people is also a form of care, as part of our shared social responsibility. But *our caregiving* warrants discussion and critique, and young people need to be part of that discussion.

It is also important to recognise that young people are fluent in caregiving, as discussed throughout this book.

Cultures of care

"Culture is ordinary: that is where we must start", said Raymond Williams in 1958 (2014). This is indeed a good place to start and fits with an *everyday practice* research agenda. Because of this, I do not begin with a strict definition of care, nor *digital cultures of care*, but will offer an account of some key discussions of care that inform this book. While interpersonal care has been discussed at length among moral philosophers (Clement, 1996; Tronto, 1993), this book focuses on care as it is practised, felt, and produced among young people through digital and social media. I argue that multiple forms of care emerge and circulate through these media and I have gained this knowledge through young people's accounts (featured within). Engaging with young people's experiences and expertise of interpersonal care, each chapter attends to different scenes of care. Through my analysis of data across each of these chapters, I trace and build the concept of digital cultures of care.

Care has an "ambivalent significance", according to María Puig de la Bellacasa (2017). Highlighting this, and the difficulties in defining care, she asks, "But what is care? Is it an affection? A moral obligation? Work? A burden? A joy? Something we can learn or practice? Something we just do?" (2017, p. 1). Further to this, she notes that "while ways of caring can be identified, researched, and understood concretely and empirically, care remains ambivalent in significance and ontology" (2017, p. 1). This book embraces this ambivalence which informs my reluctance to define care from the outset. To do so would also rob the affective force of care from young people's statements within.

It is important to note that my focus is limited to my own geo-political situation, academic training, colonial settler history, and worldview. As non-Indigenous to the continent known as Australia, I write and work from stolen and unceded land. Most of the young people who feature in this book are also non-Indigenous. Much could be said of expansive cultures of care that reverberate throughout this continent in a book such as this. Much could also be said about how cultures of care that are Indigenous to this continent have been overlooked by academic research that has adopted, reiterated, and intensified a colonial and Western imperial viewpoint (Smith, 2012). Australian academia takes its culture from European systems of imperialist knowledge that are built upon the destruction of other ways of knowing and caring about place and each other. As a book about cultures of care, this tension cannot go unstated. And while this tension is not foregrounded in any of these chapters, it has contoured my own misgivings about this project, while feeding into my ongoing interest in decolonising approaches to knowledge and place. I am in the early stages of thinking through this, so unfortunately, there is not a clear and persistent decolonising focus throughout this book.

As Leah Lakshmi Piepzna-Samarasinha points out, "White people didn't invent the concept of mutual aid – many precolonial (and after) Black, Indigenous, and brown communities have complex webs of exchanges of care" (2018), and there is an academic and social need to pay more attention to these. Importantly, informal care offers necessary safety for many Indigenous and non-White peoples in countries like "Australia". We should remember that formal care has been felt as surveillance and regulation for many QTBIPOC[3] (Piepzna-Samarasinha, 2018). This has been discussed in relation to Indigenous people's encounters with Australian health promotion (McPhail-Bell et al., 2015), and very recent histories of "Aboriginal Protection" agencies forcibly removing Aboriginal and Torres Strait Islander children from their families (HREOC, 1997).[4] These systems of trauma also speak to why formal structures of care can be distrusted and ineffective. This raises further questions about broader social and community practices of care that are not visible to outsiders and colonisers.

Throughout this book, I focus on care that is both digital and informal because this is a site of care that is largely overlooked in academic and public discussions of health and wellbeing. While there is growing academic and public health attention to "digital health" and how health knowledge and information circulates through digital and social media, there is limited attention to how young people's informal support practices are arranged in digital space and practice. This book foregrounds the ways that care encircle everyday digital interactions, highlighting how informal care is multi-directional – given and received, but also forwarded and shared indirectly. These practices of care emerge in studies of personal relationships or marginalised communities but are typically backgrounded as the common and unremarkable conditions of community, friendship, and solidarity.

In terms of care, John Silk points to the "useful distinction between benevolence, or caring about others, and beneficence, or caring for others" (1998, p. 167). This highlights different yet overlapping dimensions of care, and is a useful place to start approaching its complexity, including care's many locations, practices, and meanings. It is safe to say that we *care about* our friends, but they do not always need to be *cared for*. Some friends may, at certain times, need more care – and our care *for* such friends is informed by how we care *about* them – even though these are different modes of care, as Silk argues. Sophie Bowlby also highlights the distinction between care that is practical and care that is emotionally invested, and how these can operate on separate axes:

> [Care] can involve "caring for" – that is, tasks of care – as well as "caring about", which refers to emotional investment in another person's problems and concerns. Clearly the two are related but "caring about"

does not necessarily lead to "caring for" while "caring for" can occur without "caring about". (2011, p. 606)

As Silk and Bowlby argue, these forms of care are not mutually exclusive. If we apply these modes of care to digital intimacies, this distinction is further muddied. Caring for someone in a digital health forum, for example, may involve sharing particular information, resources, or experience-based knowledge. As strangers, we might not think that such sharing also involves *caring about* this person, if we associate such acts with friends, families, and people known to us. But this form of care can be both practical and emotional.

De la Bellacasa also notes that care is related to concern, but is more than just concern, as per its "stronger affective and ethical connotations" (2011, p. 89). She further states,

> We can think on the difference between affirming: "I am concerned" and "I care". The first denotes worry and thoughtfulness about an issue as well as the fact of belonging to those "affected" by it; the second adds a strong sense of attachment and commitment to something. (2011, pp. 89–90)

While this introduction began with a claim that care is typically understood and researched in relation to formal caregiving, as opposed to informal support, it is important to keep this distinction in tension. As Bowlby argues, while friendship provides informal care, "The social roles of friends will be influenced by the care provided from other sources such as the state, private sector or voluntary groups" (2011, p. 607). In other words, friendship care is informed by our use of, and access to, other sources of care, including formal health care. An example of this is how shared understandings of the limitations of formal health care inform our care for friends, peers, and others.

In much health research, care takes on a more specific meaning – as something administered by health professionals – persons unknown to a patient, but who can exercise the necessary expertise in diagnosing and treating patients. Academic literature on "digital care" tends to focus on digitised health care delivery and intervention. Within this, "care experiences" are discussed in relation to patient/user experiences of health care settings or systems, including the experiences of digital health tools. This focus reinstates a hierarchy of care as administered by experts and professionals, as something that "everyday people" receive but do not facilitate. Recent discussions of *digital health* typically centre the individuated health consumer who negotiates health and technology alone, in private. Discussion throughout this book speaks back to such approaches that fail to understand health and wellbeing as relationally practised among friends and peers.

"Cultures of care" is a concept used by Michael Hurley (2002; 2003) in relation to people living with HIV/AIDS, but it is more broadly deployed throughout this book, and with specific reference to digital media. For Hurley, a "cultures of care" framework is useful:

> as a way of conceptualising the social relations between health service providers, the people taking treatments, their social support networks, international media relays, community-based treatments media and the development of practices of self-care amongst people living with HIV/AIDS. (2002, p. 31)

Hurley's work informs my attention to care practices as they intermesh with, yet often depart from, public health discussion and policy. I expand and reorient this concept to engage with young people's everyday interactions, beyond the HIV/AIDS epidemic that Hurley addresses. Yet I still look across health systems (research, policy, and practice), the people engaging with and affected by these, community and public debate, and emergent, responsive, and creative cultures of care. Considering care practices among and between friends, peers, and strangers, through digital media, extends a focus beyond young people simply seeking and sourcing information for their individual needs. This approach also engages with young people's practices of caring, as well as modes of finding and/or building digital spaces to listen, share, and learn from each other's personal experiences.

Care is also gendered (Gilligan, 1993), historically and currently, though its gendered codes are contextualised differently, in different settings and relationships. Because I do not wish to define or constrain care and its practices to particular groups and functions, I am reluctant to reiterate a simplistic narrative of the gendered aspects of care. This is particularly problematic because my focus is away from families and health systems where binary gender identities, codes, and practices are more evident and enduring. In creative spaces of young people's digital peer support, however, gender can be less guiding, and it can be practised and discussed beyond binary experiences and understandings of gender. However, the difficulty of engaging cisgender straight men in digital intimacies research is evident and noted in this book. Throughout this book and the many voices that feature, female, non-binary, and queer male accounts dominate these discussions of care. This is on ongoing issue that demands ongoing consideration, yet it also tells us something about digital cultures of care and who is needing, building, and gaining from these cultures the most.

Critical health scholars often emphasise an individualising force of neoliberalism, and with that, a responsibility to *care for oneself*. While "self-care" is significant to how we might understand and theorise care cultures in digital media practice, an exploration of self-care is beyond the scope of this book. Without diminishing this discussion, I offer a parallel argument about the increasing relevance of *care for others*, as is evident in digitally mediated practices of peer support and friendship.

This book does not argue that digital media make us more caring, yet it does consider how digital media shape a range of care practices, and vice versa. This relies on the affordances of such media, and the different access points they offer to our friends, peers, and communities. The purpose of this book is modest. Like any book, it does not tell a complete story but discusses a set of social practices in the context of digital, informal care. The focus of the book is not mapping the social, political, and economic conditions of digital care practices, but expanding our view and understanding of everyday practices of digital care, friendship, and peer support.

The research

This book engages with a range of data from multiple qualitative research projects, collected from 2009–2019. Since some of the projects feature in multiple chapters, a brief overview is offered here, rather than including an overview in each chapter. Throughout the book, pseudonyms are used for all participants. Demographic information (typically age, gender, and sexuality) are provided with participant quotes throughout, though this varies due to inconsistent data collection processes.

Scrolling beyond binaries

(Chapters 1, 2, and 5)

This is a study of Australian LGBTQ+ young people's social media use. Participants were aged 16–35 years, and data was gathered through a survey (N = 1,304) and interviews (N = 23) conducted in 2016. Survey and interview questions captured a snapshot of social media used by participants (currently and previously), as well as the volume of use. Issues covered in these data include connection, belonging, identity, safety, and health and wellbeing. The project team comprises Brady Robards, Son Vivienne, Benjamin Hanckel, Brendan Churchill, and myself. Ethics Committee approval was received from the University of Tasmania (H0015362). More information is available at www.scrollingbeyondbinaries.com.

Young people, sexual health, and social media

(Chapter 3)

This study investigated Australian young people's views on the potential use of social and digital media for sexual health promotion targeting young people. The study was commissioned by a government health agency and conducted in 2011. Participants were aged 16–22 years, and data was gathered through six focus groups held in Western Sydney and a regional city in New South Wales (three each), involving 22 participants. Initial focus groups (two in each location), engaged participants aged either 16–17 or 18–22 years. Focus group participants discussed mobile phone and social media practices, sexual health, and the suitability of sexual health promotion through social and digital media. Following this, some participants returned (two groups, 16–22 years, one in each location), to workshop hypothetical sexual health campaigns that use a range of digital media. Participants were an equal mix of female and male, and while information on their sexual orientations was not collected, most "outed" themselves as heterosexual. Most participants were White. I was Research Assistant on this project led by Kath Albury, alongside Clifton Evers and Kate Crawford. This project received Ethics Committee clearance from UNSW (HREC 10232).

Practicing sexual health

(Chapter 4)

This discursive analysis of "young people's sexual health" included data from interviews with 12 young people (18–25 years), three sexual health websites, and 18 sexual health research papers (this book only reports on interview and website data). This was my doctoral research, with data collected in 2009. Interview participants were all from Sydney and had at least two years of sexual experience that included casual sex. Participants were also required to have had heterosex, since this was the focus of website and research data, as well as national sexual health policy on "young people" at this time. Not all participants identified as heterosexual, however. Semi-structured interviews covered discussion of sexual experiences, sexual relationships, and negotiations of sexual health. Most participants were enrolled in tertiary education. Six participants were Anglo-Australian, and six self-described as Middle Eastern, Asian, Jewish, or Eastern European. Seven females and five males were interviewed, and all were cisgender. Ethics Committee clearance was granted by UNSW (HREC 09026).

LGBTIQ Mental Health Help-seeking Project (MHHS)

(Chapter 5)

In this study of LGBTIQ+ young people's mental health help-seeking, data was collected through a national survey of LGBTIQ+ young people aged 16–25 years; Sydney and Perth-based focus groups with LGBTIQ+ young people (six groups) and LGBTIQ+ youth service staff (four groups); and eight interviews with health professionals. I was employed as Research Officer at Twenty10 incorporating the Gay and Lesbian Counselling Service NSW, and partnered with the Freedom Centre (Perth), Western Sydney University, and Curtin University. Data with young people is mostly discussed in this book, from the survey (N = 607) and focus groups (N = 39). Other team members were Kerry Robinson, Roanna Lobo, Dani Wright

Touissant, Sophia Rasmussen, and Brett Paradise. Ethics Committee clearance was granted by Western Sydney University (H11103) and Curtin University (HR 108/2015).

Safety, risk, and wellbeing in digital dating

(Chapter 6)

This was a study of young people's (16–35 years) uses of dating/hook-up apps in Australia, conducted from 2018–2019. The study was conducted by the Swinburne University of Technology, in partnership with Sydney University, ACON (AIDS Council of New South Wales), and Family Planning NSW. The project engaged with young people through a national survey, group workshops, and interviews. Eight workshops with young dating/hook-up app users were held in Sydney and regional New South Wales, involving 51 participants. Following these, ten interviews were conducted in Sydney. Workshops were split between Sydney and a regional city, with two in each location for straight or LGBTQ+ participants. The LGBTQ+ workshops were advertised along the lines of apps used rather than identities (i.e. Grindr and similar apps/HER and similar apps), ensuring greater participation among trans and/or non-binary young people. Workshops for straight people were not entirely straight but included participants who were agender, bisexual, and heteroflexible. The study also engaged app users and health professionals through reference groups and a workshop for health professionals, but only data from workshops and interviews with young people are discussed in this book. Ethics Committee clearance was granted by Swinburne University (SUHREC 2018/159) and ACON (RERC 2018/12).

The chapters

Chapter 1 focuses on friendship and offers a history of research approaches and theorisations of friendship. Digital and social media practices around friendship are discussed, considering how digital cultures have expanded friendships' practice and understandings, as well as opportunities for everyday care and support. Chapter 2 considers health and education research understandings of peers, particularly considering peer influence and peer education strategies. Critiques of peer education are considered and built upon, before shifting the focus to *peer support*. To demonstrate digital cultures of peer support, data are presented, including young people's statements about Tumblr, introducing the concept of *Tumblr care* in relation to LGBTQ+ young people's peer support. Chapter 3 builds on the previous chapters by considering young people's digital media expertise, with a focus on sexual health promotion via social media. Facebook is the focus of this chapter, since this is what participants were mostly using at the time of data collection, and participants demonstrate their expertise of platform cultures and the central practice of friendship. Despite the risks of sharing sexual health information in this setting, participants suggest non-disruptive strategies for promoting sexual health on social media. Chapter 4 expands the focus on friendship, discussing interview data with young people regarding sex, relationships, friendship intimacies, and sexual health. Here, close friends are argued to be sexually intimate on account of the intimate knowledge they have of each other's sexual practices, and because many participants also discussed having sex with friends. This chapter departs from a digital media focus to broaden the book's consideration of friendships, and to introduce a richer analysis of friendship care and support, drawing upon theories of intimacy. Chapter 5 focuses on digital and informal practices of peer support for mental health, drawing on data from two independent studies of LGBTQ+ young people. This furthers the discussion of *invested peers* introduced in Chapter 2 and considers how unknown and anonymous peers can offer greater mental health support than young people's close friends. Digital peers offer lived experience that is informative and supportive, and data reflects how many young people gain from this. Chapter 6 considers young people's negotiations with dating/hook-up apps. It focuses on how app use intersects with friendship – in terms of friends supporting each other's app use, but also in finding and strengthening friendships through dating/hook-up app use.

While these chapters draw from different studies undertaken at different times, with diverse groups of young people, together they illustrate common scenes and sentiments of young people's friendship and peer support practices.

Notes

1 I use LGBTQ+ as a recognisable acronym which includes, but is not limited to, lesbian, gay, trans, queer, questioning, pansexual, asexual, non-binary, and other gender and sexually diverse people.
2 I generally avoid referring to 'youth' and prefer 'young people' as this seems less entrenched in a totalising discourse of young people and is less likely to be read as commentary on *youth culture*, as though this exists in a coherent, known, sense.
3 Queer and Trans Black, Indigenous, People of Colour.
4 The removal of children continues, with recent reporting of 20,421 Aboriginal and Torres Strait Islander children currently in out-of-home care – a figure 10.2 times that of non-Indigenous children in out-of-home care (see www.familymatters.org.au).

References

Ahmed, S. (2004). *The cultural politics of emotion*. Edinburgh: Edinburgh University Press.
Albury, K., Crawford, K., Byron, P., & Mathews, B. (2013). *Young People and Sexting in Australia: Ethics, representation and the law*. Sydney: ARC Centre for

Creative Industries and Innovation / Journalism and Media Research Centre, The University of New South Wales.

Baym, N. (2015). *Personal connections in the digital age* (2nd ed.). Cambridge: Polity Press.

Baym, N., & boyd, d. (2012). Socially mediated publicness: An introduction. *Journal of Broadcasting and Electronic Media*, *56*(3), 320–329.

Berlant, L. (1998). Intimacy: A special issue. *Critical Inquiry*, *24*(2), 281–288.

Berlant, L. (2008). *The female complaint: The unfinished business of sentimentality in American culture*. Durham: Duke University Press.

Berlant, L., & Warner, M. (1998). Sex in public. *Critical Inquiry*, *24*(2), 547–566.

Bowlby, S. (2011). Friendship, co-presence and care: Neglected spaces. *Social and Cultural Geography*, *12*(6), 605–622.

Brooks, F., & Kendall, S. (2013). Making sense of assets: What can an assets based approach offer public health? *Critical Public Health*, *23*(2), 127–130.

Certeau de, M. (1988). *The practice of everyday life* (S. Rendall, Trans.). Berkeley, CA: University of California Press.

Chun, W. H. K. (2016). *Updating to remain the same: Habitual new media*. Cambridge, MA: MIT press.

Clement, G. (1996). *Care, autonomy, and justice: Feminism and the ethic of care*. New York, NY: Routledge.

de la Bellacasa, M. P. (2011). Matters of care in technoscience: Assembling neglected things. *Social Studies of Science*, *41*(1), 85–106.

de la Bellacasa, M. P. (2017). *Matters of care: Speculative ethics in More than human worlds*. Minneapolis, MN: University of Minnesota Press.

Deuze, M. (2012). *Media life*. Cambridge: Polity Press.

Dobson, A. S., & Ringrose, J. (2015). Sext education: Pedagogies of sex, gender and shame in the schoolyards of Tagged and Exposed. *Sex Education*, *16*(1), 8–21.

Dobson, A. S., Robards, B., & Carah, N. (2018). *Digital intimate publics and social media*. Cham: Palgrave Macmillan.

Foucault, M. (1978). *The history of sexuality volume 1: An introduction*. London & New York, NY: Penguin.

Foucault, M. (1991). Politics and the study of discourse. In P. Miller, C. Gordon & G. Burchell (Eds.), *The Foucault effect: Studies in governmentality* (pp. 53–72). Chicago, IL: University of Chicago Press.

Foucault, M. (2010). *The archaeology of knowledge*. New York, NY: Vintage Books.

Gilligan, C. (1993). *In a different voice: Psychological theory and women's development*. Cambridge, MA: Harvard University Press.

Grewal, K. (2007). The "Young Muslim man" in Australian public discourse. *Transforming Cultures ejournal*, *2*(1). Retrieved from https://epress.lib.uts.edu.au/journals/index.php/TfC/article/view/599.

Horst, H., & Miller, D. (2012). Normativity and materiality: A view from digital anthropology. *Media International Australia*, *145*(1), 103–111.

HREOC. (1997). Bringing them home: National inquiry into the separation of Aboriginal and Torres Strait Islander children from their families. Canberra: Human Rights and Equal Opportunity Commission.

Hurley, M. (2002). *Cultures of Care and Safe Sex amongst HIV Positive Australians: Papers from the HIV Futures I and II surveys and interviews*. Melbourne: Australian Research Centre in Sex, Health and Society, La Trobe University.

Hurley, M. (2003). Then and Now: Gay Men and HIV. Melbourne: The Australian Research Centre in Sex, Health & Society, La Trobe University.

Illouz, E. (2007). *Cold intimacies: The making of emotional capitalism*. Cambridge: Polity Press.

Jones, G. (2009). *Youth*. Cambridge: Polity Press.

Karatzogianni, A., & Kuntsman, A. (2012). *Digital cultures and the politics of emotion: Feelings, affect and technological change*. London: Palgrave Macmillan.

Kelly, P. (2001). Youth at Risk: Processes of individualisation and responsibilisation in the risk society. *Discourse: Studies in the Cultural Politics of Education, 22*(1), 23–33.

Kuntsman, A. (2012). Introduction: Affective fabrics of digital cultures. In A. Karatzogianni & A. Kuntsman (Eds.), *Digital cultures and the politics of emotion: Feelings, affect and technological change* (pp. 1–17). London: Palgrave Macmillan.

Lasén, A. (2004). Affective technologies – Emotions and mobile phones. *Receiver*, Vodaphone, 11.

Livingstone, S. (2008). Taking risky opportunities in youthful content creation: teenagers' use of social networking sites for intimacy, privacy and self-expression. *New Media & Society, 10*(3), 393–411.

Livingstone, S., & Görzig, A. (2014). When adolescents receive sexual messages on the internet: Explaining experiences of risk and harm. *Computers in Human Behavior, 33*, 8–15.

Mahdawi, A. (2018, June 22). The great Melania Trump mystery. Does she really care? *The Guardian*. Retrieved June 9, 2019 from https://www.theguardian.com/commentisfree/2018/jun/21/great-melania-trump-mystery-does-she-care.

Malik, N. (2019, March 28). With respect: How Jacinda Ardern showed the world what a leader should be. *The Guardian*. Retrieved October 17, 2019. https://www.theguardian.com/world/2019/mar/28/with-respect-how-jacinda-ardern-showed-the-world-what-a-leader-should-be.

McGlotten, S. (2013). *Virtual intimacies: Media, affect, and queer sociality*. Albany: SUNY Press.

McPhail-Bell, K., Bond, C., Brough, M., & Fredericks, B. (2015). "We don't tell people what to do": Ethical practice and Indigenous health promotion. *Health Promotion Journal of Australia, 26*(3), 195–199.

Michaud, P.-A. (2006). Adolescents and risks: Why not change our paradigm? *Journal of Adolescent Health, 38*(5), 481–483.

Moore, S. (2019, March 18). Jacinda Ardern is showing the world what real leadership is: sympathy, love and integrity. *The Guardian*. Retrieved October 17, 2019. https://www.theguardian.com/commentisfree/2019/mar/18/jacinda-ardern-is-showing-the-world-what-real-leadership-is-sympathy-love-and-integrity.

Paasonen, S. (2018). Infrastructures of intimacy. In R. Andreassen, M. Nebeling Petersen, K. Harrison & T. Raun (Eds.), *Mediated intimacies: Connectivities, Relationalities and proximities* (pp. 117–130). London & New York, NY: Routledge.

Papacharissi, Z. (2015). *Affective publics: Sentiment, technology, and politics*. New York, NY: Oxford University Press.

Pascoe, C. J. (2010). Intimacy. In M. Ito, S. Baumer, M. Bittanti, R. Cody & B. Herr-Stephenson, H.A. Horst, P. G. Lange, D. Mahendran, K. Z. Martínez &

C. Pascoe (Eds.), *Hanging out, messing around and geeking out: Kids living and learning with new media* (pp. 117–148). Cambridge, MA: MIT Press.

Piepzna-Samarasinha, L. L. (2018). *Care work: Dreaming disability justice.* Vancouver: Arsenal Pulp Press.

Senft, T. M., & Baym, N. K. (2015). What does the selfie say? Investigating a global phenomenon. *International Journal of Communication, 9,* 1588–1606.

Silk, J. (1998). Caring at a distance. *Philosophy and Geography, 1*(2), 165–182.

Smith, L. T. (2012). *Decolonizing methodologies: Research and indigenous peoples.* London: Zed Books.

Sundén, J. (2018). Queer disconnections: Affect, break, and delay in digital connectivity. *Transformations, 31,* 63–78.

Third, A., Collin, P., Walsh, L., & Black, R. (2019). *Young people in digital society: Control shift.* London: Palgrave Macmillan.

Tronto, J. C. (1993). *Moral boundaries: A political argument for an ethic of care.* New York, NY: Routledge.

Van Dijck, J. (2013). *The culture of connectivity: A critical history of social media.* Oxford & New York, NY: Oxford University Press.

Williams, R. (2014). *Raymond Williams on culture & society: Essential writings.* Los Angeles, CA: SAGE.

Wright, L. A. (2018, 22 June). What Melania Trump's "I don't care" jacket says about the state of the East Wing; if anything, the words speak to a lack of interest in the role she fills. *The Washington Post.* Retrieved June 19, 2019 https://www.washingtonpost.com/opinions/if-melania-trump-really-doesnt-care-then-who-does/2018/06/22/2bb4e9ca-762e-11e8-9780-b1dd6a09b549_story.html.

1   More than just friends

This chapter engages with recent practices and understandings of friendship in social and digital media, with a particular focus on young people. Prior to considering digital media, it is useful to consider what we know, and *how* we know this, about friendship. The first part of this chapter, therefore, considers a history of how friendship has been understood and researched, recognising the ongoing difficulties in conceptualising this elusive relationship and practice. Much recent scholarly attention to friendship has arrived through feminist and queer theory approaches to socio-political and intimate lives. Within this, friendship has been considered as a site of solidarity, shared struggle, and kinship-like relations. This work informs recent sociological approaches to friendship that I also draw upon.

Friendship remains difficult to study and this relates to its ubiquity, its variety, and its lack of recognised social norms. This poses a challenge to empirical research on friendship. As Ray Pahl states, "it is hard to get coherent information from people about something which they are barely aware exists" (2000, p. 9). However, empirical evidence presented throughout this book suggests that many young people are aware of, and fluent in discussing, friendship.

Since the 1970s, queer and feminist scholarship has examined the significance of friendship in everyday life. In their book on same-sex intimacies, Jeffrey Weeks et al. argue that "The most commonly told relationship story among non-heterosexuals is one of friendship" (2001, p. 51). Studies of queer friendship, however, have typically centred on gay men. This is likely influenced by research attention to the HIV/AIDS epidemic – where friendship played a central role in caregiving in the absence of adequate public health care. A focus on gay men is also indicative of a lack of research engagement with other queer populations, including women, until recently. As Pat O'Connor demonstrates, friendships among women were "systematically ignored, derogated and trivialized within a very wide variety of traditions" until the mid-1970s (1992, p. 9). Yet, friendships have been integral to feminist struggles and women's affective bonds for centuries (Faderman, 1981).

In early "Western thought", both Plato and Aristotle studied the meaning and practice of friendship. Plato discussed friendship as one of many forms of love and considered the connection between *philia* (meaning friendship, or brotherly love) and *eros* (associated with romantic love). His writings on this led to the later concept of "platonic friendship". Aristotle built on this work of his teacher, focusing on ethical practices necessary for "the good life" (1906). He proposed three types of friendship[1] – friendships of utility, friendships of pleasure, and "good friendships".[2] Friendships of utility, he argued, are instrumental friendships that only last as long as their offerings are useful, and he associated these with older men or businessmen. Friendships of pleasure were more fleeting and passionate, and he associated these with younger men whose passions were intense and easily aroused. Good friendships were considered both useful and pleasurable, but further to this, they were enduring friendships, built over time to become more nourishing and significant. This, he argued, was the rarest form of friendship and typically involved friends as equals who were heavily invested in each other's happiness (whereas friends of pleasure or utility were more self-focused). It is this friendship that contributes most to one's happiness, according to Aristotle (1906).

Relying on ancient theories of friendship (practised among some men), from a time that hardly resembles the present day, is questionable. Yet this understanding is still pervasive in recent sociological accounts of friendship. Aristotle associated friendship with intimacy, choice, equality, respect, and freedom – themes still used to understand friendship, including among sociologists (Adams & Allan, 1998; Blatterer, 2015). While this book's discussion of friendship does not rely on these foundations, they provide useful context to consider ongoing tensions in how we know and understand friendship, as well as what we expect from it.

The title of this chapter points to a common tendency to disavow the importance of friendship when accounting for our relationship practices. The concept of "just friends" privileges sexual and romantic relationships, positioning these as more definitive of who we are and how we orient ourselves – eros ahead of philia, in Platonic terms.[3] There are many reasons for this, but a significant reason is the social privilege assigned to "the family". Throughout Western history, the family has emerged as a model and metaphor for "the nation", underpinning our conceptualisations of gender, labour, nationalism, and more (McClintock, 1993). These understandings of "the family" also centre their role in disciplining subjects, who would become productive and useful for nation building and domestic economies (Donzelot, 1997). The Western family came to be understood as the centre of one's domestic life – as a site of nurture, care, sustenance, and personal responsibility. Love and marriage were instrumental to (and encouraged and supported for) "the good of the nation". Socio-historical narratives of social life typically assign families to the private sphere. In doing so, care and support is cordoned to the private home – yet supported by hospitals, clinics, schools, and other disciplining institutions (Rose, 1990). Less has been documented about friendship when we account for these histories, although this relationship arguably cuts through both private and public realms. Seemingly not belonging to either realm, in how they have been imagined and discussed, friendships have evaded much socio-historic analysis.

In his late interviews, Michel Foucault described friendship as a creative practice that carries the potential to generate new forms of intimacy. He argued that friendships constitute non-institutionalised relationships – that is, they are not bound to strict codes and roles found in marriage and family relations (2000a). He argued that "We live in a relational world that institutions have considerably impoverished" (2000a, p. 158), and where friendships have evaded much institutional regulation and surveillance. He saw friendship as "a way of life" in which we might create new intimacies and realities, suggesting that "after studying the history of sex, we should try to understand the history of friendship, or friendships" (2000b, p. 171). Unfortunately, he never wrote that book, but these interviews have greatly influenced queer theory (Love, 2007), as per their accounts of friendship's creative and disruptive potential to heteronormative life. As Foucault proposes, friendship's creativity is supported by its lack of recognised form, with its terms remaining open (Roach, 2012). While his focus was mostly on gay men, the potential to invent new socio-sexual relations through friendship carries to broader populations and is relevant to young people's creative engagements with digital media. This is not to suggest that traditional hetero-familial relations are no longer practised or valued by young people, but for many young people, friendships are their primary relationships, as is visible in social media publics.

Knowing friendship

Aristotle famously said: "A friend to all is a friend to none" – a statement that has resurfaced in contemporary discussions of digital practices like "Facebook friending" and common arguments that digital friendship practices are less real, enduring, or significant than traditional friendships (Bakardjieva, 2014). This criticism hinges on Aristotle's argument that a good friend prioritises quality over quantity of friends, and that good friendships are rare and long-lasting. But are young people actually interested in "friend collecting" on social media (boyd, 2006), or are social media connections more complicated than the pleasure of accumulation? Much literature reminds us that young people are predominantly not using social media to find new friends, but to further engage with friends from their everyday lives (Baym, 2015; Ellison et al., 2007).

Beyond Plato and Aristotle (yet heavily leaning into their work), are the frequently cited friendship texts of Ralph Waldo Emerson (1987) and C.S. Lewis (1960). As per many works by esteemed White male thinkers of the 19th and 20th century, they assert confident claims, seemingly based on their own experiences, yet presenting these as universal. They focus on friendships between men of common interests, and of their own calibre.

In the context of an enduring White male intellectualism, these texts held friendship away from "the everyday person" by their focus on how "great men" nourish and further each other's intellectual greatness. Their suggested neutrality demands critique,[4] yet along with the accounts of other esteemed male thinkers, these "theories" of friendship are still cited and pored over today. As with all scholarship that hinges on the viewpoint of past intellectuals, these understandings haunt how we continue to conceptualise and understand friendship. From this canon, we still focus on notions of "real", "true", or "proper" friendship – often associated with non-digital life (Cocking & Matthews, 2000; Kaliarnta, 2016).

Pat O'Connor's (1992) work on women's friendship offers a useful place to challenge how friendship has either been imagined through straight men's homosociality or disregarded entirely. She highlights an academic tendency to view friendship as "a rather trivial exercise ... [that] can be seen as reflecting a concern with the emotional, the tangential" (1992, p. 1). This is evidenced by a lack of consistent academic attention to friendship. Despite contemplations among philosophers, friendship has rarely been centred within social research. As O'Connor argues, it did not matter to scholars because it is "not concerned with the realities of sex or money" (1992, p. 1). Other sociologists similarly noted that friendship was overlooked because it was understood as having only personal, and not social, significance (Adams & Allan, 1998). Prior to recent sociological discussion, friendship was more commonly considered in psychology and the study of "interpersonal relationships" (Allan, 1998). These accounts tend to overlook the social, economic, and political dimensions of friendship, only focusing on how certain individuals experience dyadic friend relationships (Allan, 1998; Chasin & Radtke, 2013).

Decades ago, Paul Wright described friendship as "a relationship with extremely broad and ambiguous boundaries" (1978, p. 199). Comparing friendship to other social and kinship relations, including couple-based unions, he states: "friendship does not begin with a definite decision or statement of intention. Nor is an announcement or declaration necessary to bring a friendship to a close" (1978, p. 199). This matches Foucault's claims about the lack of institutional logic, concern, and regulation of friendship (2000c). Two decades later, Ray Pahl echoes that "the precise definition of a friend – as opposed to other forms of social connectedness – remains elusive" (2000, p. 8). This elusiveness of friendship seems to be a recurring problem for friendship researchers (Chasin & Radtke, 2013; Nardi, 1999). Attending to this, Pahl and Spencer (2004) found increasing suffusion between friend and family-based relationships, which led to their concept of "personal communities" that comprise *friends and family*.

In their attempts to position friendship and its social value, sociologists traditionally compare it to kinship (Allan, 1979; Pahl & Spencer, 2004; Willmott, 1987). For Graham Allan, the main difference is that friendships involve the ongoing evaluation of the relationship, whereas kinship is more fixed (1979, p. 30). This distinction reflects common understandings of friendship as voluntary, agentic, non-hierarchical, unregulated, and without expected roles. It is typical of sociological accounts to highlight the voluntary and reciprocal aspects of friendship, arguing that there is nothing beyond the relationship itself that makes it necessary (Allan, 1998). In other words, there is *no need* for friendship, but it is valuable nonetheless, as argued by C.S. Lewis (and echoed by many friendship scholars):

> I have no duty to be anyone's Friend, and no man in the world has a duty to be mine. No claims, no shadow of necessity. Friendship is unnecessary, like philosophy, like art, like the universe itself... It has no survival value; rather it is one of those things which give value to survival.
>
> (1960, 103)

As noted, Pahl and Spencer argue that "personal communities" – involving a mix of friends and family members – is a more useful concept for understanding contemporary relational intimacies (2004). They observe that relationships between family members are sometimes described as friend-like (e.g. if very close to a parent you might say you are "like best friends"), just as friends are increasingly described as one's family (2004). This suggests an erosion of traditional distinctions, which can also be seen in how friendships are performed and practised through social and digital media, where friends and family members are more horizontally arranged. While the concept of "personal communities" challenges the distinction between family and friends, it also reifies this binary, however, since these categories are used to differentiate one from the other, even when claiming their suffusion.

This co-dependent discourse of friends and family is also embedded in the concept of "families of choice" (Weston, 1991). Kath Weston highlights a lack of legal recognition (at the time of writing *Families We Choose*) for queer family structures, arguing that "just as representations are contestable, so nuclear families do not constitute the timeless core of what it means to have kin in this society" (1991, p. 7). Addressing the common vernacular of "chosen families", Weston challenges the biological underpinnings of a dominant discourse of care and nurture. She highlights a historically enduring reliance on friendship among LGBTQ+ people (1991) – all the more evident when considering histories of violence and discrimination that contour queer life, including the significant and compounding effects of social hostility, domestic violence, incarceration, medical interventions, and the HIV/AIDS epidemic. From their large-scale empirical study of "same-sex intimacies", Weeks et al. found that "Friends offer a barrier against hostility, a sense that you are part of an ongoing history, a school of manners and values, and a sense that there are others who are experiencing similar hopes and disappointments" (2001, p. 60). This highlights the strategic, reciprocal, and choice-based aspects of queer friendships. This work also conveys the significance of care roles and relationships among LGBTQ+ families, communities, and interpersonal relationships.

Like Lillian Faderman's work, Kath Weston's research on "families of choice" (1991) and Peter Nardi's work on gay male friendships (1999), have also challenged simple distinctions between sexual and friendship intimacies. But as Heather Love warns, much "families of choice" discussion romanticises friendship and avoids "the trouble and unease that are at the heart of friendship" (2007, p. 80). There has been less consistent academic attention to friendships in everyday heterosexual lives, though digital media researchers have suggested that friendship is becoming more central (boyd, 2008; 2014; Bucher, 2012).

Meanwhile, Sasha Roseneil is wary of applying a "families of choice" framework to queer friendships because of how this privileges kinship ties as the blueprint for all other forms of intimacy (2006). She argues that "what matters to people in terms of intimacy increasingly exceeds the category of 'family'" (2006, p. 339). Shelley Budgeon also challenges this hierarchy by insisting that our friendships influence how we understand other relationships, including family and romantic relationships (2006, p. 3). In other words, while notions of family, intimacy, loyalty, trust, love, etc. inform notions of friendship, this influence is bi-directional, and perhaps also multi-directional, given that we are navigating a range of intimate relationships at any given time (Budgeon, 2006). Our friendships, for example, influence our romantic and sexual relationships, and what we come to expect or want from these, as discussed in Chapter 4.

Together, Roseneil and Budgeon (2004) argue for a need to centre friendship intimacies in our academic and policy-based discussions of social life, and to expand beyond notions of "sexual/love relationships" that form our primary life narratives. They argue that a sociology of friendship enables the study of "the burgeoning diversity of contemporary practices of intimacy and care" (2004, p. 136). To date, most sociological discussions of friendship have not foregrounded friendship as a site of care, nor argued for policy reform that recognises friendship care, as Roseneil and Budgeon do. However, Anne Cronin's (2014) work on the emotions of friendship also centres care and its practice within friendships. Regarding workplace friendships, she challenges common arguments about friendship homophily, finding that "people were most likely to make friends with people who were different to them in terms of age, class and ethnicity" (2014, p. 75). Workplaces, she argues, "throw people together" (2014, p. 71), and the emotions that colleagues share in workplaces are what generate friendships in this environment, which in turn produce more emotions that strengthen the bonds of those friendships. Finding that workplace friendships offer both emotional and practical support, and that this assists in coping with workplace pressures, Cronin highlights the centrality of care in everyday friendship practices. The concept of being "thrown together" offers much potential to the consideration of particular digital spaces in which friendships develop.

Claudia Zitz et al. (2014) consider the central role of care in trans men's friendships, and how their creative and supportive roles respond to a range of social and community factors, including many trans men's re-orientations away from lesbian communities. Elsewhere, Verónica Policarpo (2017) centres the care aspects of friendships in Portugal, in the context of the economic after-effects of the 2008 global financial crisis. She found that care was synonymous with friendship for many of her participants and that even when family members were carers, this care was often conceptualised as friendship. While these are not the only examples of academic discussions of friendship care, it is noteworthy that explicit attention to this is uncommon. This is even true of digital media studies, where discussions of peer-based support groups are more dominant. Perhaps friendship care is seen as common and unremarkable. Yet, as Roseneil and Budgeon argue, friendship care warrants further analysis in the context of shifting social responsibilities and practices of support, and there is a real need for social and health policy to recognise and address this (2004).

Sociologists who are less oriented to feminist and queer theory tend to discuss the growing significance of friendship as a symptom of late modernity, citing theorists such as Ulrich Beck and Anthony Giddens. Arguments that friendships are becoming increasingly important due to socio-political infrastructure (including the break-down of families and welfare systems) suggest that friendship is necessitated by a socio-political climate in which "traditional family values" are in decline. Pahl, for example, argues that friends are increasingly "taking over various social tasks, duties and functions from family and kin" (2000, p. 8). Yet this suggests that friendship was less important until recent times, overlooking a longer history of friendship, and furthering the sociological bias in which friendship – particularly among women – was long overlooked. Claims about friendship's recent importance – despite it always existing, just never being researched – reference a denied consideration of the emotional and affective forces that embroil friendships, along with neglected attention to how these intimacies contour and give meaning to our everyday lives.

Many theorisations of late-modernity offer a top-down approach that casts our intimacies as effects of (or necessitated by) capitalism, neoliberalism, "the risk society", and other conceptual frameworks. Where such approaches examine our everyday practices and relationships, this is through the context of the "social conditions" (e.g. neoliberalism) that are the central focus of such research. Lacking here is attention to how everyday practices may co-opt strategies of late modernity or neoliberalism while still being critical of these forces. Others, such as Todd May, have claimed that friendships can cut against the grain of neoliberalism (2012). However, considering friendship as everyday practice that intersects with a range of strategies and tactics (Certeau, 1988) (i.e. forces from below, as much as above), we can develop a more rounded sense of what friendships contribute to and feel like, and the force they bring to our lives.

Discussions of friendship as voluntary, reciprocal, and without rules or structure (Allan, 1979; Pahl, 2000), suggest that friendship is malleable, open, and easy. These accounts suggest that friendships come and go with ease due to their lack of social obligation. These understandings are challenged by the empirical work of Carol Smart and colleagues who argue that because friendships provide ontological security they can be difficult to leave, and their dissolution can constitute a "break up" (2012). Smart et al. demonstrate that "movement in and out of friendship, just like degrees of closeness with kin, entails negotiation" (2012, p. 92). Further to this, when friendships are closely entwined with our self-identity (Anthony & McCabe, 2015), they cannot be abandoned without a sense of loss.

Friendship and popular culture

In the quote featuring in the previous section, C.S. Lewis states that friendship is unnecessary but adds value to life. This points to the common understanding that friendships are voluntary and that they improve and support us. Lewis explores friendship in the context of a "good Christian life" (1960), with this quote taken from his book *The Four Loves*, where he explores the four types of love discussed in Ancient Greece. He re-labels these as affection (previously storge, meaning love within families), friendship, eros, and charity (previously agape, now referring to love of God). He describes friendship as the "least natural" of these loves (1960). Like many others, he seeks to categorise and classify the types of love by giving them character and purpose. But he struggles with friendship, because it seems less natural, more peculiar, and our lives do not depend on it. He suggests that it is less valued now (than among "the Ancients") because fewer people experience it.

Several decades later, in another popular text, the Spice Girls tell a different story. Here are five friends, each one different from the next, but together they comprise a collective: the pop group. Friendship was their schtick, and perhaps the key ingredient that captured the imagination of millions of fans, from teenage girls to adult men. Friendship coded the band's identity through each member's complementary characteristics, a rhetoric of "girl power" and lyrics about solidarity. This solidarity permeated their interviews and public appearances as much as their lyrics, as found in the chorus of "Wannabe": "if you wanna be my lover, you gotta get with my friends". This positions romance as secondary to friendship, with romantic love being contingent on whether someone passes "the friend test". This lyric and song – along with the Spice Girls image, fan culture, and media narratives, suggested shifting attitudes to friendship in the 1990s – when everyday digital media communication started to take hold.

Comparing the words of C.S. Lewis (a serious philosophical man of letters) with those of the Spice Girls (a mass-marketed pop group) might be read as poor scholarship. A common tendency to situate pop culture's artefacts as trivial and base is as old as Theodor Adorno, but "low theory" (Halberstam, 2011) offers significant value when we account for what we know and how it might be known. Regardless of genre, taste, and generational differences (though these are important), what exists in these references are narratives that resonate with and give voice to our values. The historical moment that gave us the Spice Girls also generated other texts and sentiments about friendship as a primary social relationship ahead of all others – a narrative we have increasingly seen in popular culture texts that punctuate and circulate our digital media use. This is particularly the case for friendships among young women and girls (Crowley, 2010; Dobson, 2012), as also evident in meme culture (Kanai, 2017). As for the Spice Girls, it seems they maintained their central focus on friendship to the very end, as per the chorus of their final song, "Headlines (Friendship Never Ends)":

> And if I lost my way you'd carry me home
> Take me all the way to heaven, never leave me alone
> And it's just like everything matters when you are near

What could be read as a typical love song is about love between friends. Yet, this ambiguity is not new. A discourse of friendship as love features throughout many historical texts (see Faderman, 1981), including religious texts. One example is the biblical story of David and Jonathan, which speaks of the strength and passion of a friendship between two men. Today it reads as incredibly romantic, as per this excerpt:

> the soul of Jonathan was knit to the soul of David, and Jonathan loved him as his own soul … . Then Jonathan made a covenant with David, because he loved him as his own soul. And Jonathan stripped himself of the robe that was on him and gave it to David, and his armor, and even his sword and his bow and his belt.

Moving forward some centuries, we might find ourselves watching *Broad City* – a television sitcom based in New York, centring on the friendship of Abbi and Ilana. As best friends, Abbi and Ilana make sense. But neither character would be interesting, likeable, nor coherent outside of the context of their friendship. They date people, but the strongest bond lies between them. As with Jonathan and David (and perhaps the Spice Girls), there is also a queerness to their mutual affection, particularly told through Ilana's obsession with all that Abbi is and does. The opening scene of the series is a video chat between the two friends, in which Abbi (and the viewer) eventually realise that Ilana is having sex with her boyfriend while chatting. Ilana's boyfriend is loved but is not central to who she is – "this is purely physical" she tells him, after her video chat with Abbi ends. He accepts that Ilana's primary relationship is with her best friend, as do all other characters, offering us a world in which a friendship can shape our lives more than sexual intimacy.

Other scholars have also noted the value of popular culture texts to consider contemporary ideals of friendship, including discussion of the sitcom *Friends*. Pahl argued that "[t]hose in the Western world who so avidly watch the TV soap *Friends* pick up new styles and modes of friendship" (2000, p. 2). Echoing this, Roseneil argues that popular culture is well ahead of sociologists in their engagements with diverse practices of intimacy, care, and friendship (2006, p. 334). She notes that *Friends* depicted "a generation which is constructing its lives *outside* mid-twentieth-century notions of heterosexual intimate relationships" (2006, p. 337). Popular texts that centre friendship are more common than ever and constitute many of the most popular TV series today. This speaks to how we increasingly live our lives, as much as it references our relational aspirations.

My approach to friendship builds upon Roseneil's discussions (2004; 2006), including her attention to the value of queer and feminist approaches for understanding contemporary forms of friendship. Further to arguing that we must look beyond the heterosexual couple as a model for understanding intimacy, Roseneil states that "A lesson from queer theory is that we should resist the tendency to trivialize, infantilize and subordinate relationships which are not clear parallels of the conventional, stable, long-term, cohabiting heterosexual couple" (2004, p. 411). A similar argument can extend to digital friendships – that they too should not be trivialised because they seem less real, less important, and less secure than how friendship was conceptualised by past philosophers and theorists.

Friendships and social media

While this book draws more from sociological than psychological perspectives, few studies from either discipline, to date, have offered complex accounts of everyday friendship intimacies. Further still, these disciplines offer limited discussion of the integration of friendship and digital media practices. A multi-disciplinary approach is, therefore, necessary. A contemporary sociological focus on emotions, along with the "affective turn" in cultural studies, offer much to the study of friendship.

There have been countless research discussions of friendship and social and digital media, particularly relating to young people. Friendship has been discussed and contextualised throughout decades of research on online communities, social networking, mobile phones, and specific platform cultures (e.g. Facebook). Commonly, friendship is approached as a relationship that contours young people's social media practices, just as it contours their everyday lives. Many researchers account for how friendships are practised in digital spaces, sometimes compared to how they are practised "offline". Many also frame social and digital media as tools that extend existing (or "offline") friendship practices, further highlighting friendship's importance for young people's identities, connections, and support. Social media can allow friendship's continuation when geographic or emotional distances grow, such as when a friend moves away, when friends move from school to university, or from university to the workforce, or when friends simply drift apart. Friendships can be reignited too, through locating "old friends" in social media and reconstituting "idle social relationships" (Lüders, 2009). Friendship has been discussed in relation to specific platforms and how they position, prioritise, and categorise friend-based connections (boyd, 2006). Social media can also be used to find new friends, though this is less commonly researched. There has also been discussion on how friendships develop through social media, and how platform-based connections can enable the transformation of weak ties (Haythornthwaite, 2005) into close friendships, based on what is shared and discussed.

Despite frequent emphasis that friendship is freely chosen and practised, as discussed, there are some obvious limitations to this claim. As Allan and Adams argue, friendships are "none the less shaped by contextual factors that lie outside the direct control of particular individuals" (1998, p. 183). In other words, friendships are circumstantial and socially constrained and are not a matter of simply choosing anyone, anywhere, to befriend. Traditionally, friendships have formed through persistent social interactions such as among school/university peers or co-workers (Cronin, 2014; Madge et al., 2009; Rumens, 2016; West et al., 2009). Theorisation of friendship up until the 1990s (but also beyond) emphasises friendship as a face-to-face encounter – as something built and practised in shared physical space. This perspective has stubbornly persisted in many recent accounts of young people's friendships.

Social media use among young people is centrally oriented to friendship, as many researchers have demonstrated (boyd, 2006; 2008; Robards, 2012). As Brady Robards notes of popular social media platforms, "without a critical mass of known contacts on a particular social network site, its functions have no utility" (2012, 392). Since early social networking on platforms such as MySpace and Facebook, researchers consistently found that young people were using social media to connect with existing friends rather than to communicate with strangers or to seek new friends (Ellison et al., 2007; Livingstone & Brake, 2010). This research also highlighted the significance of "weak ties" (Hawthornthwaite, 2005) – where digitally connected acquaintances carry the potential for friendships to develop at a later stage. This aspect of social media "friending" complicates a sense that one is either a friend or an acquaintance, or is either part of one's "personal community" or not. In social media environments, friendships can take on more ambiguous forms, and latent/weak ties have expanded our friendship networks in ways that could not happen without social media platforms. Further to this, many Facebook friends might also be past friends – e.g. school friends who no longer engage with each other or think of each other as friends, yet there is still "a friendship". Sites such as Facebook are critiqued for weakening friendship on the basis that all connections are deemed friends (Blatterer, 2015, pp. 41–45), but young people do not lose sight of friendship diversities that offer a range of intimacies (Livingstone, 2008). As per focus group discussions in Chapter 3, young people differentiate friendships, using terms like "Facebook friends" or "friends you don't talk to", as opposed to "friend friends", for example.

The remainder of this section considers key literature on young people's social media friendship practices alongside examples of empirical data from the *Scrolling Beyond Binaries* (SBB) study (see Introduction chapter for study details). Baylee was an interview participant in this study, aged 17, female, bisexual, and city based, who described her Facebook friends as a broad network, as was common among participants:

> So I have a lot of friends from school on my Facebook page, from multiple schools from when I was in New Zealand and from here. I've got a lot of family on my page … . And I also have a lot of people I've just met in general, I guess, like at different events and things.

Older interview participants from SBB noted the changing function of Facebook over the years, which was initially felt to be a more enclosed space for friends to semi-publicly interact, much like MySpace that preceded it. But as the platform increased in popularity, Facebook friends came to include family, work colleagues, and a larger number of acquaintances and latent ties. Following this, many users were less likely to be too personal or too flippant about what they shared on Facebook. Some participants expressed nostalgia for "old Facebook" that seemed more friend based and fun. Like many participants, Alice, aged 34, who is lesbian, and based in regional Queensland, noted her acute awareness of the diversity of her Facebook friends. This limited the content she would share: "I think you can potentially lose friendships too by potentially putting the wrong thing up".

Baylee described Facebook content as more "official" and "a little bit more conservative" than Instagram content, which she considered as more personal. She suggested that Facebook was more commonly used for sharing information and news. Cami, aged 22, who is genderfluid, queer, and pansexual, and based in regional New South Wales, also associated Facebook with news. They also saw it as a site for photo-sharing, but nothing too personal:

> I use the Facebook Messenger on my phone a lot to keep in contact with my girlfriend and my friends and I have group chats with my sisters and stuff. And I just use it otherwise to keep up to date with news and current events and see the photos that my friends are posting. And if I go on a holiday or whatever I tend to post those onto Facebook.

Like other participants, Cami also shared and accessed information about the marriage equality movement through Facebook (a dominant national issue at the time of our interviews, in 2016). Elsewhere, Drew, aged 21, who is genderfluid, pansexual, and city based, describes sharing their gender identity to friends on Facebook. Before doing so, they ensured that these posts were hidden from family members:

> I have also made a few posts in the past sort of telling people, "Hey this is what I identify as. These are my pronouns. I would really like it you could please use them". but I've specifically gone into the privacy settings of those and made it so my family members can't see it.

Like other participants, Drew used "friend lists" on Facebook to ensure that more personal posts about their gender and sexuality were not visible to everyone, particularly family members. This platform affordance of audience curation (Hanckel et al., 2019) suggests that Facebook can still feel private, friend-based, and supportive for many young people, including LGBTQ+ young people who can share personal details in safer ways. Yet, nobody spoke of their Facebook disclosures as casual or easy, and there was much concern and pre-planning to ensure things would not go badly. Alex, for example, a city-based trans woman aged 32, who describes her sexuality as "open", timed her announcement (about transitioning) with going on holidays, where she could feel less concerned should there be any fallout:

> And it was also synchronised with the time that I went away with my sister on the three week holiday in New Zealand. So I effectively posted that at the airport when I was getting on the plane to go overseas. Because it was almost like a "I don't care how people react I'm going overseas" moment.

Both Alex and Drew received positive responses to coming out on Facebook. Jasmine, aged 26, who is lesbian and city based, "came out" as trans to her family first, prior to coming out to her broader Facebook networks. Unlike Drew, however, Jasmine did not filter her audience:

> I did a post on Facebook after I came out to my family and I was considerably surprised the amount of people who were supportive. Especially some people at church who I never expected to be supportive and they were amazing.

Experiences like these, as well as experiences of less positive reactions (e.g. Cami states: "my straight sister turned around to me and was like 'Why would you put that on Facebook?'"), remind us that we can never fully predict who sees our social media posts and what responses will follow. These concerns highlight the risks of posting, and these risks are no doubt greater when the information we share is more personal, more stigmatised, or more likely to be met with negative judgement. As well as coming out about one's gender or sexual identity, this can include discussions of mental health. For Colin, a city-based gay man aged 27, this happened through sharing a link to his blog on Facebook. He says, "I wouldn't really say anything about it, but I'd just be like okay, there you go. You can engage with it if you want. Or you don't have to". He had been quietly blogging about his anxiety before he decided to share the link on Facebook. For Colin, blogging assisted his recovery from being hit by a car, helping him deal with physical trauma and subsequent anxiety. He described his blog as "very blunt, where it's like 'these are all the fucked things that have happened to me'". The response from sharing his blog link on Facebook was positive and helped with his healing:

> I had lots of my friends – and the people who were sort of tangentially my friends – contact me and be like "thank you so much for talking about this. I also have anxiety, I don't know how to deal with it", all this kind of stuff … . It was great to be able to feel like, because for me it was totally at that point for myself. I didn't really care if anyone was reading it. It was part of me going through this experience, me journaling it, and being like "get this shit out of me". But as for people engaging with it, and going "fuck, thank you for talking about this" – [that] was really good.

Social media use has expanded friendship's practices, meanings, and dimensions, and the above examples demonstrate new experiments in sharing, supporting, and feeling supported through single acts of disclosure to one's broad networks. Such disclosures operate quite differently from telling a single friend or a small group of friends or telling friends *in person*. While some participants discussed keeping their health matters more private (Alice: "I think it can be quite dangerous to put too much information up on there") or preferences for sharing to smaller groups of friends offline or in private chat groups, those who publicly shared "personal information" about health, gender, or sexuality, generally reported positive experiences. For many, this brought a sense of relief and validation, and more awareness of having a support network that comprises a range of friends, close and distant, from a variety of social contexts. And among these friends were some who have had relatable experiences, or who may themselves feel supported by those disclosures and the intimacy they offer.

A diversification of friendship networks and communication styles has not diluted the value of friendships for everyday support but has seemingly broadened the scope of friendship care for these participants. Having a diversity of friendships and digital networks with whom to engage across many platforms and locations, suggests that for many young people, friendships are more present and pervasive in daily life than for previous generations of young people. There is still a tendency for young people to talk about "close friends", but interestingly, support can be found from friends who are more peripheral but are having similar experiences. Further, social media affords public disclosures that not only feel liberating through their release but also tend to generate a high volume of support along with a sense of being seen, heard, and cared for (at least for our participants). Personal announcements via a "status update" could generate a greater sense of solidarity, particularly when one is experiencing difficulties or feeling vulnerable.

The visibility of friendship networks on Facebook has been noted as a key feature of the platform since its beginning (boyd, 2006; boyd & Ellison, 2007). This visibility did not begin with Facebook, which referenced and built upon earlier social media platforms such as Friendster and MySpace. Yet there were some differences between these platforms, in terms of how visible a user wanted their interactions to be (boyd & Ellison, 2007). As boyd and Ellison note, "Structural variations around visibility and access are one of the primary ways that [social networking sites] differentiate themselves from each other" (2007, p. 213). In writing about Friendster (launched in 2003, ahead of Facebook), boyd notes how "friendship lists" were broader than one's friends: "The types of relations people included varied immensely as did the motivations for including certain people but not others" (boyd, 2006). Beyond already being friends or acquaintances, boyd's young research participants gave a number of other reasons for friending. This included feeling obliged to accept friend requests; gaining access to other people's profiles, broader networks, and friend-only features (such as other users' personal blogs); seeming more popular; and being more visibly affiliated with certain fandom communities (2006). In other words, early social media platforms that centred on friendships instigated a variety of connections, and within this, a shared acknowledgement among young people that social media friendships were not necessarily indicative of friendships, yet they could be strategically used to demonstrate affiliations and interests to gain access and insight into other people's lives and networks, or to be generative of future friendships. In such platforms, the term "friends" might stand in for "networked others". A new vernacular of "friending" has emerged to become common today, but "friending" has broader meaning and associations, beyond becoming friends.

As boyd notes, social media friending is akin to community building (2006). Friending or "following" other people on a range of platforms initiates a form of intimacy that can be generative of friendship – often in ways, and with speed, that does not happen offline. As boyd notes, "If someone seems interesting or you want to get to know them better, what's the loss in Friending them?" (2006). Once again, this highlights the role of weak ties and a familiar potential to build and strengthen relationships through connecting and interacting on social media. This practice speaks to the anticipatory pleasures of fostering new connections, while not yet knowing the strength or importance such connections may take. This new creative practice of friendship and community-building echoes the creativity of friendship intimacies that Foucault speaks of (discussed earlier in this chapter).

Early research on young people's social media friendships often focuses on the performance, display, and enactments of friendship, with less discussion about how social media practices and friendships may co-constitute each other. Arguably, a common theoretical connection to Goffman's work on performativity, and thinking through social media with reference to a front stage self-presentation as opposed to a back-stage self, produced limitations on how friendship would be discussed – mostly conceptualised as one's audience. This analytical perspective also prioritised an individualistic analysis of social media use ahead of considering these as spaces for producing new modes of interaction and collective intimacies beyond simple roles of performer/audience. For example, Julia Davies draws upon Goffman's work to ask, "Does Facebook offer new ways of friendship management?" (2012), suggesting that social media primarily offer a mode of administration. But as José van Dijck argues, "It is a common fallacy ... to think of platforms as merely facilitating networking activities; instead, the construction of platforms and social practices is mutually constitutive" (2013). As such, friendship has shaped social media platforms and cultures, as much as social media contribute to the changing landscape of friendship.

Arguably, social media have not only altered our vernacular of friendship (or our administration of them) but have furthered our sense of friendship access. For example, indirect communication to a pool of friends can generate support when needed, along with an ongoing comfort in knowing that friends are always within reach, present and listening. Not only close friends, but broader social networks have become more accessible when we require attention, support, validation, and care. Through social media, we are also finding ways to bring our friends together, enfolding and partitioning our personal communities, and bringing some friends closer while keeping others at a distance. This is particularly useful for dealing with more private or sensitive matters, or for finding personal support without sharing our emotional journeys or struggles with everyone.

Much social media research with young people suggests a utilitarian approach to communication technology, whereby we consider how media is used to communicate with friends, or what friend-based communication is made possible by a particular platform or device. This positions social media as tools. But often we use these media without specific intention – to simply browse, chat, re-blog, etc. Behavioralist approaches to media practices, however, often ask which behaviours are *caused* by social media use. This generates methods that capture and measure media use, inevitably reducing digital communication to particular techniques used for particular goals. Missing here is an array of contrasting accounts of how people conceptualise their use of, connection to, and feelings about, digital media. For example, research on young people's use of Snapchat for the sharing of ephemeral and mundane moments (Bayer et al., 2016) challenges such approaches through their attention to affect, boredom, and play. Unfortunately, research that neglects the affective dimensions of social media interactions continues to seek scientific understandings of how humans use digital technologies to communicate – i.e. What is the point of this platform? How does it serve the communicative needs of its users? Little is said about users' friendship needs or friendship as an affective force that orients our digital media practices.

Changing modes of friendship

Like all social media platforms, Facebook is changing over time – not just its interface and what it offers to users, but its cultural practices. Like all platforms, this is a dynamic space. This is obvious when we think about the range of platforms we use today, and how we take up, adapt to, and modify our use of platforms, as we move between them. A polymedia approach (Madianou & Miller, 2013) understands that the use of a particular platform (such as Facebook) is not isolated from other media use but exists in a networked media ecology. While participants in the previous section often felt uncomfortable about having broad networks on Facebook, fostering hesitancy before posting private thoughts or details, they also acknowledged other spaces where they were more likely to do so, such as Tumblr, Instagram, and Snapchat. Many participants suggested that Facebook was for presenting a more palatable version of self, since family and distant others would be seeing and judging you there. But Facebook used to be more private. For example, Anne West et al. engaged with undergraduate students in London in the earlier years of Facebook to find that most were uncomfortable about "friending parents" as this would challenge their online privacy, be felt as a form of surveillance, and open them to the risk of embarrassment if their parents start interacting with them and their friends (2009). While some of West et al.'s participants friended their parents, common concerns about privacy suggested that this was understood as a safe space when it centred on friendship and excluded parents. In my recent interviews, young people have indicated that it is now common to friend one's parents and other family members on Facebook. Therefore, many participants were unlikely to share personal information, or much information at all, compared to earlier Facebook users, as per West et al.'s participants (2009). In focus groups I facilitated with young people (16–22 years) in 2012 (discussed in Chapter 3), participants were still sharing a lot of content via their Facebook wall (available to friends, and perhaps also friends of friends or the general public, depending on their privacy settings), but this too seems outdated and distant from (Australian) young people's current Facebook practices, which is more oriented to using Messenger, Events features, and browsing and liking with little public sharing or interaction.

Implicit in much literature on social media networks is a sense that "close friends" are typically the people in our everyday lives who we engage with in person. This sense is also present among young people I interview, although many note that a close friendship does not always need this. Sam, aged 19, who is non-binary, bisexual, and lives in a city, discussed having a close friend who they have hardly met "in real life":

> Probably one of my closest friends, I think to date we've only met in real life four times, but it would be maybe four or five years now but we speak pretty much every day via Messenger and we find that we really get along. We share a lot of opinions and we use each other for support in a lot of ways. We are very close but we don't actually physically see each other a lot, just because we don't find that we need that for our relationship.

When we asked SBB participants to imagine their lives without social media, most did not enjoy this thought. Participants stated that this would challenge and reduce their friendships since they would have fewer ways to connect with friends and so would likely lose touch with many. These responses highlight the ongoing central role of friendship in social media – perhaps more central on account of a broader ecology of platforms through which to engage with friends privately, publicly, and in groups. This also emerged in participant discussions of how they "took residence" in particular platforms. More often than not, it was a friend who introduced participants to new platforms, or it was a case of most friends moving there, in a migratory sense. For example, some participants mentioned friendship-group migrations from Tumblr to Twitter. Others mentioned earlier group movements from LiveJournal to MySpace, and then from MySpace to Facebook. Along with such movements (see also Robards, 2012) comes a sense of history, nostalgia, and reminiscing that pervades a lot of current social media interactions (e.g. Tumblr nostalgia on Reddit and Twitter), and these remembrances are part of maintaining current digital friendships through shared histories of platform belonging and participation.

Missing from this chapter so far is a sense of the possible negative aspects of social media friendships. Largely, young people report on friendship as positive, though there were stories where friendships went bad, or became difficult, and where social media are seen to complicate friendships and friend break-ups. In the SBB survey, friendship difficulties emerged when we asked, "Have you ever felt rejected, excluded, or both from a community through social media?" If participants answered yes, they were invited to tell us more. Here, friends were sometimes discussed as problematic, homophobic, transphobic, or participating in forms of exclusion and bullying. Many of these stories are school based:

> My old friend group openly excluded me from group chats, where they bitched about me (that, they denied, but someone who left the group

not long before me sent me screenshots), which was some of the biggest rejection I have received on the internet. (17, female, bisexual)

[In] My friendship group … . One girl decided she hated me and cut me out of everything. (20, trans male/non-binary, queer)

I once saw a gay friend post some "joke" about bisexuality and it just reinvigorated a sense of rejection from the gay community. (17, female, bisexual)

Friendship hurt and disappointment ranged from participants' straight friends rejecting or misunderstanding them, their LGBTQ+ friends being hurtful or silencing (commonly relating to bisexuality or asexuality), not being invited to events but seeing these events play out on social media, and being excluded from friend-based group chats. Some also reported feeling hurt by being "unfriended" on social media for what seemed like an insignificant reason.

These examples demonstrate that friendship is not always wonderful and supportive and that friends can disappoint us, turn on us, or become hostile. The emphasised value and importance of friendship across the SBB data foregrounds not only our experiences of friendship but also our expectations of friendship care and support. Therefore, the hurt from bad friendship experiences is noteworthy and can be felt as more horrible and defining than the hurt experienced within other kinds of relationships, such as from unknown trolls. For many, visible exclusions through social media interactions generate a reassessment of the friendship – where friends become "supposed friends" or "people I considered friends". This is perhaps unremarkable, given our own memories of school-based friendships. Yet, these are also experiences of LGBTQ+ young people, for whom school-based friendships can take on greater significance in the context of broader exclusions and the difficulties they may face in family environments.

Across these data, it is evident that for many participants, their experiences of friendship have been intense, in both volatile and uplifting ways. But above all, friendships have been vital for the everyday support, care, and enjoyment they offer. Social media, and the ability to connect with friends beyond one's school or immediate environment, have had a significant impact, and not only for LGBTQ+ young people.

It is notable that research participants would, at times, present binary notions of online/offline, and suggest that online friendships were less nourishing, real, or supportive. These sentiments regularly emerged yet were not consistently presented. Sometimes this emerged as a sense of nostalgia for pre-digital connections and interactions that now seem more authentic. For example, Jackie, aged 28, who is female, queer, and city based, contextualised support as more than simply "liking" somebody's social media posts, but actually "turning up" and "spending time" together, as though social media interactions did not require much time or commitment:

If you liked something you would say to someone "I really like that". Or if you wanted to support somebody, instead of liking something, you might actually turn up to spend time with them or go to a thing that they're doing to show your support.

Friendship as affective practice

Much of what we "know" about friendship is presented in neutral terms, as though all people understand, practice, and value friendship in the same way. When simply understood as a voluntary, reciprocal, and interest-based relationship between two like-minded individuals, friendships' peculiarities are flattened. Anyone who has friends knows that friendships differ from one person or group to the next, and what makes some friendships work could destroy others. Seemingly there are as many styles of friendship as there are friends.

Following Aristotle's lead, friends are commonly understood as *people like us*, or *our people*, and sociologists have spent time testing this theory, noting that friendships rarely emerge between people of different social classes (Cronin, 2014). While this work offers useful clarity on the social conditions of friendship, a top-down theoretical approach (still typically informed by comparing friendship to kinship), limits the questions we can put to friendship, and fails to engage with the detours, expansions, and creative enterprises that friendships entail. This is particularly the case with *queer friendships*, including friendships that are queered regardless of the gender/sexuality of those involved. It might be said that social media itself queers friendships through disrupting the ways we have typically understood and practised it.

Throughout this book, I approach friendship at the level of everyday practice to consider its affective complexities, rather than presenting it as a stable concept. Frameworks offered by and since Aristotle are still pervasive, but we should be dubious about universalising principles that simplify vast experiences of having and being friends. Considering younger people's friendships, we should take care to listen for difference. We should also consider how digital media have invested in and exemplified friendships, and how they continue to inform and host friendship practices. Without doing so, we miss much, including how friendships generate expertise (see Chapter 3), how friendships can be sexually intimate (see Chapter 4), how friendship is practised among unknown peers (see Chapter 5), and where friendships arise through negotiating dating/hook-up apps (see Chapter 6).

Drawing from Foucault's theorisation of friendships among gay men (2000c), Tom Roach further considers the creative and political potential of friendship, stating that "In its very nature it is anti-institutional" (2012, p. 13). Sasha Roseneil also states that "right across the disciplines ... as a non-institutionalized, particularistic, affective relationship, friendship has historically been marginal to dominant themes and perspectives" (2006, pp. 324–325). Being non-institutionalised, or anti-institutional, friendships offer freedoms and creative potential that are less easily found in more formalised relationships. This freedom affords a range of friendship practices, including friendships that are sexual (as Foucault discusses), or friendships that cut across class, generations, genders, and other differences often seen as more stratified. Digital meeting spaces can further support contact across difference, where shared interests can be connection points regardless of age, gender, race, sexuality, ability, and more. Friendship's flexibility is part of its practice and being less socially ascribed than marriage and kinship ties, friendships have less defined roles. There are fewer rules as to how friendships should operate, with no clearly discernible affective norms. However, there are constraints that make friendships difficult, given how friendship bonds entwine with our sense of self (Smart et al., 2012).

It is necessary to not only explore what friendships do but also how they feel. More so, we must consider how, together, the affective and practical aspects of friendship organise, situate, challenge, and support young people in their everyday lives. The practice and emotion of friendship is social, and this sociality is evident through our digital media practices, where we emote and relate and contextualise ourselves among friends. Throughout this book I position friendship as a defining and affective aspect of young people's lives that has expanded care and its everyday practice.

As noted, historical understandings of friendship have been guided not just by class and culture (typically White cultures), but also by gender and sexuality, as per the dominant voices of affluent and scholarly White men who have carried on a long tradition of romanticising friendships among like-minded men. With a dominant focus on men's homosocial relations, here and throughout much of history, discussion of women's and/or queer friendships is quite recent. Yet literature emerging from gay and lesbian scholarship, and their re-inscription of families as voluntary, friend-based, and intensely supportive, have helped to consider friendship's creativity among and beyond contemporary queer subjects. Importantly, queer and feminist scholarship and its broader project of dismantling and challenging accepted ways of knowing (ourselves and our histories) have been pivotal in bringing friendship into focus.

Throughout historical struggles – among women, queers, Indigenous and ethnic minority groups, for example – spaces of belonging are necessarily forged, and friendship bonds are arguably much tighter and more enduring than in friendships among White, male, heterosexuals. The latter subject may have less need for strong friendships. Accordingly, such a subject may be less self-reflexive – a practice that is extended and supported by friendship (Roach, 2012). Being gay, or being a woman, or being brown, for example, one is often made aware of these "differences", making us consider where we belong. A positive aspect of this social imposition is our greater likelihood of creating strong friendship ties and solidarities (Banerjea et al., 2018; Piepzna-Samarasinha, 2018).

Platformed modes of friendship (whether on Facebook, Instagram, Snapchat, or elsewhere), can ensure that care and support are at-hand, more so than in non-digital settings. Much support offered on social media is also publicly given and "on the record", disrupting notions of friendship as private, dyadic interactions. This signals the need to consider friendship not simply as a *relationship*, but as *practice* – one that is witnessed, celebrated, learnt from, and adopted among countless digital networks, between individuals and among groups.

Importantly, social media platforms are successfully used to amplify our personal experiences and disclosures, often generating the sense of a wide support network. This is evident in Colin's experience of sharing his blog about anxiety and coming to realise that many of his Facebook friends, including distant friends, faced similar struggles. As well as offering an opportunity for Colin to find support, this disclosure offered space for others to also share their experiences and difficulties. This reciprocal sharing expands the friendship bonds and intimacies of those involved. Further to this, witnessing such sharing can build young people's knowledge and expertise about what emotions and disclosures can produce and enable in terms of friendship, care, and support. It may also offer space to develop friendships with family members and other unlikely friends.

While we do not primarily sign up to social media platforms for support and care, these are the practices we tend to find and commit to in our use of these media, as per friendship and its orientations. These contour our engagements with a range of platforms and platform-based interactions, and whether we contextualise these interactions through friendship or not, this may be inconsequential. As noted, it is perhaps more useful to think of friendship as the structuring force of many social media platforms, where all interactions suggest the practice of friendship.

When talking about young people's friendships as a key site of learning about and negotiating health and wellbeing, there is much academic slippage between discussions of friends and peers. The next chapter considers the term peers – how it is used and to what effect, taking up the question: "what do we know about peers?" That chapter will particularly focus on health research discussions of friends and peers, considering how we might differentiate these terms, while attending to their ambiguity. It considers how these terms are applied to our understandings of young people's health and wellbeing practices and how digital media practices have disrupted already unstable distinctions between young people's friends and peers.

Notes

1 See books VIII and IX of Aristotle's (1906) *Nicomachean Ethics*.
2 The latter is sometimes translated as "perfect friendship" or "virtue friendship".
3 This hierarchy was not Plato's but was developed more recently.
4 Luce Irigaray's (2002) *To Speak Is Never Neutral* is a good start.

References

Adams, R. G., & Allan, G. (1998). *Placing friendship in context*. Cambridge: Cambridge University Press.

Allan, G. (1979). *A sociology of Friendship and kinship*. London: Allen Press & Unwin.

Allan, G. (1998). Friendship, sociology and social structure. *Journal of Social and Personal Relationships, 15*(5), 685–702.

Allan, G., & Adams, R. G. (1998). Reflections on context. In R. G. Adams & G. Allan (Eds.), *Placing friendship in context* (pp. 183–194). Cambridge: Cambridge University Press.

Anthony, A. K., & McCabe, J. (2015). Friendship talk as identity work: Defining the self through friend relationships. *Symbolic Interaction, 38*(1), 64–82.

Aristotle (1906). *The Nicomachean ethics of Aristotle*. (F. H. Peters, Trans.). (10th ed.). London: Kegan Paul.

Bakardjieva, M. (2014). Social media and the McDonaldization of friendship. *Communications, 39*(4), 369–387.

Banerjea, N., Dasgupta, D., Dasgupta, R. K., & Grant, J. M. (2018). *Friendship as social justice activism: Critical solidarities in a global perspective*. London: Seagull Publications Books.

Bayer, J. B., Ellison, N. B., Schoenebeck, S. Y., & Falk, E. B. (2016). Sharing the small moments: Ephemeral social interaction on Snapchat. *Information, Communication and Society, 19*(7), 956–977.

Baym, N. (2015). *Personal connections in the digital age* (2nd ed.). Cambridge: Polity Press.

Blatterer, H. (2015). *Everyday friendships: Intimacy as freedom in a complex world*. Basingstoke: Palgrave Macmillan.

boyd, d. (2006). Friends, Friendsters, and MySpace top 8: Writing community into being on social network sites. *First Monday, 11*(12).

boyd, d. (2008). Why youth ♥ social network sites: The role of networked publics in teenage social life. In D. Buckingham (Ed.), *The John D. and Catherine T. MacArthur foundation series on digital media and learning* (pp. 119–142). Cambridge: MIT Press.

boyd, d. (2014). *It's complicated: The social lives of networked teens*. New Haven, CT: Yale University Press.

boyd, d., & Ellison, N. (2007). Social network sites: Definition, history, and scholarship. *Journal of Computer-Mediated Communication, 13*(1), 210–230.

Bucher, T. (2012). The friendship assemblage: Investigating programmed sociality on Facebook. *Television and New Media, 14*(6), 479–493.

Budgeon, S. (2006). Friendship and formations of sociality in late modernity: The challenge of "post traditional intimacy". *Sociological Research Online, 11*(3).

Certeau de, M. (1988). *The practice of everyday life*. Berkeley, CA: University of California Press.

Chasin, C. J. D., & Radtke, H. L. (2013). "Friend Moments": A discursive study of friendship. *Qualitative Research in Psychology, 10*(3), 274–297.

Cocking, D., & Matthews, S. (2000). Unreal friends. *Ethics and Information Technology, 2*(4), 223–231.

Cronin, A. M. (2014). Between friends: Making emotions intersubjectively. *Emotion, Space and Society, 10*, 71–78.

Crowley, M. S. (2010). How r u??? Lesbian and bi-identified youth on MySpace. *Journal of Lesbian Studies, 14*(1), 52–60.

Davies, J. (2012). Facework on Facebook as a new literacy practice. *Computers and Education, 59*(1), 19–29.

Dobson, A. S. (2012). "Individuality is everything": "Autonomous" femininity in MySpace mottos and self-descriptions. *Continuum, 26*(3), 371–383.

Donzelot, J. (1997). *The policing of families.* Baltimore, MD: The Johns Hopkins University Press.

Ellison, N. B., Steinfield, C., & Lampe, C. (2007). The benefits of Facebook "friends:" social capital and college students' use of online social network sites. *Journal of Computer-Mediated Communication, 12*(4), 1143–1168.

Emerson, R. W. (1987). *The essays of Ralph Waldo Emerson.* Cambridge: Harvard University Press.

Faderman, L. (1981). *Surpassing the love of men: Romantic friendship and love between women from the renaissance to the present.* New York, NY: Morrow.

Foucault, M. (2000a). The social triumph of the sexual will. In P. Rabinow (Ed.), *Ethics, subjectivity and truth: Essential works of Foucault 1954–1984* (pp. 157–162). London: Penguin Books.

Foucault, M. (2000b). Sex, power, and the politics of identity. In P. Rabinow (Ed.), *Ethics, subjectivity and truth: Essential works of Foucault 1954–1984* (pp. 163–173). London: Penguin Books.

Foucault, M. (2000c). Friendship as a way of life (J. Johnston, Trans.). In P. Rabinow (Ed.), *Ethics, subjectivity and truth: Essential works of Foucault 1954–1984* (pp. 135–140). London: Penguin Books.

Halberstam, J. (2011). *The queer art of failure.* Durham & London: Duke University Press.

Hanckel, B., Vivienne, S., Byron, P., Robards, B., & Churchill, B. (2019). "That's not necessarily for them": LGBTIQ+ young people, social media platform affordances and identity curation. *Media, Culture and Society, 41*(8), 1261–1278

Haythornthwaite, C. (2005). Social networks and Internet connectivity effects. *Information, Communication and Society, 8*(2), 125–147.

Irigaray, L. (2002). *To speak is never neutral.* London: Continuum.

Kaliarnta, S. (2016). Using Aristotle's theory of friendship to classify online friendships: A critical counterview. *Ethics and Information Technology, 18*(2), 65–79.

Kanai, A. (2017). Girlfriendship and sameness: Affective belonging in a digital intimate public. *Journal of Gender Studies, 26*(3), 293–306

Lewis, C. S. (1960). *The four loves: The much beloved exploration of the nature of love.* New York, NY: Harcourt Publishers.

Livingstone, S. (2008). Taking risky opportunities in youthful content creation: Teenagers' use of social networking sites for intimacy, privacy and self-expression. *New Media and Society, 10*(3), 393–411.

Livingstone, S., & Brake, D. R. (2010). On the rapid rise of social networking sites: New findings and policy implications. *Children and Society, 24*(1), 75–83.

Love, H. (2007). *Feeling backward: Loss and the politics of queer history.* Cambridge, MA: Harvard University Press.

Lüders, M. (2009). Becoming more like friends. *Nordicom Review*, *30*(1), 201–216.

Madge, C., Meek, J., Wellens, J., & Hooley, T. (2009). Facebook, social integration and informal learning at university: "It is more for socialising and talking to friends about work than for actually doing work". *Learning, Media and Technology*, *34*(2), 141–155.

Madianou, M., & Miller, D. (2013). Polymedia: Towards a new theory of digital media in interpersonal communication. *International Journal of Cultural Studies*, *16*(2), 169–187.

May, T. (2012). *Friendship in an age of economics: Resisting the forces of neoliberalism*. Lanham, MD: Lexington Books.

McClintock, A. (1993). Family feuds: Gender, nationalism and the Family. *Feminist Review*, *44*(1), 61–80.

Nardi, P. M. (1999). *Gay men's friendships: Invincible communities*. Chicago, IL: University of Chicago Press.

O'Connor, P. (1992). *Friendships between Women: A critical review*. Hertfordshire: Harvester Wheatsheaf.

Pahl, R. (2000). *On friendship*. Cambridge: Polity Press.

Pahl, R., & Spencer, L. (2004). Personal communities: Not simply families of "fate" or "choice". *Current Sociology*, *52*(2), 199–221.

Piepzna-Samarasinha, L. L. (2018). *Care work: Dreaming disability justice*. Vancouver: Arsenal Pulp Press.

Policarpo, V. (2017). Friendship and care: Gendered practices within personal communities in Portugal. *Journal of Gender Studies*, *28*(1), 57–69.

Roach, T. (2012). *Friendship as a way of life: Foucault, AIDS, and the politics of shared estrangement*. New York, NY: SUNY Press.

Robards, B. (2012). Leaving MySpace, joining Facebook: "Growing up" on social network sites. *Continuum*, *26*(3), 385–398.

Rose, N. (1990). *Governing the Soul: The shaping of the private self*. London & New York, NY: Routledge.

Roseneil, S. (2004). Why we should care about friends: An argument for queering the care imaginary in social policy. *Social Policy and Society*, *3*(04), 409–419.

Roseneil, S. (2006). Foregrounding friendship: Feminist pasts, feminist futures. In D. Davis, E. Evans & L. Lorber (Eds.), *Handbook of gender and women's studies* (pp. 324–343). London: Sage.

Roseneil, S., & Budgeon, S. (2004). Cultures of intimacy and care beyond "the family": Personal life and social change in the early 21st century. *Current Sociology*, *52*(2), 135–159.

Rumens, N. (2016). *Queer company: The role and meaning of friendship in gay men's work lives*. London: Routledge.

Smart, C., Davies, K., Heaphy, B., & Mason, J. (2012). Difficult friendships and ontological insecurity. *The Sociological Review*, *60*(1), 91–109.

Van Dijck, J. (2013). *The culture of connectivity: A critical history of social media*. Oxford & New York, NY: Oxford University Press.

Weeks, J., Heaphy, B., & Donovan, C. (2001). *Same Sex Intimacies: Families of choice and other life experiments*. London: Routledge.

West, A., Lewis, J., & Currie, P. (2009). Students' Facebook "friends": Public and private spheres. *Journal of Youth Studies*, *12*(6), 615–627.

Weston, K. (1991). *Families We Choose: Lesbians, gays, kinship*. New York, NY: Columbia University Press.

Willmott, P. (1987). *Friendship networks and social support*. London: Policy Studies Institute.

Wright, P. H. (1978). Toward a theory of friendship based on a conception of self. *Human Communication Research*, 4(3), 196–207.

Zitz, C., Burns, J., & Tacconelli, E. (2014). Trans men and friendships: A Foucauldian discourse analysis. *Feminism and Psychology*, 24(2), 216–237.

2 What do we know about peers?

To accommodate young people's digital cultures of care, this chapter argues for a more careful consideration of peer support in health research and promotion. Following the previous chapter's exploration of friendship, and how digital media have elaborated and complicated friendship practices, I will now explore and unpack common discourses of peers in relation to young people, health and wellbeing, and digital media. Challenging a formal discourse of *peer influence*, I argue for a need to more carefully consider the roles and practices of peer support networks, especially to gain a better understanding of how and where support is offered and found in young people's everyday media practices.

Peer influence is a dominant theme of youth research that informs health promotion and education interventions. Within this, peer influence is framed as risky. This justifies a perceived need for health educators and promoters to intervene in order to combat risks of misinformation and negative behavioural influence, often through formal peer education programmes in which young people are trained and tasked to share "good information" with peers. Formal health discourses of peer influence and peer education commonly situate peers as vectors of information sharing that are likely to trouble young people's health behaviours, and in doing so, these approaches often overlook the value of peer support. Attention to *peer support*, I argue, offers a more generous space to consider peer interactions – including, but not limited to, digital practices of learning and sharing information.

This chapter builds on existing critiques of peer education as a formal health improvement strategy. While such strategies may be useful, we should, firstly, question our understanding of who peers are, how they relate to each other, and the ways in which peer influence/support manifests in everyday digital media practice. Commonly, health researchers and promoters collapse and interchange "peers" and "friends" when engaging with the social influences of young people's health and wellbeing, indicating that peer relationships, and what these involve, are not well understood.

Beyond simply learning from and informing each other, peers can offer vital social support. Therefore, greater research knowledge of peer support practices is necessary for health promoters and researchers to accommodate, rather than overlook, digital cultures of care. Attention to everyday digital peer support can also inform public health policy and service provision, offering a greater understanding of young people's health and wellbeing needs, and where these are met or unmet through existing digital media practices. Further attention to everyday peer support can also provide more evidence of how informal care empowers young people to seek formal health care, through learning where to go and what to expect (Naslund et al., 2016).

Given the lack of clarity around what constitutes a peer, we should ask young people, when necessary, to clarify their own interpersonal relationships and support networks rather than adopting vague notions of "peers", or simply conflating peers and friends. While it seems likely that friends' carry more influence than young people's peers, this is not always the case, and will depend on the type of support that is offered or needed. For example, empirical research of Tumblr use among LGBTQ+ young people demonstrates that anonymous peers can offer more valuable support than friends, as will be discussed. This example usefully challenges the misconception that young people's close friendships are always more supportive than unknown peers they engage with through digital and social media. These data will be discussed to demonstrate that support is often sought and given by young people beyond immediate and close friendships, with digital media offering safely distant and anonymous care and support. Finding peers with lived experiences that relate to one's own experiences is now relatively easy for most young people, and certainly easier than in other everyday spaces such as schools, families, and workplaces. But once again, this will depend on the type of support that is needed. Further to this, "invested peers" willingly share their experiences and strategies with others who stand to benefit from this.

To some extent, the overlap and confusion between friends and peers tell us something useful about the complexity of peer and friendship relations, and how these can intersect or overlap and potentially expand support networks and practices. While always unclear, this distinction has been further disrupted by digital cultures of care.

Peer influence

A formal health discourse of peer influence is underpinned by a risk focus on young people's health – that is, the understanding that young people's peers are likely to negatively influence their health behaviours (Byron & Hunt, 2017). Much health promotion seeks to counter such risks through developing and delivering "proper knowledge", sometimes deploying young people to disseminate this to their peers. This is underscored by a belief in the power of peer influence among young people (Frankham, 1998; Sciacca, 1987).

Health researchers and promoters have a tendency to find young people's peer relationships problematic, typically positioning peers as a bad influence.

This rests on the key beliefs that young people lack proper health knowledge, and that young people are impressionable and easily led. Academic interest in youth cultures has also compounded a belief that peer influence is central to young people's lives, as per our collective attention to youth culture as a series of common (i.e. shared) practices and perspectives, including "risk practices" (France, 2008; Spencer, 2013). An unplanned collaborative effort among youth researchers, health researchers, health promoters, health practitioners, educators, parents, and parenting advisers supports a belief in the risk status of young people. This can amplify our negative understandings of young people's peers based on their potential influence. Young people can "fall into the wrong crowd", or be "easily led", "too naïve", or "too fearless". Or maybe they're "still learning right from wrong". These and many other familiar statements shadow how we characterise young people as vulnerable and at-risk, and how we maintain suspicion toward their peers – i.e. other young people of a similar age – who are deemed equally naïve and unknowing.

Health promoters and educators often fear that young people's peers will disrupt the knowledge and information that they offer through school-based and public health interventions. Where health professionals offer information deemed to be accurate and reliable (and founded on research evidence), the knowledge and information offered by peers are less likely to be accurate. The concept of "peer pressure" is only ever discussed in negative ways, and a discourse of "peer influence" offers much the same. Yet peers can have positive influence, as demonstrated in the latter part of this chapter. *Pressure* from peers may also, at times, be well-meaning and health supportive. And while dominant health research and education approaches are wary of peers, or co-opt peers into peer education initiatives, there is now a small but growing literature on the positive aspects of peer support – mostly in relation to mental health (Gibson & Trnka, 2020; McCosker, 2018; Naslund et al., 2016). A discourse of peer support is also more common to research on young people considered to be unsupported by mainstream schooling and health care, such as LGBTQ+ young people (Cover et al., 2020).

To further consider research discussions of young people's peers and friends, and where these are seen to differ or overlap, the following section centres on sexual health promotion and research literature that addresses peer influence. The focus on sexual health is a useful precursor to the following chapters on digital sexual health promotion (Chapter 3) and young people's sexual and friendship intimacies (Chapter 4).

Peers and friends: sexual health disruptors

While sociologists have noted the increasing social significance of friendship in the Global North (see previous chapter), many health researchers enfold young people's friendships into a discourse of peers. Literature on young people's sexual health more commonly refers to peers than friends, but often these are discussed as one and the same thing. A generous reading would be that this speaks to the complexity of young people's friendship intimacies and peer networks. Or perhaps this indicates our tendency to overlook the complexity of young people's intimacies and communication cultures. In an article about US college students' sources and perceptions of sexual health information, for example, Susan Sprecher et al. state that "Peers are another important socialization agent for teenagers. As children and adolescents try to make sense of the meaning of sexuality, they often turn to their friends" (2008, p. 18). In this statement, peers and friends are indistinct. Elsewhere, another valuable paper about friend-based sexual health support reported that "building on the good intentions of YGM [young gay men's] friends seems to be a promising avenue for increasing health behaviors. Interventions can build on peers' strong desires to help each other, enabling YGM's friends to facilitate revised sexual scripts" (Mutchler & McDavitt, 2011, p. 502). In this example, authors move from speaking of young people's friends, to their peers, and then back to their friends. Once again, this lack of distinction warrants consideration and further information from young people themselves. Arguably, the lack of clarity might be resolved if participants were invited to describe the relationship and intimacies involved.

Each of the above papers provides valuable insight into how young people's social networks influence their sexual health practices and understandings, and my point is not to discredit these articles or authors. My point is to demonstrate that even research attuned to young people's everyday intimacies often conflates young people's peers and friends, without contextualising how these categories, and their levels of influence, differ. In some cases, this overlap may be accurate (as I will discuss), but in many cases, this misses an opportunity to consider the intricacies of different relationships with different levels of influence. This overlap also fails to attend to friendship intimacies – including the specificity of these, as my research participants commonly discuss – or the broader reach and complexity of young people's support networks, particularly in view of digital cultures. Such information would be useful for health promoters developing campaigns and interventions for young people.

Much of the concern about peer influence seems to focus on the "information" young people offer each other through digital media, what they learn from this, and how it could generate "health risk behaviours". This leads us to volumes of literature on young people's "health information seeking behaviours" (discussed in the next chapter). But young people often engage with health information beyond simply seeking, finding, and assessing it. Such information is often couched in support, rather than taking on the form of instruction, as will be discussed.

As C.J. Pascoe has pointed out, a limited understanding of how young people are engaging with digital media can also generate adult fears about these media and the effects they could have on young people (2012). If young people are imagined to be blindly walking into all sorts of dark corners, and ingesting all sorts of "bad information", then this calls for more effort to educate them. As Pascoe notes, adult fears often eclipse any sense that digital media can be positive learning environments, and these can also block valuable opportunities to incorporate digital media into educational strategies (2012). Yet ideally this incorporation would involve young people's expertise (see Chapter 3 for discussion of this).

Peer education

Since peer influence is typically considered by health researchers (including health communication researchers), as risky to young people's health and wellbeing, *peer education* initiatives are developed to disrupt this risk. Commonly, this involves recruiting young people to deliver accurate and reliable health information to their peers, increasingly through digital media. As such, peer education strategies have a correctional logic in which peer influence is recognised and co-opted. In this, formal health expertise seeks to infiltrate, or present itself as, peer communication; resting on the belief that peer-delivered information will have more resonance and therefore more impact on young people's health behaviours. While peer education need not be formally arranged, it is mostly discussed as a formal health initiative. Discussion of peer education in this book will, therefore, refer to its formalised practice, orchestrated by adult professionals.

The concept of peer education dates back to the 1960s yet still lacks a common definition (Southgate & Aggleton, 2017). A frequently cited definition is that "Peer health education is the teaching or sharing of health information, values and behaviours by members of similar age or status groups" (Sciacca, 1987, p. 4). Recent accounts still cite this definition or offer something equivalent, such as "the horizontal sharing of information, values and behaviours between people of similar ages or status groups" (Cooper and Dickinson, 2013, p. 229). Each of these definitions, however, does not emphasise the formal nature of peer education strategies, suggesting that informal peer support might also constitute peer education. But we should be wary of this formal/informal distinction, as well as the ways health promotion accounts can understate this. Arguably, peer education initiatives recognise the powerful influence of young people's peers but seek to undermine its effects by introducing formally sanctioned (vertical) knowledge into informal (horizontal) practices of sharing knowledge and information. But peer education's informal conditions are constructed, its information is formally composed, and its delivery does not resemble everyday peer interaction.

Peer education has been heavily criticised (Milburn, 1995; Southgate & Aggleton, 2017), including common observations that it lacks evidence in being effective (Green, 2001; Frankham, 1998; Harden et al., 2001). While it has been found to be beneficial to peer educators themselves (Strange et al., 2002), little evidence suggests that it has benefited target populations (Milburn, 1995). Jo Frankham sought this evidence but found "a relative absence of evaluation or reflection on the educational and social premises on which the approach is based" (1998, p. 179). Despite this, she notes that a 1990s discourse of peer education had "an almost religious tenor" (1998, p. 179), with strong practitioner beliefs in this method, despite little evidence of its effectiveness. This "uncritical enthusiasm" is also noted by Mellanby et al. (2000) in their review of school-based health education programmes.

Other critiques of peer education relate to its lack of a theoretical base (Green, 2001; Milburn, 1995; Turner & Shepherd, 1999), its lack of awareness that "peer influence may operate differently with respect to different health relevant behaviours" (Milburn, 1995, p. 409), it being "overly scripted" and "relatively inflexible" (Ingham, 2005, p. 378), and its generic approach to populations, such as young people (Frankham, 1998; Kelly, 2004). The low cost of peer education initiatives is noted as a key appeal for health promoters and educators (Sciacca, 1987) since it mostly relies on the free labour of young people (Milburn, 1995, p. 409). This highlights public health's economic limitations and the common tendency to deliver cost-effective programmes despite a lack of evidence that they contribute to health improvements. The proliferation of peer education strategies also relates to public health's ready access to young people and their peers through educational settings.

Peer education strategies are commonly adopted for sensitive topics such as drug use and sexual health (Southgate & Aggleton, 2017; Green, 2001). This suggests that adult educators may feel uncomfortable or ill-equipped to engage with young people on "difficult" topics. Or perhaps it carries acknowledgement that health educators occupy different worlds to young people and that these populations discuss sex and drugs in distinct ways. In health education accounts, Frankham notes that "young people are portrayed as already engaged in free and frank discussion about issues like sex, AIDS and drugs" (1998, p. 182). She considers this claim in light of her own research where she asked young people if and how they discuss sex with their friends, finding that their friend-based conversations were more oriented to speaking about relationships rather than sex (1998, p. 183). Her participants noted that acknowledging their ignorance about sex among friends or peers carried social risks, so they more commonly learned about sex indirectly, by piecing together snippets of information from jokes and conversation (1998, p. 183). This suggests that health promoters may misconceive young people's peer-level interactions around "difficult" topics such as sex and drugs.

Elsewhere, Jackie Green has argued that much peer education is informal and happens through casual interaction (2001). This, and similar claims in the literature, suggest a common tension and overflow between "peer education" and informal peer-based learning. This is particularly true of early discussions of peer education, such as Peter Finn's claim that:

> Although structured peer education groups are sometimes established, the informal and usually spontaneous interaction that occurs in the home, on the job, or in social encounters represents the most common type of peer education. Peer education takes place constantly on an informal basis among most people. Youngsters and adults furnish each other daily with information and advice on how to promote their health and safety. (1981, p. 13)

This excerpt comes from an article written four decades ago, when health promotion was in its infancy, and prior to the Ottawa Charter that followed the first international health promotion conference (WHO, 1986). Throughout the four decades that followed, health promotion has formalised as a discipline and regime of institutional practices, values, and methodologies – including peer education. Within this history, a former sense of peer education as everyday and informal has transformed into an understanding of peer education as a public health strategy. To position these two understandings of peer education as indistinct, as many still do, overshadows young people's broader practices of peer support.

While the young people I have engaged with speak of learning from friends and peers, they rarely frame this as "education" – a term typically associated with schools and other formal institutions. As Frankham highlights, peer education is led not by young people but by adults, and young peer educators have very little control over its content (1998, p. 187). Importantly, peer education cannot resemble actual peer communication because it centres on education as a transmission of factual knowledge – firstly, from professionals to peer educators, and then from peer educators to young people (1998). As Frankham highlights, peer educators, when engaging with "peers", tend to replicate the knowledge transmission they experienced when they are trained as educators, adopting the role of expert more so than peer (1998, pp. 187–188).

It is important to remember that early peer education was focused on schools (Damon, 1984; Sciacca, 1987), and so the term itself was especially oriented to classrooms and school-aged young people. This context is often missing when peer education is used in other settings. In schools, "peers" means "peer students", but outside schools, peers (and our use of this term) are less understood. Green notes that because peer education initiatives are largely informed by "adult constructions of adolescence and adolescent health behaviour", we need to consider "whose agenda is being served by using peer education projects" (2001, p. 68). If peer education initiatives were more collaborative, where young people could lead rather than follow, and where health professionals would properly consult young people about their information and support needs, then this might offer something more useful. But as Green suggests, many peer educators are trained to transmit health messages that may not resonate with them. Central to the logic of peer education is trust in the knowledge of experts, along with trust in the value of spreading reliable and correct information. Implicit in this trust, however, is an agreement that young people have a health knowledge deficit.

Contemporary peer education initiatives are largely restricted to discussion of ambiguous peers. Mapping this idea of peers onto young people's digital media networks further complicates the notion of a peer, as a similar other. If peers are seen as people "of similar age or status groups", as per John Sciacca's (1987) definition, then whether or not young people are predominantly learning from such people in their digital interactions warrants investigation. But as Maxwell and Chase argue, "the term peer is unable to adequately capture the complexity of the different relational positions between young people" (2008, p. 310). In practice, information and support are entwined in young people's digital practices of sharing and circulating supportive content and gestures. However, a peer education model largely overlooks *support* and is more focused on *information*. A disciplinary hold on "health communication" (with its journals and practitioners publishing endless findings about "health information seeking behaviours") neglects consideration of how giving and receiving support can be a primary motivation for information sharing (McCosker, 2018; Naslund et al., 2016). Again, we return to the stubborn notion that young people are "going online" to find health information (as discussed in the Introduction chapter) and that this information often comes from peers and is therefore unreliable. This phobic understanding (of digital cultures *and* peer support) precipitates a public health need to fill this space with more factual, reliable, and instructive information. Such information is no doubt useful for some people much of the time, but it should not be designed with an aim to delegitimise or drown out other forms of knowledge that young people rely on, such as the experience-based knowledge of peers.

Returning to the common problem of conflating friends and peers, it makes sense to consider how productive each term has been. Largely, a discourse of peers has told us little about the specificities of young people's relationships and communities that influence their health and wellbeing. However, there has been useful research on friendship support, particularly regarding sexual health (Boydell, 2015; Martin, 2017). Much evidence suggests that young people are informed by the sexual practices and attitudes of their friends. As Kathryn Milburn asks, "if intimacies are shared between friends, can it be assumed that trust and confiding will simply materialise with another young person who is simply 'a peer'?" (1995, p. 416).

In her doctoral thesis, Susan Patterson[1] highlights the significant role of young people's friendships for sexual health information and support, noting that some friends more than others were more helpful and experienced in offering this (Martin, 2017, p. 11). While this may seem obvious, the specificities of young people's friendships – where specific friends are more supportive, trusted, and open to sexual health discussion than others – is rarely acknowledged in health promotion and research discussions of young people. Some of Patterson's participants also prioritised experienced-based advice from friends ahead of online information because this advice is personalised (Martin, 2017, p. 112). This suggests a key aspect of informal sexual health support that is overlooked when peers and friends are conflated. Health researchers (in discussions not limited to sexual health) have noted that young people often seek information and support from friends who are not like them. Nicola Boydell found that many young gay men in Scotland were as likely to turn to female friends for support as they would turn to other gay men (2015). That young gay men engage with female friends for sexual health support was also found by Mutchler and McDavitt (2011). But as approaches to peer education commonly state, peers are similar in age, gender, class, sexuality, and more. As such, peer education initiatives for young gay men are likely to only engage other young gay men, overlooking broader ecologies of friendship and peer support, and why young people may seek perspectives from differently identifying friends and peers.

Returning to early justifications for peer education, however, reveals that a confusion between young people's peers and friends is foundational to this concept. Sciacca, whose definition of peer education is commonly cited, rationalises peer health education through four key claims, one being that school students' "peers are frequently turned to for information and advice" (1987, p. 4). He cites four academic sources as evidence of this claim, but the first three of these relate to research claims about young people's friends rather than peers. He writes,

> For example, Kramer, Berger, and Miller (1974) reported that both male and female students chose "a friend" more frequently than official sources of assistance for help in the majority of 16 problem areas. Christensen and Magoon (1074) found that "student friends" were consulted most often for help with emotional problems. Tryon, in a 1980 review article, concluded that a friend is generally the first person students think to turn to for help with most problems. (1987, p. 4)

Evidently, this conflation is decades old and has played a key role in the peer education strategies throughout these years. This further suggests a need to define peers, as much as possible, to be able to discuss the support they offer through a more coherent common understanding.

Redefining peers

As discussed, peer education discourse often moves into discussing young people's friendships. Considering "peers", Michael Shiner writes: "Within the [peer education] literature the term is applied to describe close friends, habitual associates or relative strangers who just happen to be involved in the same activity in the same setting" (1999, p. 564). This is also true of "peer pressure" discourse, where young people are understood to be imitating their friends' behaviours or feeling the pressure to conform to the practices and values of a friend/peer group (Maxwell & Chase, 2008). This ambiguity results in a frequent slippage that is not entirely unwarranted and offers productive tension to our consideration of young people's social networks. It also speaks to the messiness of everyday communication practices, particularly digital practices, and how we participate in a range of encounters that offer different levels of support or influence. As with the very broad concept of "friends", the concept of "peers" can be a useful container for a range of allegiances, acquaintances, and support networks. A peer, in some cases, may also be a friend. However, within a formal discourse of young people's health influences, there is need for clarity, and health promoters and researchers should indicate who they refer to when they make claims about young people's peers. Further to this, it would be beneficial if they reflected on the value of this concept in relation to a given question/problem and consulted young people about their own understandings of peer influence in relation to that. Lastly, it would be useful to recognise that an unqualified reference to young people's peers fails to consider young people's more complex engagement with networked others – for information, friendship, support, and care.

In writing this chapter, I have wrestled with health research literature and its lack of definition of "peers", trying to disentangle peers from friends. On the one hand, I recognise that this confusion is reflective of human relationships, where we often do not categorise our friends and peers, or distinguish them as such, and nor do we differentiate them according to levels of influence. Further to this, we rarely refer to people as our peers, except maybe in workplace settings – such as our colleagues, co-workers, or people undertaking similar roles in different organisations, that probably have similar interests and practices. As a researcher, my peers can encompass colleagues as well as other researchers, often working on similar problems, engaging in similar activities, and employed at a similar level. We might connect at conferences, and sometimes we collaborate, and many such peers have become my friends. In some cases, however, friendships ignite from the beginning, before we establish common interests that would lead to future collaboration. Are these friends also my peers? My own experiences – such as presenting material from this book to friends and peers – are a reminder that these are overlapping entities. This example highlights a different yet related confusion, whereby peers/friends map onto formal/informal relationships. It also indicates that in certain contexts, our peers will have a greater understanding of our everyday preoccupations than our friends.

Arguably, there is less likely to be a universal definition of peers than friends, since "peership" is not a relationship we ascribe to our connections. In some cases, our peers can be acquaintances or represent "latent ties"

(Haythornthwaite, 2005), or perhaps we only know some peers by name and reputation, without ever meeting. They might be friends of friends or they may be unknown to us. Maybe we went to school with them but were never friends. Maybe we liked them, even though we were never friends. Maybe we looked up to them. Maybe we would say hello if we passed in the street, or maybe not. I mention schools intentionally since peer education was born out of school-based interventions. In schools, "peers" seems to stand in for "classmates" which will indeed include friends. Here, "peers" is a catch-all term for a captive group of young people, and the relationships among those people are of little concern. Though they should be. This tells us why the value and efficacy of peer education is still under question – because there is no sense of different affective levels of influence among young people within their broad social networks. There is also little consideration of how friendship intimacies may be more defining and influential in regard to young people's practices of health and wellbeing, or where peers may carry greater influence. When we ascribe the notion of peer to young people's digital networks (and the peer support happening there), the difference between a health promotion account of peer influence and young people's experiences of peer influence is vast.

Contemporary digital peer support practices are far from a contained reality of classmates and schoolyards. As will be discussed, peer engagements for health and wellbeing transgress the common belief that peers are similar in age, experience, identity, etc. Firstly, it is difficult to know if we are engaging with people our own age in sites such as Tumblr, Twitter, or online health forums. This is not to say that similarities and a sense of "kinship" is not felt through digital interaction with strangers. Further to this, and discussed later in this chapter, is evidence that young people often seek support from numerous people who can speak to a range of experiences – many of whom are not their "peers" in the formal understanding of the term.

Assuming we had to distinguish peers from friends, a common difference, guided by research discussions of friendship,[2] would be that friends are more intimate than peers, holding greater knowledge of each other's lives. For many, close friendships represent Lynne Jamieson's definition of intimacy, as "a very specific sort of knowing, loving and 'being close to' another person" (1998, p. 1). A close friend is likely to have more access to, and awareness of, your values, habits, and idiosyncrasies. Arguably, peers are less intimate and more distant than friends – though this does not mean they are less influential. The level of influence that peers carry will depend on a given situation and the support needed and offered, as well as how this differs from support from friends, family, health professionals, and others. For example, queer young people are often inclined to seek support for their queerness through digital interactions with strangers (peers) rather than engaging their friends – many of whom are likely to be straight.

Peer support

Research on young people's health and wellbeing has recently been more attentive to peer support, particularly in mental health research, where young people's peer interactions are recognised as valuable sites of personal support (Gibson & Trnka, 2020). Unlike other health risks such as sexual health, drug and alcohol use, and smoking, mental health promotion has not been contoured by a perceived need to promote specific health behaviours, as per "wear a condom" or "just say no". This underscores those "risks" as behavioural and therefore changeable by making "better choices". In regard to mental health, this is (mostly) not associated with bad behaviour. For mental health, the risk is less clear to health professionals and educators, and so the focus is on funnelling people into health settings if they are experiencing mental ill health, as per a discourse of "care pathways" and an Australian policy push for "digital mental health gateways" (Department of Health, 2015).

Unlike formal discussions of sexual health, peers are often recognised as a positive influence on young people's mental wellbeing. In relation to mental health, John Naslund et al. (2016) argue that the benefits of peer-to-peer mental health support outweigh the harms, and social media disclosures are doing important work of challenging stigma. They also argue that "peer-to-peer interactions will increasingly become an important part of how people with serious mental illness communicate with each other" (2016, p. 118). Elsewhere, Jane Burns et al. argue that digital mental health interventions must recognise young people's existing cultures of digital peer support in order to accommodate these (2016). Digital peer support can encompass a range of spaces, from social media (Hendry et al., 2017; Naslund et al., 2016) to online health forums (Giles & Newbold, 2013; McCosker, 2017; 2018; Prescott et al., 2017). Naslund et al. argue that social media allow us to share coping strategies and stories, and to feel less alone, though similar can be said of online forums that preceded social media and continue to be used today for mental health support (McCosker, 2018). Like forums, social media also allow some flexibility around one's involvement and participation – in both spaces one can "lurk" and listen without needing to actively respond or engage (Naslund et al., 2016).

In a study of peer mental health forums operated by beyondblue (an Australian mental health support service), Anthony McCosker engaged with peer mentors about their roles and engagements in the forum (2017; 2018). The peer mentors discuss forums as complementary to formal mental health care, since health care only provides a limited and formalised response to mental ill health, and McCosker argues that these mentors are "bridging a gap between professional mental health or organisational moderators, and the day to day support needs of those dealing with mental illness" (2017, p. 3). It is also noteworthy that mental health forums (as well as Facebook groups or subreddits)[3] are beneficial due to being freely available at any time, with no monetary cost, offering easy access to peers with lived experience of mental health issues (McCosker, 2017). While mentors often had links to the health/community service sector, they establish expertise and authority in the forums through demonstrating life experience, their development of successful coping strategies, their support of others in the forums, and their ability to build connections in the forum space (2017, p. 4). In other words, their expertise is manifold, situated in care and how mentors visibly practice this, as much as the knowledge (both personal and formal) they demonstrate.

Rob Cover and colleagues (2019) consider another example from the community sector in which the principles of peer support, and LGBTQ+ young people's expertise of social support, guides public resources. In this case, they review YouTube videos from Safe Schools Coalition Australia and Minus18 Foundation, produced by and for LGBTQ+ young people. They report that:

> Although *support* is often mentioned in literature on gender and sexual education, the term is rarely defined and often equated with "social support". With its associations of assistance and bearing the weight of something or someone, support is an intensely relational concept. (2019, p. 3, my emphasis)

Cover et al. note that a discourse of support distinguishes these YouTube videos from more typical approaches that foreground LGBTQ+ rights and choices that centre the individual. The videos analysed are not just acts of peer support, but they promote the value of peer support, and in doing so, they "shift the focus away from pedagogical norms of top-down, expert-to-novice forms of informational communication" (2019, p. 6).

Considering a UK mental health forum for young people aged 11–25 years, Julie Prescott et al. (2017) found that the main forms of support offered to forum posters were *informational support* and *emotional support*. Responses to forum posts could include either or both of these, depending on the post and what the poster asked for (2017). Further to this, they identify responses as being either directive or nondirective, where directive responses involved offering advice, and nondirective responses typically involved sharing one's own experience, or information, without offering advice (2017). However, these were not mutually exclusive. Prescott et al. also note that offering support can also be therapeutic for those who are sharing their experiences with others, suggesting "a dynamic approach to online support" (2017). As with the other examples mentioned above, Prescott et al. do not couch support in terms of education.

In another example, O'Dea and Campbell surveyed secondary students living in rural Australia, finding that most had needed mental health support and that social media commonly enabled this (2011). Of their participants who sought mental health support through social media, most believed that this was beneficial. More recently, Gibson and Trnka researched young people's use of social media for mental health peer support in New Zealand, finding that for many, these were significant spaces for building the level of trust that fostered vital support (2020). They were also impressed by the digital and emotional communication skills of their participants:

> One of the most compelling incidental findings of this research was young people's skill in communicating through social media. Participants' examples highlighted their ability to express emotion online, through words and images, and demonstrated their expertise in reading subtle expressions of distress on social media. (2020, p. 245)

Is digital support friendship?

The discussion that follows highlights how digitally mediated friendship and peer interactions challenge dominant understandings of peer influence. In everyday life, young people not only share knowledge and information with peers through digitally networked platform practices but also practice care, which takes on many forms and intensities. In other words, peers are sharing information and support, and often these are inseparable. Acknowledgement of this disrupts research attention to "health information seeking" on two levels. Firstly, information is being *shared and received*, and not necessarily actively sought, within everyday networked interactions. Secondly, information is shared alongside support, or as part of broader acts of indirect social support. As such, information is not simply passed from one peer to another but circulates widely, through digital cultures of care.

From herein, I conceptualise peers as a loose category that can involve distant or latent ties (as common on Facebook), people less intimately known to each other than friends, and strangers who may only interact through social media and other anonymous digital forums. I also introduce the term "invested peers", as those who are inclined to share information and give support to strangers and acquaintances in a range of ways, for diverse reasons that may include a sense of "giving back".

In the *Scrolling Beyond Binaries* (SBB) survey of LGBTQ+ young people aged 16–35 years, we asked participants if they thought that the benefits of social media outweigh the harms. Most participants agreed that they did. Many justified why they thought this was true, with references to "connection" being the most common reason, along with statements about feeling less isolated and having greater access to support. For example:

> social media helps people connect with like minded individuals around the world. As queer people, it teaches us we're not alone. (19, non-binary, queer)

> it's a lot easier to search and ask for help anonymously. (19, female, bisexual)

social media allows us to connect with more people like ourselves from anywhere in the world! It's an extended support network. (33, agender, unsure)

This sense of reaching others "around the world" is recurring, suggesting boundless open space through which to travel and find *your people*. In the survey, we also asked which social media platforms respondents use. The six most commonly used platforms among the 1,304 participants were (in order of use) Facebook, YouTube, Instagram, Snapchat, Tumblr, and Twitter.[4] Among participants, Tumblr was the fifth most commonly used but was more intensely used than Instagram and Snapchat – based on a higher number of hours Tumblr users spent on that platform per day, as opposed to users of Instagram and Snapchat. Its use was particularly high among trans and non-binary participants. Tumblr has been discussed as an important site of support and learning for LGBTQ+ young people (Cho, 2015; Wargo, 2015), as we also found in our data (Byron et al., 2019; Robards et al., 2020). Along with Tumblr, many participants had used private, peer-facilitated Facebook groups that supported trans, gender diverse, and/or queer young people. Jasmine, aged 26, trans, lesbian, and city based, highlights the vital sense of connection that such Facebook groups offer:

> you can easily find groups of people who have the same interests as you and it just makes you feel less alone. And that feels, yeah is amazing. Having the support groups I'm in, just feels … I don't feel like I have to worry, even if most of the people are interstate or international, it's still … there's a connection there.

As Jasmine highlights, a key benefit of such groups is their access to broad networks of support, available at any time. It also involves a range of people sharing a range of experience-based knowledge. These groups differ to discrete health-topic forums, as they are embedded in one's everyday Facebook use, as indicated by Eric, a 20-year-old trans man based in rural Victoria:

> there are a lot of groups based around video games that I follow quite actively and other support groups, Australian based, about transitioning. So they leave some really good links on there and tips and all other kind of stuff about transitioning, so that's mainly what I spend my time on Facebook looking at.

As Eric suggests, Facebook groups – whether for gaming or trans support – are part of his everyday social media practice. As such, seeking and sharing support among other trans people operates laterally, and perhaps casually, amidst other networked interactions about gaming and other interests. This everyday aspect highlights the availability of support that can exceed the support available through existing friendships. While discussions of

Facebook groups seem to suggest peer engagement rather than friendship-based support, their everydayness, their reliability, and the ongoing support and care they offer, suggest a traditional understanding of friendship. This everyday availability is also noted by Sam, aged 19, who is non-binary, bisexual, and city based. Sam refers to an "online sphere" that reminds them that "everything's going to be okay":

> I think by and large [social media] does enable wellbeing because you do feel connected and you can go into the world knowing that even if day to day, face to face, you find that things are a bit poor, you can come back, in that online sphere everything's going to be okay. Yeah, you can feel supported and you can feel connected and you can meet other people that think and feel the same way that you do.

Here, the "day to day, face to face" world is presented as potentially scary, daunting, and difficult. But experiencing the poverty of that world becomes easier with the knowledge that safer and more supportive spaces exist and are readily available. Further to this, participants noted that their need for support and connection intensified at certain times of their lives, becoming less crucial over time, or once certain journeys – such as gender transitions – had reached particular destinations. This can be seen in the following statement from Tasha, a 32-year-old trans woman who is pansexual and city based:

> It seems like there's really specific periods in your life where connecting with information and other people's experiences is really significant. Then when that stops being so significant, you move on.

Similarly, one survey participant wrote: "I used to 'live' on Tumblr, but not so much anymore". Evidently, young people are getting support from a range of networked others, not simply friends, and beyond the "day to day, face to face" world. For some participants the boundaries around whom support comes from are tight, but many (as noted in the previous chapter) found support among "Facebook friends" who were not close. Many discussed their disclosures around gender, sexuality, and mental health as a process rather than an event – one that involved sharing more information to more people each time, or testing the water among some networks, on some platforms, before broader disclosures. However, digital and "private" disclosures beyond one's friendship groups often preceded Facebook and "face-to-face" disclosures, since this afforded rehearsal, advice about what to expect, knowledge that others have experienced and survived such things, and assurance that supportive people are available if needed.

Digital interactions with invested peers enable access to the feelings and issues one may have to negotiate when coming out, for example. It also offers access to other people's experiences and strategies for prioritising safety and wellbeing. For broader populations of young people, there are manifold issues of wellbeing that are being negotiated and supported through digital media engagement with invested peers. Facebook groups, Tumblr, and health forums host a range of invested peers, some of whom are likely to have found valuable peer support through digital media and are "giving back", who support others as they also work on themselves. Either way, support is reciprocal – largely not in the sense of a dyadic exchange (e.g. reciprocal care between two friends), but reciprocal between the user of a platform/space and its "community". In this space, care circulates and invested peers offer support that can be indirect, for anyone who needs it. There seem to be no strict patterns in how invested peers support others, but the key consistency is the use of particular platforms, forums, or groups that are oriented toward informal care.

Aside from Tumblr and Facebook groups, participants mentioned online forums and other platforms such as Reddit. The following section will focus on Tumblr and how participants discuss this as a key platform for care and support. Prior to discussing Tumblr, it is important to consider the context of platform moderation cultures, particularly in light of Tumblr's moderation changes initiated in December 2018 (Byron, 2019; Tiidenberg, 2019). It is notable, too, that many participants had little faith that platforms themselves were supportive, as per experiences of harassment, trolling, and platform inaction that followed reporting other users. As such, peer-based care is further necessitated by the lack of care and support that platforms offer their users (Byron, 2019). This was noted by many SBB survey participants, for example:

> there is poor moderation of spaces and abusive accounts by Facebook, Twitter, etc. Over and over again, both companies have demonstrated they do not give a damn about more marginalised users. White supremacist, anti-Black, homophobic and transphobic users and communities run riot and prey on marginalised communities and users. Reporting does nothing – especially on FB and Twitter. (35, female, bisexual)

> Social media (especially FB) seems to silence those voices from POC/ LGBTI people while letting abuse and harassment from those in positions of privilege/ conservative continue. (29, female, butch dyke)

Tumblr care

This section introduces Tumblr as a site of care, particularly (but not only) for LGBTQ+ young people. This discussion continues in greater detail in Chapter 5, which focuses on Tumblr use for mental health support. For many young people, Tumblr has been a space to work through difficult feelings and experiences. Tumblr is less oriented to problem-solving health issues (more common to digital health forums), and typically offers a more affective space (Cho, 2015), where support cultures relate to the site's infrastructure, affordances, and established cultures of sharing feelings and experiences.

Research on Tumblr use among LGBTQ+ people and other minor sexual identity/practice groups has emphasised its "community" aspects (Renninger, 2015; Wargo, 2017), sometimes noting how users often refer to Tumblr as a community (Tiidenberg, 2016). Many of our SBB participants did the same, but some complicated the term "community" on account of their limited participation on Tumblr (Byron et al., 2019). While "community" suggests a bounded group affiliation and a sense of belonging and participation, it was suggested that a key value of Tumblr is its accommodation of anonymous interaction, and the ability to engage through quiet listening. More commonly among researchers, LGBTQ+ Tumblr interactions are contextualised as a *counterpublic* (Byron et al., 2019; Dame, 2016; Renninger, 2015) – that is, a public that is "self-creating and self-organized" and somewhat "elusive" (Warner, 2002, p. 52).

As with all major social media platforms, Tumblr use has shifted over the last decade, yet its culture of connectivity has remained different to other popular platforms. It is useful to consider LGBTQ+ young people's Tumblr practices through van Dijck's concept of "platformed sociality" (2013). Van Dijck outlines how digital media practices have quickly moved "from a participatory culture to a culture of connectivity" (2013, p. 5), through which platforms exceed the role of communication channels and come to play a greater role in organising our social connections. In doing so, participation is not always necessary in an active, content-producing sense. Given that the most common practice on Tumblr is reblogging (Kanai, 2015), this speaks to a more low-key participatory culture, but one that affords practices of care. Indeed, many of our interview participants indicated that they learned much about gender and sexuality through being on Tumblr without posting content, nor feeling part of a community (Byron et al., 2019).

Practices of following other Tumblr users offer greater space for a range of connections, including non-mutual connections (less possible on Facebook). As with most platforms, one's relationships with others can intensify, dissipate, or take on different affective dimensions over time, often due to the content users share, reblog, or respond to; or their shifting levels of platform presence. This speaks to how Tumblr differs to Facebook and other major platforms where connections are more formalised, reciprocal, and visible to our broader networks.

For each platform that SBB participants indicated using, we asked, "What is your primary motivation (if you had to choose just one) for using [it]?" Facebook and Snapchat users indicated that these were mostly oriented to communicating with friends and family[5] (83% and 87%, respectively). For Tumblr users, only 4% indicated this, with most users (65% – far more than any other platform) primarily using it to communicate with "people like me" (Robards et al., 2020). While we cannot know how those 65% of Tumblr users understood the term "people like me", and whether they understand this in terms of "peers", our follow-up interviews suggest that this refers to people who have similar identities (mostly in terms of gender and sexuality), interests (such as fandoms), or life experiences (including mental health experiences).

While acknowledging that Tumblr could at times be a toxic space, participants largely framed it as a supportive environment that was safe, as indicated by Casey, aged 20, who is agender, bisexual, and living in rural Victoria:

> No one on Tumblr is like, "We don't want you to be safe. We want you to get sick". They care. Also, they will post stuff like, "Here's what you can do to prevent HIV or AIDS" or "Here's what you should do to have better sex" and stuff like that in terms of health stuff.

Interview participants discussed Tumblr as a site for not only finding supportive people and resources but also sharing stories of their experiences – knowing that these help other people facing similar difficulties. The invested peer on Tumblr predominantly offers indirect support, such as reblogging memes and simple messages of care, as per their understanding of how support works in this space. Cami, aged 22, who is genderfluid, pansexual/queer, and living in regional New South Wales, discussed sharing their coming out story:

> I posted a story about my coming out experience to a Tumblr that's dedicated to how people come out and then had people contact me after that saying that they really liked the story and it helped them feel more comfortable in themselves. And helped them feel like maybe they could come out to their families.

While this statement suggests that Tumblr is a site of learning, we cannot relate this to "peer education" as that term is commonly understood, since this is about personal sharing and indirect support. This support offers subtle forms of information (i.e. here is how things played out for me; it could be like this for you) without claiming this to be the most correct and reputable information. Yet it is material to learn from and to feel supported by.

If we consider Tumblr as a site of peer support, the concept of peers needs to be broadened to accommodate difference, including generational differences, as per the following story from Casey. At 20 years of age, Casey speaks of engaging with someone they assumed to be aged around 60, following Donald Trump's presidential win in 2016. Casey was pleased with the solidarity and support offered here, in what they described as an emotional week on Tumblr:

One person I saw – I'm pretty sure he was like 60 – he made a post about how back in his day, when he came out, there were … like I don't think it was the Stonewall riots he was talking about, but there were a lot of riots for rights of gay people. And he was saying how he fought with his friends every day for his rights, and he's just going to have to do it again with Trump. He's like, "I'm glad that I'm here to help you through this because I know what it's like. You guys don't, because you're teenagers. It's generally been pretty okay for you guys, but I'm here to help you through this". And you've got a lot of people like that on Tumblr. Of course, every person has their own lives, and they have experiences that they can put in, and people can learn from that and share. That's what I love about Tumblr. It's a lot of times a very loving community. They all care about each other.

Again, the term community is used, alongside the notion that Tumblr is a site of care. These examples help us to think about digital peer support and how certain platforms like Tumblr become sites of care on account of their sharing cultures and affordances. This is not to say that people do not also have negative experiences of Tumblr (Byron et al., 2019). Like most counterpublics, Tumblr offered mixed experiences, and much tension exists due to the intensity of Tumblr-belonging, where users often seek to solidify and sustain Tumblr values and practices – such as care and support – while also prizing the diversity of Tumblr uses that underscore a generative and creative environment without rules or norms. Like any counterpublic, members often seek to establish and fortify cultural norms (Warner, 2002).

Tumblr connections are peer connections in which "followers" are typically unknown to each other. Yet, this seemingly brings more intimacy to many encounters – as a result of the shield of anonymity and the sense of bravery this can offer. While having limited information about the identity of other people in social media is typically presented as a risk, on Tumblr this can feel safer. As Baym notes, "The paucity of personal and social identity cues can also make people feel safer, and thus create an environment in which they are more honest" (2015, p. 10).

Many Tumblr users are invested in the wellbeing of other users, and this investment resembles friendship – commonly recognised as a site of care and dedicated support. Friendship is also evoked when Tumblr users associate this platform with a politics of care. An expertise around informal and anonymous care-giving is also evident here, as is the diversity of this care, which can be lateral, intergenerational, multi-directional, and no doubt oriented to caring for oneself (through disclosure and its personal rewards), just as much as caring for others (through disclosure and its social benefits).

Digital peer support cultures

This chapter has covered broad terrain, from formal peer education, to informal Tumblr care, encompassing peer support and influence and how these have been understood across research and health promotion and young people's everyday digital media practices. It highlights how a discourse of peer influence has informed and expanded peer education initiatives in which young people are seen as useful messengers of health information. Often, there is a lack of consideration of how peer education approaches differ from, and potentially overlook, existing peer cultures of information sharing and support. Peer education has also been informed by young people's friendship practices, yet friendship and peer relationships are not the same. While researchers and professionals often move between discussing friends as peers and vice versa, and while confusion reflects an overlap between these roles, few researchers explore the complexity of young people's digitally networked friends and peers.

Not only is a distrust of informal peer interactions symptomatic of risk-based research and its deficit approach to young people's ability to live healthy lives, but it reinforces this belief. This perspective forgoes the recognition of young people as agents invested in the negotiation of their health and wellbeing, as well as that of their friends and peers. That young people care about unknown peers has not, to my knowledge, featured in digital health promotion strategies. Given health promotion's common belief in the individualised health subject, sometimes referred to as the entrepreneurial self (Clare, 2017; Kelly, 2006), there is little attempt to consider *peer support cultures*. Yet doing so may also be complicated by the fact that many peer support spaces are not designated as spaces of support (Baym, 2015, p. 93).

Peer influence and peer support are related. In the examples of Tumblr care given, peers are influencing each other's beliefs, knowledge, and practices, but they are also supporting each other. Peer support approaches, as per the examples discussed from mental health literature, reference an assets-based approach (Brooks & Kendall, 2013) that recognises the skills and resources that community members offer to each other's wellbeing. Unlike a risk-based approach, this orients us toward researching how young people are finding, sharing, circulating, and encoding different forms and practices of peer support. Further understanding of this among researchers and health promoters can better inform future research design and health programmes (Gibson & Trnka, 2020). A move from focusing on peer influence (underpinning peer education programmes) to focusing on peer support, requires a clear break from a risk-based discourse of young people's health and wellbeing. This observation is decades old, yet this approach is still rarely adopted (Green, 2009). More focus on digital peer support also tests a common research focus on "health information seeking behaviours", revealing that young people are not simply seeking health information online, but they are sharing and finding it within everyday cultures of care.

Peer support most obviously differs to peer education in that it is informal, unstructured, less consciously practised, and it does not prioritise formally sanctioned knowledge, nor typical hierarchies of knowledge. Peer education is guided by formal expertise, along with a formal sense of method, and formal principles of education and knowledge sharing that do not translate into everyday digital cultures of care. Invested peers who have found vital support in such spaces, often return support to others, in ways they know to be useful, helpful, and *careful*. Often this support involves them accounting for their own experiences and strategies for wellbeing. For many, these are strategies for survival.

My critique of health promoters' and researchers' common understanding of young people's peer influence is not to propose an entirely new method of peer research or analysis, but to highlight a limitation of research that acts from stubborn beliefs about youth – as vulnerable, unknowing, and easily, negatively influenced. But there is space to revise peer education approaches, allowing young people to translate health information and potentially lead such projects. More health-based research that expands rather than limits our ways of engaging with young people's everyday practices would certainly be valuable. Without innovative approaches, or greater attention to young people's digital support practices, however, health initiatives and policy will continue to reinscribe negative perceptions of youth into the public imagination; ensuring more of the same, including peer education programmes that have little value.

Fears of peer influence precede digital media practices, and the concept of young people's peers has rarely been questioned or remediated through closer academic attention to digital cultures. We need to consider what our reliance and insistence on certain research methods and paradigms – including, but not limited to, peer education – does to our understandings of young people. Given that there is much evidence that young people practice peer support, we need young people to be involved in designing and leading social media research about their health and wellbeing. We should also pay attention to how we interchange the terms "friends" and "peers" throughout discussions of young people's social networks and influences. While this signals the difficulty of differentiating these overlapping relations, it also references our thin engagement with young people's social networks.

Health professionals' and educators' limited access to young people's digital support networks, as well as to young people's understandings and negotiations of health and wellbeing, ensures that many attempts to educate young people through digital and social media platforms are unsuccessful, as discussed in the following chapter. Given contemporary flows of information and knowledge, no "health expert" can control the concept of health and what this means, and any attempt to speak over everyday practices of health support is futile. Further attention to existing peer-level discourse, and what this tells us about young people's concerns and negotiations of wellbeing, will equip health professionals and educators to better engage with and support young people.

Tumblr interactions among invested peers offer evidence as to why we should consider peer support as a key aspect of peer influence in young people's everyday digital media practices. This challenges the steadfast belief among many adults and professionals that peer influence primarily signifies risk. Also, the common understanding that peers are similar in age or status (Sciacca, 1987) is troubled by digital practices that widen the frame of peer engagement. As foregrounded in young people's statements about Tumblr use, peer support can come from many people, including people of different generations and experiences, and the sharing of personal stories constitutes new forms of expertise. Arguably, these aspects of peer exchange on Tumblr not only borrow from friendship practices but also expand and modify the practice of friendship.

Notes

1 Formerly publishing material as Susan Martin.
2 I base this on discussions of friendship because very few young people have explicitly discussed peers in my research. 'Someone I know' or 'someone I know of' seems to be a more commonly used equivalent.
3 A subreddit is an open community forum thread on Reddit that has a dedicated theme. Subreddits are moderated by community members and usually have explicit rules on what can or cannot be shared.
4 Most of these were used by more than 50% of participants, with Twitter use being just below 50%. The next five most commonly used platforms were used among 10–21% of participants, including Pinterest, Tinder, WhatsApp, Reddit, and Grindr. As the survey was conducted in 2016, this will have likely changed.
5 This was the first time we ran this survey, so of course there are things we would improve next time. One thing we would do is not include 'friends and family' as a single category.

References

Baym, N. (2015). *Personal connections in the digital age* (2nd ed.). Cambridge: Polity Press.

Boydell, N. (2015). *Personal communities and safer sex: A qualitative study of young gay and bisexual men in Scotland.* University of Glasgow. Retrieved from http://theses.gla.ac.uk/6345/.

Brooks, F., & Kendall, S. (2013). Making sense of assets: What can an assets based approach offer public health? *Critical Public Health, 23*(2), 127–130.

Byron, P. (2019). "How could you write your name below that?" the queer life and death of Tumblr. *Porn Studies, 6*(3), 336–349.

Byron, P., & Hunt, J. (2017). "That happened to me too": Young people's informal knowledge of diverse genders and sexualities. *Sex Education, 71*(3), 319–332.

Byron, P., Robards, B., Hanckel, B., Vivienne, S., & Churchill, B. (2019). "Hey, I'm having these experiences": Tumblr use and young people's queer (dis)connections. *International Journal of Communication, 13*, 2239–2259.

Cho, A. (2015). Queer reverb: Tumblr, affect, time. In K. Hillis, S. Paasonen & M. Petit (Eds.), *Networked affect* (pp. 43–58). Cambridge, MA: MIT Press.

Clare, S. D. (2017). "Finally, she's accepted herself!" coming out in neoliberal times. *Social Text, 35*(2), 17–38.

Cooper, S., & Dickinson, D. (2013). Just jokes! Icebreakers, innuendo, teasing and talking: The role of humour in HIV/AIDS peer education among university students. *African Journal of AIDS Research, 12*(4), 229–238.

Cover, R., Aggleton, P., & Clarke, K. (2020). Education and affinity? pedagogies of sexual citizenship in LGBTIQ youth support videos. *Journal of Youth Studies, 23*(2), 221–236.

Dame, A. (2016). Making a name for yourself: Tagging as transgender ontological practice on Tumblr. *Critical Studies in Media Communication, 33*(1), 23–37.

Damon, W. (1984). Peer education: The untapped potential. *Journal of Applied Developmental Psychology, 5*(4), 331–343.

Department of Health. (2015). *Australian Government response to contributing lives, thriving communities – Review of mental health programmes and services.* Canberra: Commonwealth of Australia.

Finn, P. (1981). Teaching students to be lifelong peer educators. *Health Education, 12*(5), 13–16.

France, A. (2008). Risk factor analysis and the youth question. *Journal of Youth Studies, 11*(1), 1–15.

Frankham, J. (1998). Peer Education: The unauthorised version. *British Educational Research Journal, 24*(2), 179–193.

Gibson, K., & Trnka, S. (2020). Young people's priorities for support on social media: "It takes trust to talk about these issues". *Computers in Human Behavior, 102*, 238–247.

Giles, D. C., & Newbold, J. (2013). "Is this normal?" the role of category predicates in constructing mental illness online. *Journal of Computer-Mediated Communication, 18*(4), 476–490.

Green, J. (2001). Peer education. *Promotion and Education, 8*(2), 65–68.

Green, J. (2009). Is it time for the sociology of health to abandon "risk"? *Health, Risk and Society, 11*(6), 493–508.

Harden, A., Oakley, A., & Oliver, S. (2001). Peer-delivered health promotion for young people: A systematic review of different study designs. *Health Education Journal, 60*(4), 339–353.

Haythornthwaite, C. (2005). Social networks and Internet connectivity effects. *Information, Communication and Society, 8*(2), 125–147.

Hendry, N. A., Robards, B., & Stanford, S. (2017). Beyond social media panics for "at risk" youth in mental health practice. In S. Stanford, R. Heller, E. Sharland & J. Warner (Eds.), *Beyond the risk paradigm in mental health policy and practice* (pp. 135–154). London: Palgrave.

Ingham, R. (2005). "We didn't cover that at school": Education against pleasure or education for pleasure? *Sex Education, 5*(4), 375–388.

Jamieson, L. (1998). *Intimacy: Personal relationships in modern societies.* Cambridge: Polity Press.

Kanai, A. (2015, November 23–26). *Laughing through the discomfort: Navigating neo-liberal feeling rules in a Tumblr attention economy.* Paper presented at the Refereed Proceedings of TASA's 2015 Conference, Cairns.

Kelly, J. A. (2004). Popular opinion leaders and HIV prevention peer education: Resolving discrepant findings, and implications for the development of effective community programmes. *AIDS Care, 16*(2), 139–150.

Kelly, P. (2006). The Entrepreneurial Self and "Youth at-risk": Exploring the Horizons of Identity in the twenty-first Century. *Journal of Youth Studies, 9*(1), 17–32.

Martin, S. (2017). *Young people's sexual health literacy: Seeking, understanding, and evaluating online sexual health information* (PhD). University of Glasgow, Glasgow. Retrieved from http://theses.gla.ac.uk/8528/.

Maxwell, C., & Chase, E. (2008). Peer pressure – Beyond rhetoric to reality. *Sex Education, 8*(3), 303–314.

McCosker, A. (2017). *Networks of advocacy & influence: Peer mentors in Beyondblue's mental health forums.* Melbourne: Swinburne Social Innovation Research Institute. Retrieved from http://apo.org.au/node/97236.

McCosker, A. (2018). Engaging mental health online: Insights from Beyondblue's forum influencers. *New Media and Society, 20*(12), 4748–4764.

Mellanby, A. R., Rees, J. B., & Tripp, J. H. (2000). Peer-led and adult-led school health education: A critical review of available comparative research. *Health Education Research, 15*(5), 533–545.

Milburn, K. (1995). A critical review of peer education with young people with special reference to sexual health. *Health Education Research, 10*(4), 407–420.

Mutchler, M. G., & McDavitt, B. (2011). "Gay boy talk" meets "girl talk": HIV risk assessment assumptions in young gay men's sexual health communication with best friends. *Health Education Research, 26*(3), 489–505.

Naslund, J. A., Aschbrenner, K. A., Marsch, L. A., & Bartels, S. J. (2016). The future of mental health care: Peer-to-peer support and social media. *Epidemiology and Psychiatric Sciences, 25*(2), 113–122.

O'Dea, B., & Campbell, A. (2011). Healthy connections: Online social networks and their potential for peer support. *Studies in Health Technology and Informatics, 168,* 133–140.

Pascoe, C. J. (2012). Studying young People's new media use: Methodological shifts and educational innovations. *Theory into Practice, 51*(2), 76–82.

Prescott, J., Hanley, T., & Ujhelyi, K. (2017). Peer communication in online mental health forums for young people: Directional and nondirectional support. *JMIR Mental Health, 4*(3), e29.

Renninger, B. J. (2015). "Where I can be myself... where I can speak my mind": Networked counterpublics in a polymedia environment. *New Media and Society, 17*(9), 1513–1529.

Robards, B., Byron, P., Churchill, B., Hanckel, B., & Vivienne, S. (2020). Tumblr as a space of learning, connecting, and identity formation for LGBTIQ+ young people. In A. McCracken, A. Cho, L. Stein & N. Indira (Eds.), *A Tumblr book: Platform and cultures.* Iowa City, IA: University of Iowa Press.

Sciacca, J. (1987). Student peer health education: A powerful yet inexpensive helping strategy. *Peer Facilitator Quarterly, 5*(2), 4–6.

Shiner, M. (1999). Defining peer education. *Journal of Adolescence, 22*(4), 555–566.

Southgate, E., & Aggleton, P. (2017). Peer education: From enduring problematics to pedagogical potential. *Health Education Journal, 76*(1), 3–14.

Spencer, G. (2013). The "healthy self" and "risky" young other: Young people's interpretations of health and health-related risks. *Health, Risk and Society, 15*(5), 449–462.

Sprecher, S., Harris, G., & Meyers, A. (2008). Perceptions of sources of sex education and targets of sex communication: Sociodemographic and cohort effects. *The Journal of Sex Research, 45*(1), 17–26.

Strange, V., Forrest, S., & Oakley, A. (2002). Peer-led sex education – Characteristics of peer educators and their perceptions of the impact on them of participation in a peer education programme. *Health Education Research, 17*(3), 327–337.

Tiidenberg, K. (2016). Boundaries and conflict in a NSFW community on tumblr: The meanings and uses of selfies. *New Media and Society, 18*(8), 1563–1578.

Tiidenberg, K. (2019). Playground in memoriam: Missing the pleasures of NSFW Tumblr. *Porn Studies, 6*(3), 363–371.

Turner, G., & Shepherd, J. (1999). A method in search of a theory: Peer education and health promotion. *Health Education Research, 14*(2), 235–247.

Van Dijck, J. (2013). *The culture of connectivity: A critical history of social media.* Oxford & New York, NY: Oxford University Press.

Wargo, J. M. (2015). "Every selfie tells a story …": LGBTQ youth lifestreams and new media narratives as connective identity texts. *New Media and Society, 19*(4), 560–578.

Wargo, J. M. (2017). #donttagyourhate: Reading Collecting and curating as Genres of Participation in LGBT Youth Activism on Tumblr. *Digital Culture and Education, 9*(1), 14–31.

Warner, M. (2002). Publics and counterpublics. *Public Culture, 14*(1), 49–90.

World Health Organization. (1986). *Ottawa charter for Health Promotion.* Geneva: World Health Organization. Retrieved from http://www.who.int/healthpromotion/conferences/previous/ottawa/en/.

3 Young people's social media expertise[1]

This chapter makes a case for researchers and health promoters to consider young people's digital media expertise. This expertise, I argue, is more than technological but encompasses a rich understanding of platform cultures and knowledge of where health discussion can and cannot operate in social media. Young people's knowledge of social media platform cultures typically surpasses that of health promoters, educators, and researchers. Therefore, there is a need to more carefully consider partnerships between health promoters, researchers, and young people whom health professionals are seeking to support.

Young people's digital media competencies are underpinned by friendship and peer-based interactions, but health promotion strategies often fail to engage with these. Rather than addressing digital media broadly, this chapter focuses on social media that is central to the data presented, particularly Facebook. This data is taken from focus groups with young people (16–22 years) based in urban and regional New South Wales, discussing the potential use of social media for sexual health promotion.[2] Participants discuss and reflect upon their everyday social media use, as well as their understandings of sexual health as a complicated and stigmatised topic, offering vital insight into the feasibility of promoting sexual health through social media.

Health promoters understand that social media are integral to most young people's everyday lives, as per common goals to capitalise on this by developing platform-based interventions. Most commonly, this has involved Facebook (Gabarron & Wynn, 2016). Within "digital health" research and policy, however, there is narrow attention to young people's use of social media for friendship, peer support, and informal care. Too often, this is missing from public health policy and research, as discussed in Chapter 2. Also missing is an engagement with young people's competencies and expertise in negotiating these spaces (Ito et al., 2010), including their skills in building intimate networks. In social media environments (as in everyday life), young people engage with, trust, support, and listen to their friends. Friendship plays a central role in young people's social media practices, as discussed. Friendship also ensures that social media use is an everyday practice for most young people, and this everydayness generates and constitutes young people's digital expertise.

This chapter analyses discourses of *social media use* by comparing researcher accounts of digital health interventions with young people's discussions of social media use. On the one hand, researchers consider *social media use among health promoters* as a strategy to reach and engage with expansive audiences of young people, and on the other hand, *social media use among young people* is presented as everyday and oriented to friendship practices. Attention to these two discourses of use allows us to see how they operate on different axes – as instrumental, goal-oriented, and designed to "reach" others (in the case of formal health interventions), or as pervasive, everyday, and intimate (in young people's practices).

After considering how *social media use* can be everyday or targeted and instrumental, this chapter brings recent health promotion research into conversation with ethnographies of young people's digital cultures. Ethnographic studies and their centring of young people's social media practices offer valuable disruption to health literature that focuses on "harnessing" social media as spaces ripe for intervention. I highlight how social media is commonly approached by health promoters as a "setting" for the dissemination of information and how this neglects the participatory cultures of platforms. Traditional dissemination of a clear and simple health message – from expert to consumer – does not translate to social media environments, as will be discussed.

Young people's digital media expertise is further analysed through attention to poststructural theories of knowledge (Certeau, 1988; Foucault, 2004; Lyotard, 1991) that trouble traditional notions of expertise. This problematisation of expertise is warranted, given the discursive tensions of *social media use* between the axes of health promoter's professional practices and young people's everyday practices. Dialogue between these axes requires rethinking expertise in the space of *social media use*. Theorisations of knowledge, practice, and power from Certeau, Foucault, and Lyotard are useful here for their focus on how knowledge that is scientific and/or institutionally sanctioned becomes esteemed through its subjugation of informal knowledge and expertise – in this case, young people's expertise of digital cultures, and how these support sexual health promotion (or not). This dynamic presents an impasse for sexual health promoters that seek to engage young people through social media without acknowledging young people's expertise in platform negotiations, interactions, and networks of intimacy.

This chapter explores two key themes of focus group data. Firstly, how participants foregrounded friendship as the central component of their social media use (particularly Facebook use), and secondly, how participant discussions of social media use can be understood as *expertise* – an expertise that health promoters do not have but could engage with to better guide and situate digital health interventions. This is particularly the case for sexual health promotion, given the notable issue of stigma that prevents many young people from publicly discussing this topic.

Social media use

Public health professionals increasingly consider the value of promoting health through social media, especially when seeking to engage with young people. This is evident in sexual health promotion literature that commonly reports on the use (or proposed use) of social media to *reach* young people (Burgess et al., 2018; Pedrana et al., 2013). Despite common statements about the importance of social media in young people's lives, few health researchers report on implementing sexual health strategies that engage with the participatory cultures (Jenkins et al., 2015) of social media, nor do they engage with media theories of platform connectivity (van Dijck, 2013). Social media research engaging with young people's practices of identity, self-presentation, and friendship (Marwick, 2005, 2013) are also rarely discussed in health promotion literature. Rather, social media platforms are commonly approached as "settings" through which to reach health consumers (Bull et al., 2012; Loss et al., 2014), preserving a model of one-way health messaging that is devised and delivered by health "experts".

For almost two decades, digital media scholars and ethnographers have highlighted young people's use of social media for negotiating identities, self-representation, gender, sexuality, intimate relationships, friendship, politics, and more (Baym, 2015; boyd, 2008; Gray, 2009; Green & Brady, 2013; Marwick, 2005; Marwick & boyd, 2014a). Many of these cited studies are ethnographic, and many point to or suggest young people's digital media competencies (boyd, 2008, 2014; Ito et al., 2010; Pascoe, 2012). Such research provides valuable evidence of the complexities of young people's digital media interactions, including sensitivities to different platform cultures and affordances, diverse networks, context collapse (Marwick & boyd, 2011), and how digital communication practices continue to shift across a range of dynamic media sites and practices.

As with public health discussion, these ethnographic studies offer a discourse of *social media use*, yet this discourse of use operates differently. Digital media ethnographers typically centre young people's media use as everyday – with close attention to the communities, networks, and relationships involved. Public health research, however, more simply implies that young people's use of social media is important because this is where they congregate and can be reached. Health researchers less commonly consider the intricacies of how young people occupy, engage with, and relate to others through their social media networks. Swiftly moving to questions about how health professionals and organisations can (and many say *should*) use social media to reach young people, volumes of public health literature have failed to consider the intimacies within young people's social media cultures.

To consider a discourse of use that operates across these two discussions, I draw upon Certeau's theorisation of everyday practice, particularly his attention to the production that occurs within everyday uses of media, language, and discourse. Certeau asks the following question, which guides my consideration of how health promotion has sought to engage with young people via social media to date:

> The thousands of people who buy a health magazine, the customers in a supermarket, the practitioners of urban space, the consumers of news-paper stories and legends – what do they make of what they "absorb", receive, and pay for? What do they do with it? (1988, p. 31)

This provocation suggests the importance of (and neglected attention to) the production that occurs in everyday consumption, as elsewhere highlighted by the term *produsage* (Bruns, 2006). Of the health messages that are devised and delivered to young people via social media, how do we know what is done with them? How does counting "likes" on Facebook posts (Kite et al., 2016; Syred et al., 2014) differ from counting the number of newspapers sold? This quantification of "engagement" tells us little about how this material is read and its impact if any. We cannot presume to know why a social media post was liked, nor whether its message impacted its reader in any particular way. The simple fact of seeing or purchasing media tells us neither about how these media are used nor whether they are, in fact, *useful*.

Certeau's emphasis on the productions that take place within consumption, and how these are two co-present aspects of everyday practice, help us to think beyond a media effects model still common to much health communication scholarship – as though we simply "absorb" the messages put before us. Further, the productive aspects of social media "consumption" are more evident than in our consumption of "old media", as per visible user practices of producing, sharing, narrating, and re-inscribing media content. The productive aspects of social media use can be seen in Deborah Chambers' account of how social media have expanded the ways we do intimacy (2013), and danah boyd's argument that social media have generated new forms of community, particularly among young people (2008). More broadly, almost two decades of ethnographic work on young people's social media practices attest to how these have productively expanded the contours of young people's everyday lives and intimacies (boyd, 2014; Marwick, 2005; Pascoe, 2010), including their friendships. However, the cultural aspects of these practices are often unavailable to outsiders, as boyd argues, who are also "ill prepared to understand the context" (2008, p. 133). This includes health promoters, researchers, and policymakers.

Thinking beyond "health information seeking"

While research on health promoters' use of social media to engage with specific populations continues to grow, this has largely been observational – focusing on the feasibility of such engagement and how to measure and evaluate the impact of digital health interventions (Capurro et al., 2014; Lim et al., 2016). Despite decades of attention to digital health, and the focus on social media that expanded previous discussions of eHealth and mHealth,[3] questions of how best to *use* social media for improving health behaviours still abound. The behavioural approach that dominates much health communication scholarship seems to be part of the problem. Ongoing research into *health information seeking behaviour*, encompassing *online health information seeking*, primarily consider digital and social media (whether this constitutes websites, apps, digital forums, or social media platforms) as sites of information. Further to this, these are contextualised as sites that health consumers actively visit in order to find health information.

Literature on health information seeking presents the "health consumer" as actively and knowingly entering digital spaces (i.e. "going online") in search of health information. This imagined practice is no doubt scripted by surveys and research questions that (changing little over the years) ask health populations *where* information is found. While health information is indeed found in social media (as discussed throughout this book), often this is not actively and intentionally sought and found. As discussed in the previous chapter, health information is often indirectly shared and found, couched in peer support.

Further emphasising the notion that young people are seeking and finding health information online, including through social media, are dominant research questions about young people's skills in determining the validity and reliability of this information (Gray et al., 2005; Hu & Shyam Sundar, 2010). Research on young people's health information seeking often considers key sources to be friends and the internet (Patterson et al., 2019), and sometimes health professionals. Other sources mentioned in the literature include families/parents, and in terms of sex education, pornography is frequently discussed as a source of information (Löfgren-Mårtenson & Månsson, 2010). When information sources are questioned for their reliability and accuracy, young people's friends and peers are easily deemed as "bad sources", as noted in the previous chapter.

Too often, health researchers discuss "online information" without clarifying the communities, networks, participants, interactions, or styles of communication involved in the circulation of particular forms of information. Much of this health research, as with peer education approaches previously discussed, is correctional. That is, upon discovering that many people are finding health information online, a need for the development of new digital resources or interventions emerges to compensate for, and possibly eclipse, "bad information" (Cole et al., 2016) produced and shared by unreliable and non-expert sources. Much of this work seeks to promote health literacies, where good health information seekers will know to only trust "reputable sources" such as state-based, state-funded, or research-led health websites. Research on online health forums also considers the reliability of information shared here (Cole et al., 2016; Lederman et al., 2014), while also often acknowledging the supportive role of community forums. Yet concerns about young people's ability to appraise health information online are commonly expressed (Eysenbach, 2008), along with the belief that young people's peers are unlikely providers of accurate and reliable health information (Wang et al., 2008). Much of this research neglects consideration of how young people typically build their knowledge of health issues from a range of sources, digital and otherwise (Fergie et al., 2015; Fox & Jones, 2009).

Moving away from studies of static websites or digital health forums, researchers have increasingly indicated that health information is sourced through social media (Thackeray et al., 2013). Such research has largely maintained its "health information seeking behaviours" approach, transplanting this to social media. But social media practices are less informationally oriented than a simple web search and the browsing that follows. Young people are often not actively seeking health information when they find it through social media. Such information circulates and presents itself through the combined force of friends, peers, and algorithms. Its presence and availability also speak to digital cultures of care. Health information is not central to, nor an addition to, social media content – it circulates like all other information, and often emerges through support. Therefore, a need exists to expand and diversify research approaches to digital health information, in ways that do not present a simple account of how information is transmitted, as though simply passing from educator to student, or doctor to patient.

Sexual health promotion and social media

Public health's focus on the use of social media to reach young people deploys what Deborah Lupton describes as "instrumental and technological solutionist approaches" (2015, p. 175). Here, social media and associated technologies are used as tools to deliver existing models of health promotion. In doing so, health messages are not necessarily revised to accommodate new media practices. Literature reviews of sexual health promotion through social media have found that young people are most commonly targeted (Gabarron & Wynn, 2016; Gold et al., 2011) and that such interventions mostly involve the dissemination of static information, often referred to as "passive" approaches (Capurro et al., 2014; Clar et al., 2014; Gold et al., 2011). Sexual health promoters have often seen social media as a tool for "reaching" young people (Lim et al., 2016), as per the following example:

> Professionals concerned with promoting sexual health for adolescents are beginning to take advantage of technology and to use readily available online and mobile networks to extend their reach and communicate with young people about critical health information. (Levine, 2011, p. 18)

In "taking advantage" of social media spaces that are "readily available" to them, professionals can apparently "extend the reach" of health promotion.

But how these spaces are readily available to professionals is not discussed, nor are the ways in which young people may engage with health promotion content or not, which can be considered as intrusive (Byron et al., 2013). Elsewhere, Lauren Ralph et al. also discuss the utility of social media, describing the internet as "a key venue for delivering health-related messages and interventions to adolescents" (2011, p. 39). Like others (Bull et al., 2012; Dunne et al., 2014), they conceptualise social media as a "venue" where health professionals can successfully connect with target populations: "where they live, learn, work, and play" (2011, p. 46). This is core to a settings-based approach commonly deployed by health promoters (Poland et al., 2009). The notion of health professionals "harnessing" technology is expressed by Susannah Allison et al.:

> there is still a considerable need for high-quality research to understand the impact of different forms of new media use on youth sexual health, as well as to determine the best ways to harness technology to promote safer sex behaviors. (2012, p. 208)

This statement highlights a two-pronged health-based approach to young people's social media use. Firstly, it considers social media's *impact* on sexual health, and secondly, how social media can be *harnessed* and incorporated into public health strategies. This correlates with a model of peer education (see the previous chapter) that seeks to challenge peer influence by generating peer communication that aims to co-opt this form of influence. Allison et al. propose developing an understanding of social media risks, then intervening to remediate these through formal health intervention, thus diffusing the risks. The second part of this equation speaks of health professionals "harnessing" young people's social media, but without further considering the feasibility of supplanting formal health messages into media environments oriented to informal communication among friends and peers.

Julika Loss and colleagues challenge this public health consideration of social media as a "site" or "venue" (2014) by returning to Poland et al.'s definition of a settings-based approach (2009). For Poland et al., a settings-based approach centres on "the physical, organizational, and social contexts in which people are found as the objects of intervention" (2014, p. 161). Here, workplaces, community organisations, and schools are typical settings that have hosted health promotion interventions (2014, p. 161). As a non-physical venue, social media have been conceptualised as a "novel setting", but Loss et al. argue that having a geographical locus with physical boundaries is an important feature of a "health setting" (2014, pp. 163–164) as understood by Poland et al. (2009). Social media platforms are unbounded spaces where messages cannot be contained and controlled, nor can they offer a uniform sense of engagement. Further to this, these are not sites through which impact can be easily measured – this being a core principle of settings-based health promotion interventions (Loss et al., 2014).

A public health report from the UK contemplates the value of social media use for HIV prevention work by engaging with the practices and obstacles of health workers in this field (Mowlabocus et al., 2014). Sharif Mowlabocus et al. note the importance of engaging with gay men in digital media spaces yet highlight the difficulties that workers face when integrating social media into their professional practice (2014). The authors state, "In contrast to general assumptions that digital work can offer a 'quick fix' for health promotion, health workers often have to develop deep and lasting relationships with users of a site", and that "[m]ultiple forms of literacy (informational, technological, cultural) are increasingly required of workers as they move towards more online forms of outreach" (2014, p. 2). In this rare example of health promotion research that considers the digital media practices and capabilities of health promoters, concerns are expressed for staff privacy as well as for the accuracy of information that staff are able to quickly provide in these dynamic spaces. These findings suggest that digital outreach is unmanageable and unlikely through a current paradigm of formal health promotion, where expertise is shared carefully and must remain unchallenged. It also speaks to the hierarchies, audit culture, and risk management within health organisations, where public-facing messages must be checked and approved by senior officials prior to release. This slowness is somewhat surpassed by digital health stories and information that circulate beyond health promotion sign-offs. As Kath Albury argues, health promoters must recognise that their social marketing efforts are in competition with a range of material that young people are likely to find more engaging and informative, as per social news produced by *Vice*, *Buzzfeed*, and similar outlets (2019).

Significantly, a risk framing prevents health promotion researchers from properly considering young people's digital media competencies in navigating a range of health information, formal and otherwise. A risk approach also prevents further attention to the health benefits of digital media use, beyond simply accessing information. While the health benefits of young people's digital media use have been documented (Collin et al., 2011; Third et al., 2017; Third et al., 2019), these fall away when the question moves to risk and how to deal with risks (of misinformation and negative health outcomes). Once again, we need to move beyond a risk paradigm of young people's health if we wish to engage with young people's digital cultures rather than seeing digital cultures as a risk to health behaviours. The "riskness" that encapsulates much discussion of young people's digital media practices, often fanned by news media stories that feed anxieties of parents and other educators, can influence health promotion (Albury & Byron, 2019). But these narratives of young people's risky media practices close off much useful discussion about the skills, competencies, and expertise that young people bring to (and develop within) their social media use, and how these can usefully inform their health knowledge and practices. Taking an assets-based approach (Morgan & Ziglio, 2007) to young people's health and wellbeing allows us to be more attuned to young people's competencies.

Friendship and social media use

In the first of two phases of this project's focus groups, participants were separately engaged in school-age (16–17 years) and post-school-age (18–22 years) groups, with two focus groups each in Sydney and a regional city in New South Wales. In these groups, young people discussed their social media and mobile phone practices and the suitability of sexual health interventions using social and digital media. In the second phase, one focus group was held in each location, with returning participants aged 16–22 years. These two groups reviewed key discussion points from the initial focus groups and mapped potential social media strategies for hypothetical Australian sexual health campaigns. The only requisites were for their campaigns to involve social media and to promote condom use and sexual health testing among young people. Participants were asked not to develop campaign content but to develop models for campaign delivery. Suggested interventions were not implemented but were fed back to government funders for consideration.

Discussion covered a range of social media but mostly centred on Facebook, as this was the most frequently used platform among participants at this time. While Facebook is the focus of the following discussion, the argument presented here – for greater consideration of young people's social media expertise – is also useful for considerations of other social media platforms and networked media practices.[4]

Stated reasons that Facebook was the most used and favoured platform among participants included it being "straightforward", "easy", "user-friendly", "cheaper" (than text messaging and phoning), and that "it doesn't cost you anything" and "everyone has it". When asked what Facebook was used for, the most common response was "to keep in touch with friends", and other responses included "talking", "socialising", "to chat", "find out about parties", "seeing what everyone is up to", "communication", "photos", "organising social events", "making friends, keeping friends", and "remembering birthdays". Evidently, Facebook was primarily used to practice and administrate friendships, as other researchers discuss (boyd, 2006; Niland et al., 2015; Robards, 2012). A commonly noted negative aspect of Facebook among participants was that it holds "too much drama" in terms of gossip, bullying, and falling out with friends. Since participants' use of Facebook centred on friendship, including friendship dramas and difficulties (see also boyd, 2008; Marwick & boyd, 2014a), health promoters should consider how these particular "risks" may be exacerbated by proposed social media interventions.

The use of platforms such as Facebook involves the curation of one's public/semi-public self, where users conduct themselves with an awareness of being seen by others in their social networks as well as the networks of their friends (boyd, 2008). In participant discussions of "Facebook friends", this included "close friends" and others considered as "not really friends", or friends "you don't even talk to" (urban, 18–22). Many stated that they were "always on" Facebook on account of having the app on their phone. Some noted compulsive tendencies in how they and their friends used Facebook. While there was a suggestion that its use could be a distraction from daily life, it was evident that "Facebooking" was a key feature of everyday life. This can be seen in the following statements:

> I use Facebook heaps, like, way too much for communication. (regional 16–17)

> I'm on Facebook while I'm doing uni work as well. (urban, 18–22)

> I'm always on my laptop so, basically, I'm always on Facebook. (urban, 18–22)

> I probably couldn't live without it because I'm so used to it – it's part of everyday life now. (urban, 18–22)

> I'm on it, like … now. (regional, 16–17)

As an everyday and seemingly constant media practice, young people's use of social media across a range of locations (including school and work), speak to their competencies in negotiating co-presence and polymedia practice (Madianou & Miller, 2013). Throughout group discussions, the terms "public", "private", and "personal" were used inconsistently, complicating a traditional public/private binary and suggesting that intimacies need not be private (Baym & boyd, 2012; boyd, 2008); or indeed, that the concept of privacy is malleable. Young people's concerns about privacy have been noted as inconsistent with "adult concerns" for their privacy (Livingstone, 2008; Marwick & boyd, 2014b), and this research has highlighted cultural and generational differences regarding privacy, whereby social media privacies operate differently to earlier understandings of private/public. In earlier conceptualisations, privacy would best be practised by non-participation in social media due to their seemingly public nature. To ask or expect this from young people is of course not feasible and nor would it be healthy if it reduced their access to friendship and peer-based support. As we know, young people's friendship intimacies, social connections, and cultural practices typically involve social media presence (Balleys & Coll, 2017; boyd & Hargittai, 2010; Livingstone, 2008; Marwick & boyd, 2014b).

Participants from all focus groups noted that sexual health information is sought and appreciated by young people but that the stigma of STIs make social media an improbable space for seeking and sharing this information. This was reinforced by participant concerns for privacy, and how this would be undermined if sexually suggestive material (including sexual health information) became associated with them on Facebook. However, while it was often said that sexual health discussions do not belong on Facebook, participants did not fully reject the possibility of this. All groups noted the benefits of Facebook advertisements which would be visible to individual users but not to one's networks (Byron et al., 2013; Evers et al., 2013).

The use of humour was also discussed in all groups as an avenue whereby the seriousness of sexual health topics could be tempered, along with the personal risks in posting/receiving this content among friends and social networks (Byron et al., 2013; Evers et al., 2013). Participants pointed to the sociality of Facebook as a rationale for not posting things "too heavy", political, or educative, as "no one wants to get a lecture whilst they are online and trying to be doing their social thing" (regional, 18–22). Doing one's "social thing" refers to a range of communicative and participatory practices that centre on friendship ties, and any dissemination of material seeking to educate their friends (and implicate themselves as being too serious, or too health-concerned) could betray this standard practice. Sharing sexual health information with friends on Facebook was deemed unlikely as this held social risks and certain connotations: "Again with the stigma of, if you found something about a sexual health infection, then you don't really want to be like, hey it's made me think of you. It just has that connotation" (regional, 18–22).

Participants felt that sexual health was "a taboo subject" (urban, 18–22) that "heaps of people don't talk about" (urban, 16–17). Stigma and embarrassment surrounding sexual health ensure not only its absence on social media but its non-discussion among peers. Participants noted that "people push it away", and "people are scared about that stuff; they don't want to know about it" (urban, 16–17). Given the replicability of online messages (boyd, 2008), and the potential for friendship fallouts and ensuing drama (Marwick & boyd, 2014a), this material was considered to be too risky for Facebook.

Asked about the likelihood of discussing sexual health matters with friends more generally, participants felt that it would depend on the form of communication and who was involved. While the public sharing of sexual health information on Facebook was deemed possible if part of a humorous post (see also Burgess et al., 2018; Pfeiffer et al., 2014), discussion of personal sexual health matters was deemed as likely to occur between "close friends" offline (see also Divecha et al., 2012). This highlights young people's expertise about the different spatial arrangements of friend-based caregiving, where certain topics are only permissible among certain friends, in settings that are more supportive and private. Posting personal sexual health matters on Facebook walls would be "weird" (urban, 16–17) and inappropriate: "It's like, you don't really want that on your wall" (urban, 18–22). There was disagreement about the likelihood of privately messaging about sexual health matters, which many participants felt was also too risky since it could be forwarded to, or found by, unintended recipients: "because everyone gets their hands on it and everybody knows", and "confidential things can spread like wildfire" (urban, 16–17). This references a common "context collapse" that takes place on social media (Marwick & boyd, 2011), as well as a familiarity with "drama" (Marwick & boyd, 2014a).

In stage two focus groups, one person proposed a sexual health promotion strategy involving a video-making competition where films could be produced by young people who would not only create but disseminate these through their social media networks. This was seen by participants as a good strategy to generate a range of peer-produced material that would offer various perspectives and genres, likely to encompass serious, personal, and humorous messages. Being self-produced, participants felt that such material would most likely be shared among peer networks, as per existing cultures of sharing one's creations. Such a strategy would encompass a form of peer education that poses less risk for young people than the dissemination of formal sexual health media that they were not involved in producing. This example highlights young people's awareness of existing cultures of health promotion, whereby the message is fixed, not co-produced, and not up for discussion or remediation. In other words, young people are very aware of the dynamics of traditional health messaging in which they are constituted as a passive audience. Sharing such messages does not resonate with digital sharing cultures and would confuse their friends while also implicating themselves as concerned about STIs (Byron et al., 2013).

This suggestion for the development and dissemination of peer-generated content also offers the potential of multiple user-generated messages that can diversify sexual health discussions – "they could do animated video, real video, and I guess they could take it any way they want. Like funny, serious, real life story ... you'd have a lot of different views" (regional, 16–22). This is arguably more compatible with social media flows of content and messaging, whereby a singular narrative frame is incongruent with platform feeds and interactions, as well as broader cultures of social media sharing and interaction.

In devising campaign strategies, most participants suggested resources that would lead to a central campaign website. This reflects Gillian Fergie et al.'s finding (2013) that young people more often associate factual and reliable information with websites produced by reputable organisations, whereas social media offers something more dynamic, responsive, and peer-led. Elsewhere, it has been reported that young people feel more comfortable accessing sexual health information through websites rather than social media (Lim & Eaton, 2014). This suggests that social media interventions should not replace the provision of information found in formal websites, but supplement these, or offer something that is more suitable to the communicative cultures of these media.

Experience-based knowledge offered by young people constitutes a valuable form of expertise that could have prevented numerous failed public health attempts to involve young people in sexual health discussions on social media. But unfortunately, young people's expertise has rarely been deployed when developing digital health interventions – at least not in a substantial, collaborative sense.

A crisis of authority and the changing nature of expertise

Following the consideration of public health and media researchers' attention to young people's social media use, and statements from young people that demonstrate their cultural expertise of social media and how platforms such as Facebook could accommodate sexual health promotion, the final section of this chapter proposes a theoretical approach to understanding young people's digital expertise. Drawing upon poststructuralist theories of knowledge to consider the gaps between health promotion expertise and young people's everyday practice, I argue that we need to consult the expertise that young people have in negotiating these spaces, along with a need for health promoters to work with young people if they wish to produce valuable and effective digital health interventions. When analysing the above data, I found little evidence of mainstream public health promotion and research that engages with young people's everyday aspects of social media use. This neglect partially reflects a risk-based agenda that apportions limited agency to young people. It also signals an incompatibility between formal health promotion systems and digital media cultures. Seemingly, formal approaches to health communication cannot accommodate young people's social media expertise. Attempts to marry these two modes – each with their own systems of communication and knowledge transfer – can result in a crisis of authority.

This is also a matter of different, incompatible knowledges. Of scientific discourses, Foucault asked, "What theoretico-political vanguard are you trying to put on the throne in order to detach it from all the massive, circulating, and discontinuous forms that knowledge can take?" (2004, p. 10). This can be asked of formal health discourses and the expertise that these not only enact but also protect through health promotion's standard practice of information delivery; buttressed by health communication research focusing on "online health information seeking". Sanctioned forms of sexual health knowledge are embedded in professional networks and are further legitimised through a commitment to scientific knowledge. As Certeau argues, expertise operates as a specific form of practice that legitimates both its knowledge and "the Expert" (1988). In its sanctioned forms, expertise is not only produced but performed in research statements that iterate their truth while reinforcing a system of authority through which expert claims can continue to be made and understood as such (Law, 2004). This system protects certain knowledges and excludes other ways of knowing, as evident in research discussions of young people's lack of sexual health knowledge (Moore & Smith, 2012; Wadham et al., 2019). In delivering this knowledge, "the Expert" reminds young people of the limitations of their knowledge and the persistent need for health education and promotion to be produced and delivered to them by formal, reputable institutions. Here, expertise is only aligned with the professional roles of people who speak from "legitimate" sites of knowing. This ensures a continued risk framing that does not (and cannot) invite engagement with young people's practical knowledge, including their know-how in managing digital communication risks to privacy, social status, identity, and friendships.

Formal health communications' narrow scope of how media is used is foregrounded in much of the health literature mentioned. As such, young people's expertise in digital communication (Third et al., 2019), along with their competencies in negotiating a range of digital platforms and intimacies, rarely feature in public health discussions. In grappling with this problem, I find value in Lyotard's work on the interplay and hierarchy between "scientific knowledge" and "narrative knowledge". He states that

> scientific knowledge does not represent the totality of knowledge; it has always existed in addition to, and in competition and conflict with, another kind of knowledge, which I will call narrative in the interests of simplicity. (1991, p. 7)

For Lyotard, narrative knowledge is constituted by *know-how, knowing how to live,* and *knowing how to listen* (1991, p. 18) – as such, this encapsulates social competencies. Lyotard argues that knowledge is more akin to a game in which moves are negotiated (1991, p. 16), rather than being confined to fixed and reliable nodes of information produced by the knowing expert. Narrative knowledge is generated beyond the scope of scientific statements, is less concerned with accuracy, and involves the exercise of competent negotiation. This form of knowledge is more oriented to having the skills and faculties of knowing – i.e. knowing how to find and assess information, as necessary. Narrative knowledge has some similarity to Foucault's concept of subjugated knowledges – as "ways of knowing" that are typically discredited by scientific discourse (2004). An example of this knowledge can be seen in young people's everyday negotiations of identity, self-presentation, and friendships in social media. Professional attempts to inject "scientific knowledge" into young people's social media interactions – such as fact-based knowledge about the health risks of STI transmission, therefore poorly translate into these media environments and cultures. As one focus group participant said, "No one wants to get a lecture whilst they are online and trying to do their social thing".

Certeau considers how "experts" commit to a particular genre of expertise through which they claim a specific "place" of knowledge that is distinct from other sites, and uninhabitable by other people. Accordingly, formal sexual health knowledge, as well as a current professional understanding of health communication, is not available to young people, and young people's direct input into this knowledge is not sought. According to Certeau, knowledge is strategic in the sense that "every strategic rationalization seeks first of all to distinguish its 'own' place" (Certeau de, 1988, p. 36). As such, the place of health professionals is formalised through claims to legitimacy that effectively delegitimise other ways of knowing. Also delegitimised is knowledge that is co-produced and curated through friendship and peer support – as central to much social media interaction. For public health knowledge institutions to maintain their expertise, informal knowledge systems, as found in everyday care and support among friends and peers, must be overlooked or undermined. For health promoters, this ensures that most social media interventions are bound to fail.

Partnering with experts

A public health tradition of targeted health promotion strategies has carried into sexual health promotion online, where "harnessing" social media spaces is presented as key to ensuring that health promotion messages reach young people. In the health literature discussed, social media platforms are commonly presented as "settings" amenable to targeted interventions like those administered in schools, universities, or youth services (Loss et al., 2014). Furthermore, health promoters are encouraged to enter social media spaces without unpacking the obstacles and ethical issues in doing so (Mowlabocus et al., 2014). In not engaging with the participatory aspects of social media (Albury & Byron, 2019) in which young people are knowledgeable "produsers", the effects of such health interventions are limited.

Young people's discussion of Facebook in this chapter suggests a complex arrangement of social and interpersonal practices whereby sexual health content is risky and, in most cases, unlikely. All groups considered stigma, alongside privacy risks inherent to social media, and the likelihood of sexual content generating drama, as prohibitive factors for sharing sexual health content. This practice-based knowledge is valuable to current health promotion strategies seeking to engage with young people via social media.

Health promoters and professionals must remember that social and digital media environments are not separate from offline worlds, but these are integrated spaces for young people (boyd, 2014; Pascoe, 2011). These spaces also centre on friendship and its practice. Social media profiles, content, and interactions serve as a form of social identity and are managed accordingly (Davis, 2014; Marwick, 2013), and young people use a range of platforms to share and produce media content for audiences comprised of friends and broader networks (Niland et al., 2015). Through social media, friendship networks have become increasingly visible and central to the formation of a public identity (Baym, 2015; boyd, 2006). As well as to friends, young people's social media interactions are visible to extended networks, as per boyd's concept of *networked publics* which highlights the impossibility of containing communication within "structurally enforced borders" (boyd, 2008, p. 131). Therefore, sharing "controversial" media, such as sexual health messages, carries broader social risks beyond immediate friendship networks.

As CJ Pascoe has argued, social media play a significant role in "connecting youth to communities and information that might not be available elsewhere" (2011, p. 12), and this includes opportunities for expansive access to a range of experience-based knowledge. Despite adult concerns, privacy is not neglected by young people in their practices of public sharing but is carefully managed in ways that trouble traditional notions of public/private communication, complicating the notion of "publicness" (Baym & boyd, 2012). Young people's management of privacy does not simply involve withholding personal information, but carefully choosing to disclose information about themselves to some people and not others (Livingstone, 2008), often through the use of careful language that can exclude parents and adult onlookers (Marwick & boyd, 2014b).

More interdisciplinary approaches to health promotion are needed, where health agendas are informed by digital ethnographies of young people's social media use. Findings from ethnographic research can inform new health communication strategies that recognise how media production occurs through media use, generating new modes of friendship, intimacy, and community. To date, most mainstream public health implies a "media effects" approach that considers its messages as having a uniform meaning and trajectory, from sender to receiver. This disregards what is known about communication practices in digital environments (as well as in pre-digital environments), and young people can provide much expertise on this.

While young people's health knowledges can be informed by health professionals, they are also informed by other relationships and significant sites of care, including friendships. As such, young people's expertise is not simply garnered from top-down education but is increasingly lateral. Young people gather health knowledge that is both scientific and narrative based, and they engage with a range of knowledges, both sanctioned and subjugated by health professionals. In today's knowledge economy, trust is placed not only in professionals but in one's social and intimate networks, and it is encoded in shared stories of "lived experience", as discussed throughout this book. Despite this, young people are rarely engaged as research partners, stakeholders, or co-producers of digital health interventions. Yet they could be, if their cultural expertise of social and digital media use was recognised and respected in health and research settings. As Albury (2018) notes, while formal health projects sometimes invite young people to sit on advisory committees, this rarely extends to involving young people in decision-making. She asks, "how might young people participate in sexual health practice as experts, partners, policy-makers and/or researchers, rather than simply as clients, research subjects or 'target populations'…?" (2018, p. 1334).

Health promoters and professionals should consider ways in which health interventions can further support young people's social media practices of friendship and peer support. It may be the case that most young people are well placed (and well practised) to be able to source, manage, and disseminate sexual health information within existing networks of care and support. This is not to suggest that health promotion strategies are redundant but that they might gain leverage from existing cultures of care, of which many young people have considerable expertise. Accordingly, health promoters could also invest more resources in young people's own mediated practices of care, support, and information sharing – including sexual health information and support. As already noted in this book, peer support and information sharing cannot be disentangled, and support – among friends and invested peers – increases the likelihood of engaging with, learning from, and further building everyday health knowledge.

Notes

1 This chapter was originally published as the following article but has been revised and updated for this book: Byron, P. (2015). Troubling expertise: social media and young people's sexual health. *Communication Research and Practice*, 1(4), 322–334.
2 See Introduction chapter for more information about this study.
3 eHealth (electronic health) initially focused on internet-based health information delivery but is used more broadly today, and mHealth (mobile health) initially focused on mobile phone messaging interventions, but would later include mobile phone app interventions.
4 Notably, Facebook is not as actively used by young people today.

References

Albury, K. (2018). Young people, digital media research and counterpublic sexual health. *Sexualities*, 21(8), 1331–1336.

Albury, K. (2019). "Recognition of competition" versus Will to App: Rethinking digital engagement in Australian youth sexual health promotion policy and practice. *Media International Australia*, 171(1), 38–50.

Albury, K., & Byron, P. (2019). Taking off the risk goggles: Exploring the intersection of young people's sexual and digital citizenship in sexual health promotion. In P. Aggleton, R. Cover, D. Leahy, D. Marshall & M. L. Rasmussen (Eds.), *Youth, sexuality and sexual citizenship* (pp. 168–183). London & New York, NY: Routledge.

Allison, S., Bauermeister, J. A., Bull, S., Lightfoot, M., Mustanski, B., Shegog, R., & Levine, D. (2012). The intersection of youth, technology, and new media with sexual health: Moving the research agenda forward. *Journal of Adolescent Health*, 51(3), 207–212.

Balleys, C., & Coll, S., S. (2017). Being publicly intimate: Teenagers managing online privacy. *Media, Culture and Society*, 39(6), 885–901.

Baym, N. (2015). *Personal connections in the digital age* (2nd ed.). Cambridge: Polity Press.

Baym, N., & boyd, d. (2012). Socially mediated publicness: An introduction. *Journal of Broadcasting and Electronic Media*, 56(3), 320–329.

boyd, d. (2006). Friends, friendsters, and MySpace top 8: Writing community into being on social network sites. *First Monday*, 11(12).

boyd, d. (2008). Why youth ♥ social network sites: The role of networked publics in teenage social life. In D. Buckingham (Ed.), *The John D. and Catherine T.*

MacArthur foundation series on digital media and learning (pp. 119–142). Cambridge: MIT Press.

boyd, d. (2014). *It's complicated: The social lives of networked teens*. New Haven, CT: Yale University Press.

boyd, d., & Hargittai, E. (2010). Facebook privacy settings: Who cares? *First Monday, 15*(8), 2.

Bruns, A. (2006). *Towards produsage: Futures for user-led content production*. Paper presented at the Cultural Attitudes towards Communication and Technology. Tartu, Estonia.

Bull, S. S., Levine, D., Black, S. R., Schmiege, S. J., & Santelli, J. (2012). Social media–delivered sexual health intervention: A cluster randomized controlled trial. *American Journal of Preventive Medicine, 43*(5), 467–474.

Burgess, J., Osman, K., McKee, A., & Hall, N. (2018*). 7 Funny guys talk Sex: An entertainment-education model for reaching young men with sexual health information through digital media*. Brisbane: Digital Media Research Centre, Queensland University of Technology & True Relationships and Reproductive Health.

Byron, P., Evers, C., & Albury, K. (2013). "It would be weird to have that on Facebook": Young people's use of social media and the risk of sharing sexual health information. *Reproductive Health Matters, 21*(41), 35–44.

Capurro, D., Cole, K., Echavarría, M. I., Joe, J., Neogi, T., & Turner, A. M. (2014). The use of social networking sites for public health practice and research: A systematic review. *Journal of Medical Internet Research, 16*(3), e79.

Certeau de, M. (1988). *The practice of everyday life*. Berkeley, CA: University of California Press.

Chambers, D. (2013). *Social media and personal relationships: Online intimacies and networked friendship*. New York, NY: Palgrave Macmillan.

Clar, C., Dyakova, M., Curtis, K., Dawson, C., Donnelly, P., Knifton, L., & Clarke, A. (2014). Just telling and selling: Current limitations in the use of digital media in public health. *Public Health, 128*(12), 1066–1075.

Cole, J., Watkins, C., & Kleine, D. (2016). Health advice from internet discussion forums: How bad is dangerous? *Journal of Medical Internet Research, 18*(1), e4.

Collin, P., Rahilly, K., Richardson, I., & Third, A. (2011). *The benefits of social networking services: Literature review*. Sydney: Cooperative Research Centre for Young People, Technology and Wellbeing.

Davis, K. (2014). Youth identities in a digital age: The anchoring role of friends in young People's approaches to online identity expression. In A. Bennett & B. Robards (Eds.), *Mediated youth cultures: The internet, belonging and new cultural configurations* (p. 11). Hampshire: Palgrave Macmillan.

Divecha, Z., Divney, A., Ickovics, J., & Kershaw, T. (2012). Tweeting about testing: Do low-income, parenting adolescents and young adults use new media technologies to communicate about sexual health? *Perspectives on Sexual and Reproductive Health, 44*(3), 176–183.

Dunne, A., McIntosh, J., & Mallory, D. (2014). Adolescents, sexually transmitted infections, and education using social media: A review of the literature. *The Journal for Nurse Practitioners, 10*(6), 401–408.

Evers, C. W., Albury, K., Byron, P., & Crawford, K. (2013). Young people, social media, social network sites and sexual health communication in Australia: "this is funny, you should watch it". *International Journal of Communication*, 7, 263–280.

Eysenbach, G. (2008). Credibility of health information and digital media: New perspectives and implications for youth. In M. J. Metzger & A. J. Flanagin (Eds.), *Digital media, youth, and credibility, the John D. and Catherine T. MacArthur foundation series on digital media and learning* (pp. 123–154). Cambridge: MIT Press.

Fergie, G., Hilton, S., & Hunt, K. (2015). Young adults' experiences of seeking online information about diabetes and mental health in the age of social media. *Health Expectations*, 19(6), 1324–1335.

Fergie, G., Hunt, K., & Hilton, S. (2013). What young people want from health-related online resources: A focus group study. *Journal of Youth Studies*, 16(5), 579–596.

Foucault, M. (2004). *'Society must be defended": Lectures at the Collège de France, 1975–1976*. London: Penguin.

Fox, S., & Jones, S. (2009). *The social life of health information*. Washington, DC: Pew Internet & American Life Project. Retrieved from http://www.pewintern et.org/Reports/2009/8-The-Social-Life-of-Health-Information.aspx.

Gabarron, E., & Wynn, R. (2016). Use of social media for sexual health promotion: A scoping review. *Global Health Action*, 9, 32193.

Gold, J., Pedrana, A. E., Sacks-Davis, R., Hellard, M. E., Chang, S., Howard, S., ... Stoove, M. A. (2011). A systematic examination of the use of online social networking sites for sexual health promotion. *BMC Public Health*, 11(583), 1–9.

Gray, M. L. (2009). Negotiating identities/queering desires: Coming out online and the remediation of the coming-out story. *Journal of Computer-Mediated Communication*, 14(4), 1162–1189.

Gray, N. J., Klein, J. D., Noyce, P. R., Sesselberg, T. S., & Cantrill, J. A. (2005). The Internet: A window on adolescent health literacy. *Journal of Adolescent Health*, 37(3), 1–7.

Green, L., & Brady, D. (2013). Young people online. In J. Hartley, J. Burgess & A. Bruns (Eds.), *A companion to new media dynamics*. West Sussex: Wiley-Blackwell.

Hu, Y., & Shyam Sundar, S. (2010). Effects of online health sources on credibility and behavioral intentions. *Communication Research*, 37(1), 105–132.

Ito, M., Baumer, S., Bittanti, M., Cody, R., Herr-Stephenson, B., Horst, H. A., ... Pascoe, C. (2010). *Hanging out, messing around, and geeking out: Kids living and learning with new media*. Cambridge: MIT Press.

Jenkins, H., Ito, M., & boyd, d. (2015). *Participatory culture in a networked era: A conversation on youth, learning, commerce, and politics*. Cambridge, UK: Polity Press.

Kite, J., Foley, B. C., Grunseit, A. C., & Freeman, B. (2016). Please like me: Facebook and public health communication. *PLoS One*, 11(9), e0162765.

Law, J. (2004). *After method: Mess in Social science research*. London & New York, NY: Routledge.

Lederman, R., Fan, H., Smith, S., & Chang, S. (2014). Who can you trust? Credibility assessment in online health forums. *Health Policy and Technology*, 3(1), 13–25.

Levine, D. (2011). Using technology, new media, and mobile for sexual and reproductive health. *Sexuality Research and Social Policy*, 8(1), 18–26.

Lim, M., & Eaton, K. (2014). *Sexual health & youth (SHY) SMS project: Final report*. Melbourne: Burnet Institute. Retrieved from https://www.burnet.edu.au/projects/156_sexual_health_youth_shy_project.

Lim, M. S. C., Wright, C. J. C., Carrotte, E. R., & Pedrana, A. E. (2016). Reach, engagement, and effectiveness: A systematic review of evaluation methodologies used in health promotion via social networking sites. *Health Promotion Journal of Australia, 27*(3), 187–197.

Livingstone, S. (2008). Taking risky opportunities in youthful content creation: Teenagers' use of social networking sites for intimacy, privacy and self-expression. *New Media and Society, 10*(3), 393–411.

Löfgren-Mårtenson, L., & Månsson, S.-A. (2010). Lust, love, and life: A qualitative study of Swedish adolescents' perceptions and experiences with pornography. *The Journal of Sex Research, 47*(6), 568–579.

Loss, J., Lindacher, V., & Curbach, J. (2014). Online social networking sites – A novel setting for health promotion? *Health and Place, 26*, 161–170.

Lupton, D. (2015). Health Promotion in the digital era: A critical commentary. *Health Promotion International, 30*(1), 174–183.

Lyotard, J.-F. (1991). *The postmodern condition: A report on knowledge*. Manchester: Manchester University Press.

Madianou, M., & Miller, D. (2013). Polymedia: Towards a new theory of digital media in interpersonal communication. *International Journal of Cultural Studies, 16*(2), 169–187.

Marwick, A. (2005). *"I'm a lot more interesting than a friendster profile": Identity, presentation, authenticity and power in social networking services*. Paper presented at the Conference of the Association of Internet Researchers 6, Chicago, IL. Retrieved from http://papers.ssrn.com/sol3/papers.cfm?abstract_id=1884356.

Marwick, A. (2013). Online identity. In J. Hartley, J. Burgess & A. Bruns (Eds.), *A companion to new media dynamics* (pp. 355–364). West Sussex: Blackwell Publishing Ltd.

Marwick, A., & boyd, d. (2011). I tweet honestly, I tweet passionately: Twitter users, context collapse, and the imagined audience. *New Media and Society, 13*(1), 114–133.

Marwick, A., & boyd, d. (2014a). "It's just drama": teen perspectives on conflict and aggression in a networked era. *Journal of Youth Studies, 17*(9), 1187–1204.

Marwick, A., & boyd, d. (2014b). Networked privacy: How teenagers negotiate context in social media. *New Media and Society, 16*(7), 1051–1067.

Moore, E. W., & Smith, W. E. (2012). What college students do not know: Where are the gaps in sexual health knowledge? *Journal of American College of Health, 60*(6), 436–442.

Morgan, A., & Ziglio, E. (2007). Revitalising the evidence base for public health: An assets model. *Global Health Promotion, 14*(2_suppl), 17–22.

Mowlabocus, S., Harbottle, J., Dasgupta, R., & Haslop, C. (2014). *Reaching out online: Digital literacy and the uses of social media in health promotion*. Sussex: Cultures and Communities Network + & University of Sussex.

Niland, P., Lyons, A. C., Goodwin, I., & Hutton, F. (2015). Friendship work on Facebook: Young adults' understandings and practices of friendship. *Journal of Community and Applied Social Psychology, 25*(2), 123–137.

Pascoe, C. J. (2010). Intimacy. In M. Ito (Ed.), *Hanging out, messing around and geeking out: Kids living and learning with new media* (pp. 117–148). Cambridge, MA: MIT Press.

Pascoe, C. J. (2011). Resource and risk: Youth sexuality and new media use. *Sexuality Research and Social Policy, 8*(1), 5–17.

Pascoe, C. J. (2012). Studying young people's new media use: Methodological shifts and educational innovations. *Theory into Practice, 51*(2), 76–82.

Patterson, S. P., Hilton, S., Flowers, P., & McDaid, L. M. (2019). What are the barriers and challenges faced by adolescents when searching for sexual health information on the internet? Implications for policy and practice from a qualitative study. *Sexually Transmitted Infections, 95*(6), 462–467.

Pedrana, A., Hellard, M., Gold, J., Ata, N., Chang, S., Howard, S., … Stoove, M. (2013). Queer as F** k: Reaching and engaging gay men in sexual Health Promotion through social networking sites. *Journal of Medical Internet Research, 15*(2), 25.

Pfeiffer, C., Kleeb, M., Mbelwa, A., & Ahorlu, C. (2014). The use of social media among adolescents in Dar es Salaam and Mtwara, Tanzania. *Reproductive Health Matters, 22*(43), 178–186.

Poland, B., Krupa, G., & McCall, D. (2009). Settings for Health Promotion: An analytic framework to guide intervention design and implementation. *Health Promotion Practice, 10*(4), 505–516.

Ralph, L. J., Berglas, N. F., Schwartz, S. L., & Brindis, C. D. (2011). Finding teens in TheirSpace: Using social networking sites to connect youth to sexual health services. *Sexuality Research and Social Policy, 8*(1), 38–49.

Robards, B. (2012). Leaving MySpace, joining Facebook: "Growing up" on social network sites. *Continuum, 26*(3), 385–398.

Syred, J., Naidoo, C., Woodhall, S. C., & Baraitser, P. (2014). Would you tell everyone this? Facebook conversations as health promotion interventions. *Journal of Medical Internet Research, 16*(4), e108.

Thackeray, R., Crookston, B. T., & West, J. H. (2013). Correlates of health-related social media use among adults. *Journal of Medical Internet Research, 15*(1), e21.

Third, A., Bellerose, D., De Oliveira, J. D., Lala, G., & Theakstone, G. (2017). *Young and online: Children's perspectives on life in the digital age (The State of the world's children 2017 companion report).* Sydney: University of Western Sydney.

Third, A., Collin, P., Walsh, L., & Black, R. (2019). *Young people in digital society: Control shift.* London: Palgrave Macmillan.

van Dijck, J. (2013). *The culture of connectivity: A critical history of social media.* Oxford & New York, NY: Oxford University Press.

Wadham, E., Green, C., Debattista, J., Somerset, S., & Sav, A. (2019). New digital media interventions for sexual health promotion among young people: A systematic review. *Sexual Health, 16*(2), 101–123.

Wang, Z., Walther, J. B., Pingree, S., & Hawkins, R. P. (2008). Health information, credibility, homophily, and influence via the internet: Web sites versus discussion groups. *Health Communication, 23*(4), 358–368.

4 Friendship and sexual intimacy[1]

This chapter takes a step back from the book's focus on digital cultures to look at young people's friendships more broadly. Here, I report on data collected in 2009, as part of my doctoral research project on sexual health and its negotiations. Interviews with 12 young people, aged 18–25 years, were part of a broader discourse analysis (Foucault, 1991) of *young people's sexual health*, where I looked across three datasets to consider the discursive elements of this concept that is now embedded in health policy in Australia and many other countries. The three datasets comprised a selection of sexual health research papers, sexual health promotion websites targeting young people, and interviews with young people. Through comparison of these data it became evident that young people's friendships were a significant aspect of their sexual health negotiations and that research and health promotion accounts of young people's sexual health barely acknowledged this. As such, the space and practice of young people's friendships represented a rift between formal and informal understandings of young people's sexual health. This rift represents a significant problem when we consider how health promoters seek to digitally engage with young people alongside health professionals' tendencies to see young people as having a health knowledge deficit, as discussed in previous chapters.

To engage with the centrality of friendship in young people's everyday lives, it is necessary to also consider less digital interactions. Further to this, it is useful to consider other points in time (in this case, ten years prior to writing this book) to reflect on how young people's friendship practices may change but also remain consistent. Interestingly, the friendship stories told throughout this chapter have much in common with the friendship stories shared with me throughout the next decade, while researching digital intimacies. This consistency includes the ways friends support each other, and how this support is structured through intimate knowledge that we have of our friends – thereby increasing the trust and comfort in disclosing and workshopping personal experiences, thoughts, and worries. Of course, digital and non-digital spaces are entangled, even in 2009. Yet this was a time before Instagram, Snapchat, TikTok, and a range of other social media existed – media that are now integral to many young people's friendships.

But of course, these are not the only sites of young people's friendship practices.

Presenting a discursive analysis of the 12 interviews along with three Australian sexual health websites for young people, this chapter considers the relationship between sexual health and friendship intimacies. Participants were not representative of a general population and were mostly university educated.[2] All participants voluntarily participated in the study, and when asked why, most indicated an interest in sexual health, sex, and sexuality. Within the interviews, many indicated that they were "that friend" who advised and supported their friends about sex and sexual health issues. Part of being "that friend" was being sex positive, non-judgemental, and enthusiastic about discussing sex. As such, participants' input offered a useful starting point for expanding health promotion considerations of young people's sexual health expertise, along with important insight into young people's friendship cultures.

Throughout the interviews, explicit references to "intimacy" and/or "closeness" were made by most participants. This was unexpected. I had framed many questions around a discussion of sexual pleasure, since I had assumed this was how sex would be more oriented, rather than in terms of "intimacy". My expected focus on pleasure was informed by common research statements about pleasure's absence in sexual health promotion and sexualities education for young people (Fine, 1988; Fine & McClelland, 2006). But in responding to questions such as "How did you learn what you like, sexually?" and "Do you always enjoy the sex you have?" participants had more to say about intimacy. While it was often stated that better sex occurs in the space of romantic/partner relationships, intimacy was also central to sexual encounters between friends and casual partners. The following statements illustrate the diversity of intimacy discourse.

Betty (age 25): I guess I'm at a point where I'd prefer to be with someone on that sort of level of intimacy more so than it being about the sex. You know what I mean? Just more about friendship and intimacy on a companionship level rather than on a sex-based level.

Jack (age 24): I can have a pretty great time without penetrative sex ... . Like I don't have any qualms about [giving oral sex]. For me, I like the intimacy and that wholly knowing of another person. I find that really exciting and arousing.

These statements highlight how intimacy discourse accommodates a range of sexual encounters, whether casual, part of an ongoing or long-term relationship, or friend based. In Betty's statement, intimacy is more than sex and is aligned with friendship and companionship. But in Jack's statement, intimacy is enhanced through sex, including oral sex with casual female partners. In these examples, intimacy operates at different proximities to sex and is forged through sex as well as peripheral to sex. While illustrating a broad operation of intimacy discourse, these statements do not discount the importance of pleasure, yet they challenge assumptions that pleasure is the primary motivation for young people's sexual practices.

More than simply focusing on young people's *experiences of intimacy*, this chapter considers a socio-cultural *discourse of intimacy* common among research participants and later considers what this offers to recent discussions of digital intimacies. Throughout interviews, references to friends and friendship were common, highlighting friendships' influence on young people's sex and relationship practices. This influence has not been well handled by sexual health promoters to date, aside from the provision of "peer education" strategies which seem to reference, but depart from, young people's friendships (see Chapter 2). Throughout these interviews, however, friendship is presented as a space of shared values, identity work, and non-judgemental listening and support regarding sexual experiences and relationships.

This chapter argues that health promotion should be more responsive to the contextual spaces of young people's sexual intimacies, and the sexual intimacies of close friendships where sexual health is often negotiated. While no single theory adequately corresponds to intimacy discourse in these data, contemporary feminist and queer approaches highlight changing landscapes of public intimacies (Berlant, 1998; Illouz, 2007; Roseneil & Budgeon, 2004). That digital communication technologies have introduced new practices of intimacy (Chambers, 2013) also provides rationale for rethinking the importance of intimacy in young people's sex and relationship practices.

This chapter adds context to previous discussions of friendship support in this book. Firstly, I consider how negotiations of sex (including sexual health) are supported by friends. Secondly, I argue that friendship intimacies include sexual intimacy, as per many participants' experiences of sex with friends. Thirdly, I argue that many close friendships are sexually intimate regardless of whether these are sexual friendships, on account of friends mutually sharing their sexual experiences and interests. For most participants, sex was negotiated through friend-based communication, and much of this happened in-person. Highlighting the porousness of sexual and social networks among young people, this chapter is a useful precursor to Chapter 6, on young people's friendships in the context of dating/hookup app use. That chapter explores how social and digital media contribute to this porousness – where social media and sexual media overlap due to friendship practices. The following sections of this chapter look closely at the different themes of intimacy from my interviews with young people about their sexual health negotiations.

Intimacy, bodies, and feeling

At the beginning of this study, my expectation was for interview participants to highlight the importance of pleasure in their sexual negotiations, and how this might disrupt "safe sex". However, far more was said about "intimacy" and "closeness". For many participants emotional connection was a useful (sometimes necessary) precursor for experiencing sexual pleasure. In many accounts of negotiating sex, participants expanded "safe sex" to include feelings of personal safety and comfort. In doing so, it was commonly suggested that sexual pleasure was often greater and more likely when non-physical intimacy had already been established with partners, including through friendship. This data sits apart from the health promotion websites I will discuss, where intimacy is barely acknowledged in sexual health material designed for young readers.

While key sociological accounts of intimacy conflate this with love, and typically contextualise intimacy's practice in terms of romantic partnerships (Beck & Beck-Gernsheim, 1995; Giddens, 1992), participants rarely did so.[3] More often, they discussed how intimate relationships expand the range and availability of sexual pleasures. For example, Lily (age 21), discussed a range of sexual scenarios in which she and her partner aim to please each other – sometimes forfeiting or minimising one's own sexual pleasure:

My current boyfriend, he'll finger me and bring me to orgasm. He knows what he's doing, and that's ... it's different emotionally, in terms of the closeness, but physically it's just as powerful, if not sometimes better because you can reach places and get specific things done that aren't otherwise.

Lily suggests that while fingering is not as emotionally close (as vagina-penis sex), it can lead to greater physical pleasure for her. Through the intimacy of their relationship, she and her partner have expanded their sexual repertoires to produce new pleasure practices. Here, distinctions between physical and emotional closeness are paradoxical, since it is only through an established closeness that practices described as less intimate become more available, and through which physical pleasures are enhanced. Further reflecting upon her closeness with her partner, Lily states, "even if I'm not aroused it's still fun and closeness ... even if just the other person's enjoying it, it still makes it worth my time". Here, Lily notes a pleasure in pleasuring that is fostered by, and enhanced through, intimacy. Charlie (age 24) also reflects on a sexual experience where he found greater pleasure in intimacy than sex, saying, "I feel that probably the intimacy and just her presence was probably 100 times more enjoyable than sticking it in".

This discourse of intimacy extends to discussions of friendship, including experiences of sex with friends. Amanda (age 22) described an occasion where she had sex with a close friend but later regretted this. She suggests an ambiguous relationship between pleasure and intimacy, where intimacy can be furthered through sex that is unenjoyable.

> I regret sleeping with my friend last year because it wasn't incredibly enjoyable because I knew that I shouldn't have been doing it. And then, you know, afterwards his awkwardness has made it, you know, like counter-productive of the whole experience. Even though I feel like, I do actually feel like we became closer because of it, there's still the awkwardness.

Despite describing sex with this friend as not particularly enjoyable, and generating a current awkwardness, Amanda notes how the experience also made their friendship closer. Here, intimacy is produced through sex regardless of pleasure and can therefore create space for acceptable non-pleasure.

Commonly, the discursive proximity of pleasure and intimacy within casual sex differs to partner-based sex, though there is no agreement on this. Oliver (age 19) states that for him, seeking intimacy through casual sex is problematic. This is illustrated in a story he shares about having sex with a work colleague, stating, "I was sort of at a weird stage. My brother had died about a month before and I think I just needed, I just wanted to feel close to someone". But Oliver did not find this to be a positive experience, and he suggests that he was supplanting his need for intimacy with casual sex. Meanwhile, Jack's earlier statement about the intimacy of "wholly knowing" another person through oral sex suggests that intimacy need not precede sex but can be forged through sex. Jack states that oral sex not only offers a form of safer sex (in the absence of condoms) but enhances sexual intimacy.

Elsewhere, pleasure and intimacy are considered as less mutually supportive, such as when Brad (age 23) discusses seeking sexual pleasure that is free of emotion, stating, "I've been considering going and seeing, paying for sex, because then it would be like, I just feel like there would be no emotion and … because I, I'd like to have sex". Brad's experiences of being a sex worker inform his knowledge of the affordances of purchased sex, and his consideration of paying for sex offers a scenario in which unemotional sex with an unknown person can afford emotional safety.

These accounts point to the slipperiness of intimacy and the difficulty in locating or identifying it (or not) in sexual practices. This is important context for other discussions of intimacy throughout this book – particularly the discussion of digital intimacies. These accounts draw our attention to intimacy as a complex structure of feelings, bodies, and relationships (including friendships). To think about "digital intimacies", it is useful to consider the uneven, shifting, and sometimes contradictory narratives of closeness, proximity, comfort, and care. Notably, there is no agreed-upon ideal of sexual intimacy. As Lauren Berlant has argued, "While the fantasies associated with intimacy usually end up occupying the space of convention, in practice the drive toward it is a kind of wild thing that is not necessarily organized that way, or any way" (1998, p. 284). This lack of organisation can be further considered in relation to the context in which interview participants' accounts are doing the labour of producing a coherent account of intimacy – for themselves and their own reflective benefit, but also for me, as the researcher asking difficult questions.

Friendship and sex

In stories of sex between friends, participants suggest more complex arrangements of intimacy. In some accounts, sex between friends is said to offer greater safety through increased condom use but also through a broader sense of safety attributed to established trust and intimacy. Sometimes the pleasure of sex is heightened by such intimacies. Elsewhere, sex with friends is presented as risky. In discussing an occasion where she "cheated on" a former partner by sleeping with her friend, Cathy (age 20) stated that she preferred sex with her friend.

Paul: Why was it better?
Cathy: Because he knew what he was doing and I actually liked him.
Paul: Okay. And so that guy you slept with many times?
Cathy: Just once, actually, because we were friends and then it got weird.

This suggests that friendship makes for better sex, yet that sex can complicate the friendship. This echoes Amanda's story discussed earlier, in which sex challenged her friendship, while also strengthening its intimacy. Literature on "friends with benefits" (FWB) relationships (Bisson & Levine, 2009; Wentland & Reissing, 2014), notes that sexual friendships are increasingly common among young people and that these afford sex that is intimate, respectful, and carries less obligation than sex within "a relationship". The FWB relationship troubles distinctions traditionally made between young people's relations of romance, casual sex, and friendship (Bisson & Levine, 2009; Epstein et al., 2009; Hughes et al., 2005). Health promotion accounts, however, tend to benchmark sexual safety with reference to heteronormative, monogamous partnerships (Allen & Carmody, 2012), as per common sociological accounts of intimacy (Roseneil & Budgeon, 2004), and also found in the sexual health websites reviewed later in this chapter.[4]

Public health literature and health promotion messages often suggest that young people's use of condoms is challenged by their prioritisation of sexual pleasure (Braun, 2013; Measor, 2006). But condom use is not only a "pleasure risk", as it can also threaten the *intimacy* of sex, according to several participants. For example, Betty states that stopping sexual activity to put a condom on "can ruin the moment of intimacy". Lily makes a similar claim but notes that this is not the case when having sex with friends.

With a new partner kind of thing there's this expectation to be constantly pleasing them. And if you have to stop to put on a condom it's like, it's like you build up your thing. You're like, "oh man, I'm losing fuel" … and it can be quite stressful. Or like, if you're not comfortable talking with them, there's awkward silence while you do the whole routine. But if you're mates … if you're friends anyway, you're comfortable being in each other's company and it's just another step in the process.

Here, the pressures of wanting to please a new partner, and the pause and awkward silence in applying a condom, present a risk to the flow (and pleasures) of sex. However, the space of friendship makes condom use less disruptive. Further to this, friendship can offer a safer space for sexual experimentation, as Lily stated elsewhere:

> During high school and early uni I'd do things with friends for the pleasure kick, but it had to be a friend who I was at least close with, kind of thing. I'd have to feel quite close with them.

Lily also refers to her experiments with bondage and how this is best facilitated with friends rather than her current partner who feels uneasy about these practices. She says, "It's taking a while to sort of ease him into that kind of thing because he's terrified of hurting me. He's very protective". Thus, the intimacy of a partner relationship may be more restrictive to sexual pleasures that are better supported by friends, with friendship offering a wider range of negotiations of pleasure through more open and creative forms of intimacy.

Safe intimacies

Participants suggest that intimacy enables safer sex to happen – not just in terms of condom use but in feeling safe and comfortable within one's sex practices. Natalie (age 25) recounts an experience of having sex in a park while drunk, saying she was "relatively inexperienced" at the time and "just going along with it". She states that she regretted it the following day, and in describing why, she highlights the kind of sex she would prefer:

> It wasn't a very sort of intimate sort of caring experience. It was just sort of quite sort of rough sex … no foreplay; no sort of making sure I was enjoying it; no sort of checking in with the other person saying, "Does this feel good?" Any of that. Like none of that. It was just sort of like quick, over and done with. Not particularly pleasurable for me.

Suggested here is a preference for sex that is more intimate and caring, with more communication to ensure pleasure and comfort. Natalie states that she would have better managed this situation had she been more sexually experienced. Following this, I asked her to describe "good sex", which she notes as variable:

I think you can have great sex without any foreplay, if that's what you're both in the mood for at that point in time. Then you can have other sex where you have lots of foreplay. In the same way that you can have really gentle sex with one partner one night and then with the same partner the next night have really sort of rough sex. And that can all be pleasurable as long as it's kind of communicated either verbally or non-verbally.

In this statement, the spatial arrangements of pleasure are quite open, but this openness is contextualised through established intimacy, along with respect and communication. Natalie's statement does not situate intimacy or pleasure within a particular mode of sex practice, however, nor a particular kind of sexual relationship, given that "the same partner" does not necessarily imply a monogamous partner. This account also suggests levels of trust and intimacy that interviewees elsewhere commonly associate with friendship. Such intimacy accommodates both sexual pleasure and safety, as also noted by Lily when she discusses her tactics for negotiating safety with new partners:

Paul: You mentioned [with] the three guys you've had sex with that you asked about their sexual history. How do you do that?

Lily: Well, like I said, I generally know them beforehand. And usually there's ... you feel close enough as friends, you're hanging out, you're talking ... I find that if you keep talking through, like you know, you show interest by touching and stuff ... you keep talking for a bit until you have all the information that you need, then it draws you closer, because you're like, you're telling things about yourself.

Drawing partners closer through conversation, disclosure, and touching has a twofold effect for Lily; getting to know their sexual history as well as furthering an intimacy in which sexual pleasure will be enhanced. Lily's tactical approach simultaneously enhances the pleasure, safety, and intimacy of a sexual event, where pleasure and safety are not antithetical. For a young person, tactics such as these are more likely to be shared among friends, rather than formal sources of education, since friends have more knowledge of, and concern for, the details of one's intimacies. Yet these tactics for managing sexual safety are also offered by peers through anonymous discussion in digital media forums.

The distance of sexual health promotion

This section considers data from three websites that provided sexual health information to young people at the time this research was conducted. These were produced by the Australian Government (Department of Health and Ageing), a non-government organisation (Marie Stopes), and an Australian university (University of Melbourne). These websites were selected because each targeted an audience of young people living in Australia, each comes from a different institutional setting – crossing public and private sectors – and each addresses a range of sexual health and STI prevention practices. These websites largely offer a sex-positive approach since they are not framed by a sexual abstinence agenda, nor do they discuss sex as a moral problem. The websites also do not explicitly discuss how intimacies, including friendship intimacies, can support young people's negotiations of sexual health.

The following statement from *Your Sex Health* was the most explicit reference to intimacy given in any of these sites, yet it focuses on gender differences, stating that intimacy is more prevalent and available among girls:

> Experts suggest that it's partly because the sexes have different capacities for intimacy at different stages. Teenage girls may be better equipped to handle intimate relationships because of the kinds of close friendships they've had with girlfriends. Girls talk to girls about their problems, share emotions and support each other. Boys have a joke together but generally don't reveal as much when they talk to their mates. (University of Melbourne)

By gendering intimacy in this way, this statement forgoes a deeper understanding of how intimacies play out beyond a measure of sexual difference. At the same time, this statement notes the value of intimacy for supporting young people's sexual negotiations. Unfortunately, this supportive space is not discussed further. In such examples, a discourse of intimacy not only falls short of promoting or situating it as health enabling but also binds intimacy practices to gender in a simplistic way, where intimacy belongs to female friendships. While acknowledging friendship in a potentially useful way – as a key site of emotional support – a hierarchy of intimacy is also present here. It is implied that friendship intimacies inform one's "relationship" intimacies, with the latter implied to be the primary relationship that young people seek. As such, and through an otherwise lack of attention to friendship intimacies, these intimacies are characterised as temporary – as something that one experiences before moving into the space of intimate (heterosexual) relationships. Perhaps this seems too harsh a reading of health promotion resources, given that their focus is on sex, presumed to be between couples. Yet, as my research here suggests, along with further evidence (Bisson & Levine, 2009; Furman & Shaffer, 2010), friendships are often sexually intimate. It therefore seems necessary to incorporate friendship intimacies into sexual health promotion resources.

In a section of the *Your Sex Health* site titled "Accelerating Intimacy", young readers are warned against "dating" practices that take place via email, mobile phones, and text messaging. Readers are told, "This trend towards accelerating sexual intimacy demands new social skills. Perhaps the most important one is the ability to slow it all down, if you feel rushed" (University of Melbourne).[5] This statement brings gravity to sexual intimacy, suggesting a need for its careful management and slow development. Given the broader health focus of this particular website (it offers a more holistic account of health, sex, and relationships), this "danger" correlates a need to manage one's sexual intimacies as part of one's management of sexual health. Statements such as these are somewhat redundant in a culture where digital intimacy is everyday practice. Though young people too, often note a need for a more careful negotiation of sex and intimacy found through digital communication and a range of platforms (see Chapter 6 on negotiating dating/hook-up apps).

In the Stancombe Research qualitative report that informed the government website,[6] young people's practices and understandings of sex are questioned in relation to their "base language", and their references to "friends with benefits" and "fuck buddies".

> When all group discussion participants focussed specifically on the meaning of sex, it was unanimously described in raunchy, physical terms, and often with base language. Talk of "fuck buddies", "booty calls", and "friends with benefits" was common. There was little mention of romance or love (except amongst some gay men) and most language focussed on the convenience aspects of no-strings attached sex or the physical act. (2008, p. 18)

This statement provides a moral critique of the language used by young people rather than unpacking these discussions to consider the sexual cultures these terms relate to. That young people are discussing sex in relation to "friends with benefits" points to practices beyond simply seeking love and romance (implied here to be the norm) but involve sexual friendships. Aside from its moralising, and the inadequacy of sexual health promotion that is informed by doing so, this statement fails to engage with the overlap between sexual and friendship cultures. Here, the important role friendships can play in young people's sexual health negotiations – as sex partners, sexual advisers, or both – are overlooked. By overlooking sexual friendships, the care-giving – and potentially health-promoting – aspects of friendship are also not addressed. Yet this aspect of sexual health support would be useful for health promoters to know about and learn from.

While mentioned in these websites, friendship is rarely discussed in relation to sexual health. Rather, "safe sex" is presented to readers as an individualised practice that they must manage alone, or with their sexual partners, with guidance from formal health information. In the websites' promotion of young people's need for professional sexual health information, friendships are sidelined as potentially disruptive to sexual health knowledge. The government website does not discuss young people's friendship or peers at all, perhaps on account of the Stancombe Research reports

(2008, 2009) that position friendships as risky and likely to corrupt young people's knowledge and practice of sexual health. The quantitative report that informed this website states:

> A significant proportion of sexually active 16-29 year olds would talk to their friends / partner. Given the lack of detailed knowledge regarding STIs among this group, this could potentially give rise to an element of "the blind leading the blind". (2009, p. 22)

While the three sexual health websites certainly offer information that would be useful to young people, they do not reflect the range of intimacies that young people seek and enjoy throughout their sexual lives. Warning readers about the inexperience and limited knowledge of their friends or peers, and/ or suggesting that a young reader must manage their sexual health alone, fails to acknowledge young people's need for support beyond simply ingesting information or attending clinical settings for STI testing and treatment. Throughout these websites is a consistent dislocation of sexual acts from the context and relations in which they unfold.

Sexual information sharing

When interview participants were asked where they sourced information about sex and sexual health, the most common sources named were friends, pornography, and the internet. Formal sexual health information was not rejected but used in tandem with informal sources. Reference to the experience-based knowledge of friends suggests that this is highly valued and trusted, and many noted their comfort in asking friends about sex. When asked about sexual information seeking, Brad stated, "[I'd] probably ask my friends. Because I feel they're experienced. And there's a good dialogue around that stuff". Suggested here is an accessible and trustworthy expertise that friends provide that is safe to seek. Brad's reference to dialogue suggests a two-way communication around sex that differs from information sourced from a GP or a website (but he also mentions using these). A similar response is given by Amanda, who states: "I'd probably ask a friend, like a close friend … there's lots of questions about that that I get from those people because they're so open with it. So it's easy and it's normal to ask them".

Participants mostly sourced sexual information from their friends, whereas sexual health information was primarily sought online. The likelihood of discussing sexual health with friends depended on who the friend was. Some friendships were particularly useful for offering information about sex, including sexual moves and techniques one might try to increase sexual pleasure. Oliver states that with his religious friends, "the topic of sex will never come up", yet he frequently discussed sex with his "women's studies" friend. This suggests that sexually intimate friendships (whether sex happened in those friendships or not), relied on having shared values around sex, and mutual comfort in openly discussing sexual experiences, relationships, problems, and pleasures. As Oliver states:

> I have some friends who, like, who're quite comfortable talking about sex and stuff, and so you know, they'll be like "Oh yeah, he did that and that felt good. You should try that". Or like, you know "I did this and she seemed to like it. Do that".

That participants' negotiations of sexual pleasure were often supported by advice and counsel from close friends, indicates that sexual pleasure is not only produced through sex, or between sexual partners, but within friendships that offer support, reflection, and disclosure. For example, Cathy tells a story about having drunken sex in an electrical closet with a bartender while he was on-duty. She was encouraged to approach the man by her friends in the bar that evening and discusses how she recounted the story to those friends the following day. She says: "I was kind of just very surprised at myself the next morning. My friends thought it was really funny". She describes the event as something she is not proud of: "Makes for a good story, but not my best decision". Arguably, Cathy found greater pleasure in sharing the story with her friends than in the sex itself. Such anecdotes demonstrate how "private" sexual encounters are often de-privatised through friendship-based storytelling.

There was variation among participants about whether talking about sex was easier among same/different gender friends, and many noted that this might depend on what they wanted to learn or reflect on. Participants also discussed their friends' sexual predicaments and how the space of friendship offers a site of workshopping and problem-solving. For example, Natalie tells a story about her friend figuring out how to enjoy sex with her partner:

> I was speaking to one friend who was going out with a guy who was not particularly well endowed. And so her response was, "Alright, I'm just gonna go online and I'm gonna Google the best sex positions for having sex with somebody to make it the best sex possible".

Here, Natalie's friend shared not only her sexual issue but her method of problem-solving. In such discussion, friends are acquainted with the intimate details of each other's sexual lives and can therefore be considered *sexually intimate*. They also gather insight into friends' strategies for addressing sexual problems. Furthermore, by being privy to a friend's experiences, including the sexual anatomy, preferences, and quirks of their partners, a friend becomes a more dependable source of support based on their intimate knowledge of your sexual history and practices. Friendship advice is therefore tailored. It can also provide safety from judgement, as highlighted by Betty (age 25), who states that male partners and male health professionals have judged her negatively for having had many sex partners, but that her friends are reliably non-judgemental:

> My close friends don't judge me. And that's why I find it hard when other people do. It's like, why judge me, you know? What did I do to you? But yeah, they don't, it doesn't bother them at all that I've been and done whatever.

A similar discourse of non-judgement is expressed in relation to STIs. For example, Brad is open with friends and housemates about having herpes, saying that he does not believe it should be taboo. Yet this openness does not extend beyond his close friends. A space of non-judgement is also reflected where friends have non-traditional sex and relationship practices. While Oliver notes his need to only have relationship-based sex, he states, "I have some friends who are like 'yeah, [casual sex is] beautiful and you know, you meet strangers and you share this moment' and yeah, that sounds sort of nice". Elsewhere, Lily defends her friends who are judged negatively for having an open relationship:

> I know people in an open relationship and they seem to have things quite well worked out, so everyone is like "[gasp] sleeping with more than one person at the same time". But hey, they're happy, and have a very emotionally rewarding relationship.

Both Oliver and Lily defend the sexual practices of their friends, despite these contrasting with their own relationship preferences. This suggests that being acquainted with your friends' sexual and romantic relations allows you to consider and accept a range of relational and sexual possibilities. In effect, the openness of friendship discussions of sex and relationships can also open us up to a range of intimate possibilities, beyond the limits of our own experiences.

Sex with friends

As noted, literature on friends with benefits relationships points to a range of intimate relations among young people that operate beyond categories of casual or regular sex partners (Bisson & Levine, 2009; Erlandsson et al., 2013). Bisson and Levine (2009) note that 60% of the US college students they sampled had such relationships, and a decade earlier, Afifi and Faulkner (2000) claimed that more than half of all US college students have sexual relations with "otherwise platonic" friends. Erlandsson et al. (2013, p. 55) describe FWB relations as a hybrid of independence and commitment that are useful for attaining "physical and psychological intimacy without expectations and demands". For Bisson and Levine (2009, p. 67), an FWB relationship resembles neither a hook-up nor a traditional romantic relationship, but "combines the psychological intimacy of a friendship with the sexual intimacy of a romantic relationship". Their research participants note the advantages of established trust and comfort with sex partners, along with avoiding romantic commitment that would complicate their friendships. This locates friendship as the primary and most valued aspect of these relationships (2009).

Participants situate sex with friends as both safe and risky, depending on context, timing, and the type of friendships involved. As noted, Amanda spoke about having sex with a friend, and her regret in doing so. She further states:

> we've been friends for so long that when we slept together he actually realised that he shouldn't have done that. He realised that. We're still friends now. It's slightly hard because I don't think he's told his current girlfriend that that occurred. But we're quite good friends. So it makes it difficult.

This account points to how sex among friends can sometimes negatively affect one's social and friendship networks, with this resulting in Amanda having an uneasy friendship with this guy's current partner. Natalie similarly speaks to how sex with some friends can compromise an established friendship intimacy, as discussed in relation to a sexual experience with her friend:

> I would never have had sex with that person under sober circumstances. And I've just felt like, particularly when it was a friend, because then it's like, well you can't really undo that and that could potentially change our friendship, and the dynamic of that.

Elsewhere, Natalie recalls her first experience of sex with a man who was her work colleague and her friend's older brother. She describes it as "a good first experience" due to their "pre-established friendship". Paired with her previous example, Natalie demonstrates the different contexts of sex with friends, and how this can offer both safety and risk. Evidently, friendship intimacy can make sex more comfortable and pleasurable, but friendship intimacy may also be disrupted by sex. Risk of friendship loss through sex was a common concern among participants, further indicating a high regard for friendship. Sam (22, gay) gave an example of sex with a friend in which he "didn't feel comfortable about that experience", and said: "as I expected, our relationship, I mean the friendship, is kind of destroyed".

But not all accounts of friend-sex were described as risky. Discussing a sexual "trade off" with her friend in secondary school, Lily notes the learning opportunities found in negotiating sex with friends. Here, friendship offered a safe space for sexual experimentation where Lily was able to receive oral sex in exchange for her male friend getting to experience anal sex. She describes the arrangement as two one-sided events in which the anal sex was a detached experience for her.

Lily: As I said, we were friends, not anything else. It's something he wanted to try out. I'm like "Okay. I'll just be here. Let me know when you're done back there".
Paul: So there was no pleasure for you?
Lily: No. … And it was important that there wasn't any. It was a friend thing.

Being a "friend thing" suggests that the success of this arrangement was in the negotiated exchange, where trust enabled each friend to trade acts of non-reciprocal pleasure. While Lily's friend may have enjoyed the oral sex, this seemed inconsequential to Lily in the context of this arrangement. In such a scenario, a shared experience of pleasure might challenge the friendship that was necessary for the experiment to take place. Here, friendship offered safe sexual experimentation.

Friendship as health promoting

For participants, sexual disclosure among friends is predicated on trust and intimacy, where discussion and advice regarding one's practices are informed by the intimate knowledge that close friends share. This relies on established spaces of dialogue (Brad), openness (Amanda), and non-judgement (Betty). Here, young people are not simply seeking factual and biological information, as commonly offered by health promotion and sexualities education, but they speak with friends to learn about and better understand sex (including sexual health and pleasure) and to further consider their sexual experiences, tastes, and identities.

Wanda (age 23) discusses friendship as a site where she actively promoted sexual health at school, stating, "I was always the one that was like, 'Are you using a condom?'" Situating herself as a sexual health promoter of sorts, Wanda's encouragement of her friends' condom use was a valuable asset to public health strategies. Oliver also refers to taking on an informal role of *friend educator*, telling his friends where to go for sexual health check-ups and for online information, based on his own experiences: "I said, you know, 'Go here, go there, do that', you know, 'don't look at that website, look at this website'". This highlights informal practices of friendship-based care that sit apart from, yet are informed by, formal sexual health strategies. From an experience of being falsely diagnosed with herpes, and sourcing additional information online that led him to attend a sexual health clinic for a second opinion, Oliver presented his acquired sexual health expertise to friends. In this space, he and Wanda reinforced official sexual health narratives yet also challenged the authority of these through their informal, intimate, and tailored dissemination of this knowledge.

Participants also brought their friends' sexual experiences into interview discussion, further highlighting their access to their friends' sexual intimacies. For example, Natalie shared a story about a female friend whose male sex partner initiated penetration without a condom. She re-told the story told by her friend, including details of her friend's reaction and her own response to this. In the re-telling, Natalie shared her friend's anger and told me how she reassured her friend of the appropriateness of her response:

> She was saying, "Do you think I overreacted?" And I was like, "No, I don't think you overreacted. And I'm annoyed that he made you feel that way. Like I'm not only annoyed that he did that to you, I'm annoyed that he made you feel that there's something wrong with you for insisting on being careful".

This is an example of how friends check in with each other about sexual experiences, their reactions to these, and their uncertainties about doing "the right thing" in sex and relationships. This is a service that formal health promotion cannot offer young people through its one-way dissemination of information, its generic advice, and its lack of intimate sexual knowledge. This story also highlights the connections between different sexual safeties, where negotiations of consent, contraception, and sexual health are entwined.

Attending to intimacy

This chapter considers young people's discourses of intimacy and friendship against sexual health promotion resources. A missing discourse of intimacy in sexual health websites for young people not only overlooks this key aspect of young people's sex but forecloses opportunities to discuss how intimacies (including friendship intimacies) can support negotiations of safer sex. As Carmody and Ovenden argue, an awareness of the complexities of young people's sexual intimacies demands a reconsideration of how health and education professionals engage with this population (2013).

While the term "intimacy" has a broad scope, this chapter prioritises intimacy as discussed by young participants, commonly presented as offering comfort, safety, trust, closeness, pleasure, and friendship. Interview data highlight how intimacy and pleasure practices imbricate and support each other, whereby intimacies – whether forged through sex or established prior – can expand pleasure practices between partners who are regular, casual, and/or friends. Young people's statements also demonstrate how intimacy enables sex that need not be pleasurable, and how one's sexual pleasure can be willingly compromised, or found in non-mutual pleasures, rather than in one's own satisfaction. Evidently, intimacy can both accommodate and eclipse sexual pleasure, and friendship can offer space where sexual experimentation (with or without pleasure) is viable and feels safe.

Interview statements offer varied discursive associations between intimacy, pleasure, safety, and risk. This warrants reflection on how intimacy can be theorised in the context of young people's negotiations of sex and sexual health. Recent decades have seen increasing sociological attention to intimacy (Crowhurst et al., 2013), sometimes considering intimacies beyond heterosexual couple relationships and their associated family structures (Roseneil & Budgeon, 2004; Weeks, 2007). Many scholars draw upon theories of intimacy from Giddens (1992), Beck and Beck-Gernsheim (1995), and Bauman (2003), yet these accounts offer limited value to my consideration of the intricacies of young people's sexual relations, and nor do they translate well to an understanding of digital intimacies (that Bauman in particular was very cynical about). The late-modern subject of these theories is implicitly adult and heterosexual, as problematised by feminist and queer scholars (Illouz, 2007; Jamieson, 1998; Roseneil & Budgeon, 2004).

Interview participants' accounts of intimacy do not simply reflect Giddens' concept of the *pure relationship* that prioritises the romantic couple above other intimate relationships (1992). Writing against Giddens, Jamieson usefully defines intimacy as "a very specific sort of knowing, loving and 'being close to' another person" (1998, p. 1). This extends beyond traditional sociological attention to hetero-familial relations and supports a greater diversity of intimacies. It also suggests a need for health and social policy to engage with this diversity. As Roseneil and Budgeon argue in relation to social policy reform, "to understand the current state, and likely future, of intimacy and care, sociologists should decentre the 'family' and the heterosexual couple in our intellectual imaginaries" (2004, p. 135).

This decentring can be found in Lauren Berlant's argument for "rethinking intimacy" beyond dualistic notions of private and public lives (1998). This rethinking is necessary to engage with public practices of intimacy that traditional sociological approaches overlook. For Berlant, "intimacy builds worlds" and "creates spaces" (1998, p. 282); it is productive, involved in both the production of ourselves and other selves and the relations we produce between us. This intersubjective understanding breaks from Giddens' account of intimacy as a property of "the couple" that is privately produced through partner/romantic interactions. Berlant argues that intimacy discursively "links the instability of individual lives to the trajectories of the collective" (1998, p. 283), and so its practice is not limited to private negotiations. By theorising intimacy as a set of cultural practices in which individual and collective agendas merge and entangle, Berlant renders the separation between public life and private intimacies as untenable. This work informs much recent scholarship on digital intimacies and their affective aspects (Dobson et al., 2018; McGlotten, 2013; Karatzogianni & Kuntsman, 2012).

Berlant's account of individual lives connecting to collectives can be traced through the stories of sexual and friendship intimacies in this chapter. Evidently, nobody is keeping intimacy private, and the space of friendship offers greater insight into cultures of intimacy. In digital spaces, media practices themselves (messaging, liking, reblogging, etc.) can also produce and further intimacies, whether based in friendship or the care of strangers. These are also sites of storytelling (Plummer, 1995), and stories expand our intimacies just as they expand our knowledge of the intimacies available to us.

Eva Illouz also troubles the association of intimacy with private lives by offering the concept of "public privacies" (2007). Considering the mechanics of intimacy beyond the individual and their relationships, Illouz highlights a broader constitution of socio-cultural practices in which a discourse of intimacy is publicly produced through a range of social relations and systems (2007). She argues that therapeutic discourse has generated cultural repertoires of intimacy through which new social ideals of "emotional competence" have emerged (2007, p. 21). In theorising how emotion has become known a form of capital, she argues that through its connection to economic and feminist discourse, therapeutic discourse "has made emotions into micro public spheres" (2007, p. 37). Emotions, she argues, are discussed and regulated publicly, through shared procedures and cultural values, as per an "emotional competence" discourse where emotionality is publicly discussed and reproduced. Illouz's excavation of contemporary intimacies not only highlights how intimacy and emotions circulate beyond a private sphere but emphasises an expanding discourse of intimacy, as found in data discussed throughout this chapter.

In addition to these queer and feminist approaches, and their useful rethinking of intimacy as both *public and private*, is the growing literature on digital intimacies cited throughout this book. The project of rethinking intimacy is far-reaching and interdisciplinary. It also needs to be factored into health programmes, and sexual health research, given the proliferation of friendship intimacies practised through a range of digital and non-digital sites that inform and overlap with young people's sexual intimacies.

These data demonstrate some of the ways that young people incorporate notions of safety into sexual health practices. As Fine argues, sexual health is not isolated from young people's broader negotiations of sex, desire, and pleasure (1988, p. 38), and so young people should not be seen as inexperienced subjects with no regard for their sexual safety. For some participants, sexual experimentations more readily emerge in friendship spaces due to the safety of established intimacy. Lily particularly reflected on how friendship intimacies allow easier integration of condom use and a heightening of sexual pleasure. Tactics she discussed – for condom use and partner assessment – could feature in health promotion campaigns to better support young people's plural agendas of safety.

Because "intimacy only rarely makes sense of things" (Berlant, 1998, p. 286), any public health attempt to factor young people's cultures of intimacy into health strategies will not be easy and requires more "openness" than health promotion tends to offer. Berlant's observation that "virtually no one knows how to do intimacy" (1998, p. 282) certainly includes sexual health promoters and educators. Such professionals need not *know* intimacy, however, nor seek to instruct young people on how to best practice it (young people can manage this). More simply, health professionals should consider intimacy's significance and recognise how it entangles with discourses (and practices) of sexual pleasure and safety. The diversity of intimacy's practice does not weaken its importance but connotes its integral role in young people's negotiations of sex, relationships, and sexual health. This discussion of intimacy and friendship, and the relationship between these, offers a useful foundation for engaging with digital negotiations of sex and dating, as discussed in Chapter 6.

As evident in these data, sexual support and advice among friends is afforded through established care and intimacy and has no equivalent formal source. It is informed by an intimate knowledge of the friend's sexual values, history, preferences, and support needs. While participants note their appreciation and use of formal sexual health information, this does not provide all that is needed to negotiate safer sex. While young people's practices of safety differ from professional health discourses of "safe sex", further attention to everyday intimacies can draw useful links between these safeties; recognising safety as an always contextual and negotiated practice rather than an overarching strategy (e.g. condom use) that is evenly applied to all sex practice. Through greater engagement with friendship intimacies, these issues can be further explored to produce sexual health strategies that are more connected to young people's understandings and practices of safety.

Since young people commonly engage with friends to negotiate their sexual practices and identities, friendship might itself be seen as a tactical response to more limited accounts of sexual relations; whether from traditional narratives of heterosexuality, or limited approaches to sexualities education (Forrest et al., 2004; Ingham, 2005). Self-invention through friendship, Foucault argues (2000), is what made homosexuality "disturbing". Similar can be said of sexually intimate friendships among young people and their potential to disrupt heteronormative systems that still pervade public health discourse. Health promotion's neglected discussion of friendship as a mode of social support underscores friendship's disturbance to institutional agendas and norms, as well as to formal health knowledge.

Close friendships offer multiple spaces for sexual negotiation, through talk and/or sex – and any such distinctions are less relevant to health promotion agendas seeking to resource young people to negotiate sex safely. In the context of these data, close friendships are sexually intimate regardless of sex, and so sexual health promotion that discourages friendship advice misses an opportunity to engage with and resource young people's friends. Furthermore, a current public health emphasis on the need to promote sexual health to young people via social media (Gilliam et al., 2014; Levine,

2011) exacerbates the need for a better consideration of young people's friendship cultures.

Throughout this chapter, interview data reflects recent queer and feminist studies' claims about friendship's increasing role in everyday care and support (Roach, 2012; Roseneil & Budgeon, 2004), troubling clear distinctions between sexual and friendship intimacies. Throughout, close friendships are presented as dialogical, open, and non-judgemental. Sexual storytelling among friends produces a range of ways to negotiate sexual experiences, relationships, and futures, and these are not isolated to individuals but are socially produced through friendship and its cultural practice. Further work needs to be done to track these intimacies through digital media spaces. While I have not accounted for digital forums for sex and relationship advice and support among peers, these would be valuable sites to consider in relation to social narratives of sexual intimacies. The following chapter, however, returns to explore peer support among strangers in relation to mental health. This usefully expands the discussion of care in this chapter, to sites beyond, yet sometimes resembling, close friendships.

Notes

1 This chapter merges work from the following two journal articles: Byron, P. (2017). Friendship, sexual intimacy and young people's negotiations of sexual health. *Culture, Health & Sexuality*, 19(4), 486–500; and Byron, P. (2017). The intimacies of young people's sexual health and pleasure. *Journal of Youth Studies*, 20(3), 332–348. This work has been updated and considerably revised.
2 See Introduction chapter for an overview of these research participants and more information about this study.
3 Only one participant (Charlie) spoke of experiencing love, while Wanda discussed the context that love brings to sex, as did Betty and Natalie, but each only refers to love on one occasion, with little discussion.
4 On two occasions, the *Your Sex Health* website states, "Unless you're in a long-term, monogamous relationship or doing it on your own, there's no such thing as 'safe sex'" (University of Melbourne).
5 This demonstrates that this website is now very outdated, though it was also outdated at the time I initially reviewed it in 2009, and it remained active for several years afterwards. In 2009, smartphones were increasingly common in Australia (though still quite expensive), and Grindr also became available in 2009, existing alongside web-based sex and dating platforms that had existed for two decades.
6 Stancombe were commissioned by the Department of Health and Ageing to undertake qualitative and quantitative research with young people to inform the national campaign that this website is part of. This resulted in two reports (qualitative and quantitative) that were also downloadable from this website.

References

Afifi, W. A., & Faulkner, S. L. (2000). On being "just friends": The frequency and impact of sexual activity in crosssex friendships. *Journal of Social and Personal Relationships*, 17(2), 205–222.

Allen, L., & Carmody, M. (2012). "Pleasure has no passport": Re-visiting the potential of pleasure in sexuality education. *Sex Education, 12*(4), 455–468.

Bauman, Z. (2003). *Liquid love: On the frailty of human bonds.* Cambridge: Polity Press.

Beck, U., & Beck-Gernsheim, E. (1995). *The normal chaos of love.* Cambridge: Polity Press.

Berlant, L. (1998). Intimacy: A special issue. *Critical Inquiry, 24*(2), 281–288.

Bisson, M., & Levine, T. (2009). Negotiating a friends with benefits relationship. *Archives of Sexual Behavior, 38*(1), 66–73.

Braun, V. (2013). "Proper sex without annoying things": Anti-condom discourse and the "nature" of (hetero)sex. *Sexualities, 16*(3–4), 361–382.

Carmody, M., & Ovenden, G. (2013). Putting ethical sex into practice: Sexual negotiation, gender and citizenship in the lives of young women and men. *Journal of Youth Studies, 16*(6), 792–807.

Chambers, D. (2013). *Social media and personal relationships: Online intimacies and networked friendship.* New York, NY: Palgrave Macmillan.

Crowhurst, I., Roseneil, S., Hellesund, T., Santos, A. C., & Stoilova, M. (2013). Close encounters: Researching intimate lives in Europe. *International Journal of Social Research Methodology, 16*(6), 525–533.

Department of Health and Ageing. (2009, May 29). STIs are spreading fast, always use a condom. Retrieved May 12, 2012, from http://www.sti.health.gov.au/.

Dobson, A. S., Robards, B., & Carah, N. (2018). *Digital intimate publics and social media.* Cham: Palgrave Macmillan.

Epstein, M., Calzo, J. P., Smiler, A. P., & Ward, L. M. (2009). "Anything from making out to having sex": Men's negotiations of hooking up and friends with benefits scripts. *The Journal of Sex Research, 46*(5), 414–424.

Erlandsson, K., Jinghede Nordvall, C., Öhman, A., & Häggström-Nordin, E. (2013). Qualitative interviews with adolescents about "friends-with-benefits" relationships. *Public Health Nursing, 30*(1), 47–57.

Fine, M. (1988). Sexuality, schooling, and adolescent females: The missing discourse of desire. *Harvard Educational Review, 58*(1), 29–54.

Fine, M., & McClelland, S. (2006). Sexuality education and desire: Still missing after all these years. *Harvard Educational Review, 76*(3), 297–338.

Forrest, S., Strange, V., & Oakley, A. (2004). What do young people want from sex education? The results of a needs assessment from a peer-led sex education programme. *Culture, Health and Sexuality, 6*(4), 337–354.

Foucault, M. (1991). Politics and the study of discourse. In P. Miller, C. Gordon & G. Burchell (Eds.), *The Foucault effect: Studies in governmentality* (pp. 53–72). Chicago, IL: University of Chicago Press.

Foucault, M. (2000). Friendship as a way of life (J. Johnston, Trans.). In P. Rabinow (Ed.), *Ethics, subjectivity and truth: Essential works of Foucault 1954–1984* (pp. 135–140). London: Penguin Books.

Furman, W., & Shaffer, L. (2010). Romantic Partners, friends, friends with benefits, and casual acquaintances as Sexual Partners. *The Journal of Sex Research, 48*(6), 554–564.

Giddens, A. (1992). *The Transformation of Intimacy: Sexuality, love and eroticism in modern societies.* Oxford: Polity Press.

Gilliam, M., Chor, J., & Hill, B. (2014). Digital media and sexually transmitted infections. *Current Opinion in Obstetrics and Gynecology, 26*(5), 381–385.

Hughes, M., Morrison, K., & Asada, K. J. (2005). What's love got to do with it? Exploring the impact of maintenance rules, love attitudes, and network support on friends with benefits relationships. *Western Journal of Communication, 69*(1), 49–66.

Illouz, E. (2007). *Cold intimacies: The making of emotional capitalism*. Cambridge: Polity Press.

Ingham, R. (2005). "We didn't cover that at school": Education against pleasure or education for pleasure? *Sex Education, 5*(4), 375–388.

Jamieson, L. (1998). *Intimacy: Personal relationships in modern societies*. Cambridge: Polity Press.

Karatzogianni, A., & Kuntsman, A. (2012). *Digital cultures and the politics of emotion: Feelings, affect and technological change*. London: Palgrave Macmillan.

Levine, D. (2011). Using technology, new media, and mobile for sexual and reproductive health. *Sexuality Research and Social Policy, 8*(1), 18–26.

Marie Stopes. *Like it is*. Retrieved May 12, 2012, from http://www.likeitis.org.au/.

McGlotten, S. (2013). *Virtual intimacies: Media, affect, and queer sociality*. Albany: SUNY Press.

Measor, L. (2006). Condom use: A culture of resistance. *Sex Education, 6*(4), 393–402.

Plummer, K. (1995). *Telling sexual stories: Power, change and social worlds*. London & New York, NY: Routledge.

Roach, T. (2012). *Friendship as a way of life: Foucault, AIDS, and the politics of shared estrangement*. New York, NY: SUNY Press.

Roseneil, S., & Budgeon, S. (2004). Cultures of intimacy and care beyond "the family": Personal life and social change in the early 21st century. *Current Sociology, 52*(2), 135–159.

Stancombe Research & Planning. (2008). *Formative research for the national sexually transmitted infections (including HIV/AIDS) prevention program*. Paddington, NSW: Stancombe Research & Planning, for Department of Health and Ageing.

Stancombe Research & Planning. (2009). *Measuring awareness and attitudes among young Australians towards STIs, including HIV/AIDS*. Paddington, NSW: Stancombe Research & Planning, for Department of Health and Ageing.

University of Melbourne. Your sex health. Retrieved May 12, 2012, from http://www.yoursexhealth.org.au/.

Weeks, J. (2007). *The world we have won: The remaking of erotic and intimate life*. London & New York, NY: Routledge.

Wentland, J. J., & Reissing, E. (2014). Casual sexual relationships: Identifying definitions for one night stands, booty calls, fuck buddies, and friends with benefits. *The Canadian Journal of Human Sexuality, 23*(3), 167–177.

5 LGBTQ+ peer support for mental health

In this chapter, I consider LGBTQ+ young people's accounts of digital media use for mental health support. I engage with data from two separate Australian studies of LGBTQ+ young people. The first is the *LGBTIQ Mental Health Help-seeking* (MHHS) project that I worked on in my former community research role with Twenty10, a Sydney-based organisation that supports queer and gender diverse young people in New South Wales. The second is the *Scrolling Beyond Binaries* (SBB) study of LGBTQ+ young people's social media practices. While the former study centred on young people's mental health help-seeking, and particularly their experiences of engaging with formal health care services and professionals, many survey and focus group participants (aged 16–25 years) discussed support found through friends and digital media. And while SBB particularly focused on the social media practices of LGBTQ+ young people (aged 16–35 years), statements about mental health and everyday emotional support were common. It is therefore useful to pool these data, which offers the experiences of up to 2,000 young people in Australia.[1]

From my involvement in these and other studies that engage with LGBTQ+ young people and their digital media use, I have found that digital cultures of care operate in diverse ways, depending on the people, issues, and platforms involved. Through digital media, care is offered as much as it is found, as evident in many LGBTQ+ participants discussing not only the support found but also the support they offer to friends and unknown peers. Data from heterosexual and cisgender young people would likely differ to these, but the accounts of personal experience in this chapter offer useful insight to all health promoters and researchers about digital interactions that are health supporting.

The literature on LGBTQ+ young people's use of the internet and digital media for connection to peers, identity, and community is vast. This chapter acknowledges but builds on that work to consider not just how young people access peer communities, but how peers support each other beyond traditional roles of friendship, as per everyday practices of anonymous care and support among invested peers. To illustrate these cultures of care, I particularly focus on participant experiences of Tumblr use.

Young people's use of Tumblr is more than simply finding "safe spaces" or a "safety net" (Hillier et al., 2012) and constitutes something as mundane as it is vital. Many described this platform as intense, enlightening, affirming, fun, and political. The support that many LGBTQ+ young people offer and find through Tumblr and other social media seemingly filters into broader digital cultures of care, as per meme cultures that may form on Tumblr, 4chan, or Reddit (Shifman, 2014), but seep into more popular platform cultures.

While existing and solid friendships are significant to LGBTQ+ young people in my research, many indicated that friends were not always the best people to offer mental health support. In part, this is because friends without lived experience of mental health issues do not always have the knowledge or skills to handle these issues. In other cases, friends who are also facing mental health issues may not have the capacity to offer support. In addition, some participants expressed reluctance to "contaminate" their friendships with mental health issues. Evidently, many LGBTQ+ young people have broader access to invested peers and digital support hubs that offer ongoing access to informal care and support.[2]

This chapter will first consider research discussions of LGBTQ+ young people's information and support seeking, and how a discourse of "help-seeking" may limit the ways we understand digital and social media interactions and networks and how these foster cultures of care. Further to this, I consider recent research reports on mental health to consider how these discursively represent LGBTQ+ young people and their care practices. Following this, I draw upon research data to discuss digital cultures of care. These data paint a more complex picture than often presented in public statements of LGBTQ+ young people as vulnerable and in need of protection.

Digital information and support

Echoing sentiments expressed throughout this book, it is important to remember that young people are not "going online" to find support, as they already occupy digital spaces and platforms. Unfortunately, our language around digital media practice is spatially coded in ways that position platforms, websites, forums, and even our phones, as "places we go" to search for information. This spatialised logic is particularly pervasive within formal health discourse. Public health systems and their institutionalisation of health practice – i.e. hospitals, clinics, and other formal settings that we *attend* to be consulted with, assessed, diagnosed, and treated – influence our understandings of care. A spatialisation of health care also pervades research discussions of young people's informal support practices, where "online" is constructed as a place young people visit, or retreat, to find support (Gowen, 2013). Further to this, adult anxieties discussed in previous chapters (i.e. imagining digital space as unregulated and therefore risky) amplify concerns about the dangers young people contend with online, and the sense that this is not a safe space. For some, "online" is imagined to house countless trolls, bullies, scammers, and people sharing false information under the cover of anonymity. As such, there is concern that young people needing health information, particularly when these young people are imagined or described as collectively vulnerable and at risk (Bryan, 2017; Cover, 2012, 2013), may be exploited, misled, or victimised online.

Young people sourcing online health information has been a dominant concern among health practitioners and researchers since "online" became on option, as evident in the volumes of literature on *health information seeking* (Eysenbach, 2008; Gray et al., 2005), as discussed in Chapter 3. A primary concern in this literature that extends beyond young people is whether or not health consumers can adequately judge information and its sources as accurate, credible, reliable, and trustworthy (Fergie et al., 2013; Gray et al., 2005). This relates to previously discussed concerns about peer information, that might misinform young people, and result in negative health effects. Much research literature on "online health information seeking" also focuses on digital health forums. Typically, this literature considers peer support in terms of helping others with similar health needs or conditions, including discussion and advice on how to navigate formal health care systems. Much of this literature focuses on "patient communities" or "shared patient experience" (Sillence et al., 2013), or discusses "expert patients" (Fox & Ward, 2006). This literature typically focuses on adults living with chronic illness or specific health conditions, considering these sites as bounded community spaces that offer valuable support alongside forum users' engagements with formal health care. As such, these differ from more subtle and less advice-driven practices of digital support.

As discussed in Chapter 3, there is a need to question a discourse of "going online" for information and support – a focus of much literature regarding LGBTQ+ young people's health. In terms of information seeking, if we consider our own digital media practices, we see that phones, platforms, and websites are not arranged as simple tools to manage our daily lives, nor as tools for simply seeking and finding information (although some apps and platforms may promise this). While health information can be found from a simple web search, it also presents itself to us as we browse, chat, and scroll through social media on an everyday basis. At times when the health information we see is pertinent, we are likely to engage. This is the stuff of digital marketing, algorithms, and targeted content. At other times, information can present as interesting but not be useful right now – for example, a health organisation telling us that syphilis is trending again might be something to note as we keep scrolling. And perhaps we will revisit this information later if a concern or symptom arises. Other information might be disregarded entirely. And some information may seem useful to a friend, in which case we could forward it, or read and relay it to them. This is variable, of course, depending on the user, their friends, the health topic, and more. Though we can see common practices, such as young people not sharing sexual health information to friends on Facebook, as discussed in Chapter 3.

In conjecturing toward expansive practices of knowledge and information sharing, my point is that the internet is not a library. It can be used as one, and while we often search for particular information, this is far from the extent of digital health practices. For most young people, digital media practices are heavily embedded in their daily movements to the point that this is not a separate sphere to "real life" (Deuze, 2012).

It is problematic to suggest that online health information seeking deters or limits support seeking in formal health care settings, though this will depend on the severity of the issue and whether medical intervention is necessary. In the MHHS study, 67% of those who completed our survey indicated that they had sought professional help for mental health, in addition to sourcing informal care (Byron et al., 2017, p. 26). As we know, a general practitioner has a specific role and purpose and it is not feasible or cost effective to attend a clinic for every health concern or discomfort. A doctor will not provide endless information about all possible explanations of a symptom and is unlikely to discuss their own experiences of a health problem and how they dealt with it. A doctor will not usually refer patients to non-professional others, networks, or digital forums where further discussion can be found. They are also unlikely to discuss how to deal with health systems, treatment costs, insurance, and more. A doctor is likely to only give us 15 minutes and will facilitate those minutes. A doctor may also be transphobic and confused by a patient's sexual orientation and spend a good portion of those 15 minutes asking them to explain their bodies or sexual practices despite these being irrelevant to the support needed. This was noted by MHHS survey participants:

> That's the main one I've been asked. It's like "what's pansexual?" Then I explained it's like I do not care about their gender, it's more of who they are … . They just go on and ask, "Aren't you just bi? Isn't it the same as bi?" and it's like no. (17, genderfluid, pansexual)

> You shouldn't ask a trans woman about her breasts when she wants to talk about her depression. (16, trans genderfluid, asexual)

These are just two of many examples of young people's clinicians fixating on their gender or sexual identities ahead of their mental health needs. Participants often found themselves frustrated by having to educate health professionals on matters of gender and sexuality, or spending most of a consultation justifying their identities, particularly when seeking mental health care (Byron et al., 2017).[3] This shows how formal health care can sometimes be more detrimental than supportive of one's health. Fear of discrimination is an often-cited barrier for LGBTQ+ young people seeking formal mental health support (McNair & Bush, 2016), and this fear is often informed by young people's negative experiences with mainstream health professionals/services (Byron et al., 2017). In part, this explains why many LGBTQ+ young people seek less judgemental support through digital media (Lytle et al., 2018; McDermott, 2015), including information about which health care providers and services are going to be supportive and non-discriminatory.

Digital care structures

For many decades, researchers have addressed LGBTQ+ young people's use of digital media and "online spaces" in relation to finding support, community, identity, and friendship. Much of this work presents an account of "the online" as a safe space for LGBTQ+ young people, as illustrated by Hillier et al.'s conceptualisation of the internet as a "safety net" (2012). Research on LGBTQ+ young people's use of social media has expanded this work, with continued attention to young people's use of these media for establishing identities (Cavalcante, 2016; Craig & McInroy, 2014), community building (Hanckel & Morris, 2014; Jackson et al., 2017), coming out (Clare, 2017; Lovelock, 2019), and other forms of self-expression (Jenze, 2017; Wargo, 2017). Importantly, a sense of being out/closeted has been challenged by different practices across different social media platforms, given the varying degrees of anonymity and visibility they offer. But these are always less straightforward than we think, given young people's expertise in "socially mediated publicness" (Baym & boyd, 2012).

A proliferation of research on trans young people's use of digital media has also diversified a literature that was more focused on community building and "coming out" in terms of sexuality or sexual orientation. Much of this literature is supported by close attention to platforms like YouTube (Dame, 2013; Horak, 2014; Raun, 2015), Tumblr (Cavalcante, 2018; Fink & Miller, 2014), Twitter (Jackson et al., 2017), and Facebook (Haimson et al., 2015). In much of this work, the focus is not simply on identity and community building, nor "coming out", but includes attention to how platformed networks foster peer support – practices enabled by the platforms discussed, but also sometimes complicated by their affordances, norms, and cultures, such as per Facebook's "real name" policy (Haimson & Hoffman, 2016) which challenges the safety that many trans young people feel through anonymity. However, digital trans support did not begin with social media, as evident in Andre Cavalcante's discussion of *Susan's Place* (2016) and Avery Dame-Griff's research on Usenet (2019). *Susan's Place*, started by Susan Larson in the mid-1990s, offers forums, resources, and information for trans people, and is described by Cavalcante as a *care structure*, citing Paddy Scannell (2014). For Cavalcante, care structures are "architectures of organized care and concern, created and maintained by collective and cumulative practices of human thought, effort, and creativity" (2016, p. 110). In his research on Usenet,[4] Dame-Griff illustrates how transgender discussion and organising was happening there in the early 1990s, and that "recent" terms like cisgender first appeared on Usenet in 1994 (2019, p. 224). Considering newsgroups such as alt.transgendered, beginning in 1992, Dame-Griff notes the values of anonymity and unregulated digital space, and how community factions generated breakaway newsgroups, thereby expanding networks (2019). Together, Cavalcante and Dame-Griff's work demonstrates that digital trans communities, activism, and knowledge building is as old as the internet and that today's social media platforms are recent sites of a much longer history. As such, queer and trans digital interactions today are embedded in longer histories of organised care and support.

Much of the above literature comes from media studies, where mental health consideration features, but is more informed by socio-cultural (non-medical) perspectives of health. While digital and social media certainly intersect with mental health negotiations among LGBTQ+ young people, there is limited cross-disciplinary work in this space. As someone more oriented to digital media and cultural studies research, I too am hesitant to present myself as knowledgeable on mental health, including what this means and why we conceptualise it as such. Most research that centres on LGBTQ+ young people's mental health comes from health researchers, where friendship and peer support through digital media is often noted but is largely peripheral to a focus on public health, medicine, or psychiatry. Unfortunately, much of this seems to report on the value of "online communities" and online peer support, without collecting data on what this looks and feels like. Elsewhere, LGBTQ+ focused community organisations (often partnering with academics) have produced numerous reports on LGBTQ+ young people's mental health. The following section considers such reports and their engagement with friendship and digital peer support.

Community reports: friends and peers

To consider the present state of knowledge about the mental health support that LGBTQ+ young people give and receive among friends and peers, this section considers recently published and freely available research reports. From my involvement in the community health sector, I am aware that such reports are key documents for this sector – given their embeddedness in LGBTQ+ community organisations as well as their accessibility to community members and policy advocates alike. The ten reports I consider below were published in the last two decades and mostly come from Australia, but also from Canada, Ireland, Scotland, the United Kingdom, and the United States.

One of the first studies of Australian young people that allowed participants to self-define their gender identities is reported on in *From Blues to Rainbows* (Smith et al., 2014). Researching the mental health and wellbeing of trans and gender diverse young people (aged 14–25), this study engaged almost 200 young people through surveys and interviews. Most participants did not feel supported by their families, and when asked about strategies used to "feel better", the most common responses selected were to "Spend time with friends" (77%), "Chat with friends online" (70%), and "Text and call friends" (66%) (2014, p. 78). The fourth most common response (45%) was to "Chat with a health professional" (though 36% indicated they would not do this). While 37% of participants indicated that spending time with family made them feel better, more commonly this was reported as unhelpful or not practised, with 28% indicating that this was likely to make them feel worse (2014, p. 78). These findings offer important insight into the role of friendship support among LGBTIQ+ young people and how this often contrasts with other potential sources of care.

The most recent *Writing Themselves In* report, which engaged "same sex attracted and gender questioning" young Australians aged 14–21 years, found that "Friends continue to be the most popular choice as confidantes for young people disclosing their sexual feelings" (Hillier et al., 2010, p. 67). This was the only key finding relating to young people's friendships, yet participant quotes throughout the report indicate that friends played a key role in assisting participant negotiations of gender and sexuality. The report also discusses the wellbeing aspects of digital peer support: "Connecting with others (often in the form of reading others' blogs or stories) provided a sense of being less alone, and provided hope and possibility for the future" (2010, p. 63).

A survey of Canadian trans young people found that when younger participants (14–18 years) asked for help they most commonly asked a "friend" (87%) followed by a "family member" (56%) (Saewyc et al., 2015, p. 62). A follow-up question asked which sources of support were found to be helpful, with "friend" being the most common response (81%) (2015, p. 63). Participants were asked if they had ever requested to be addressed by a name or pronoun different to what was assigned to them at birth, and those most commonly asked to do so were trans friends (85%), "people online" (84%), non-trans friends (79%), and a spouse or partner (79%) (2015, p. 66). Despite these findings, the significance of support from friends or "people online" did not feature in this report's key findings.

The Australian *Growing Up Queer* report also discussed friendship as an important source of support for young LGBTIQ participants, but this, too, is not presented as a key finding (Robinson et al., 2014). Like many such reports, friendship features heavily in the data, and often friendships are addressed with reference to institutions that house them, such as schools. For example: "Schooling for many was generally an unsupportive environment, except for a few close friends who accepted them for who they were" (2014, p. 26). Elsewhere, the authors found that: "The internet was a place where [participants] 'can find friends they can trust' (49%) or a place where they 'feel accepted' (78%)" (2014, p. 31), and online friendships were noted as particularly supportive for many (2014, p. 35).

The Scottish *Trans Mental Health Study*, in which participants ranged from 18–78 years (but where the highest age group was 21–25 years), found that "When participants did need urgent support they were most likely to contact their friends, followed by their GP or partner" (McNeil et al., 2012, p. 52). Rates of friendship support were lower than in other studies (only 35–36%), presumably relating to this study's broader age range.

The Australian *Trans Pathways* project surveyed young trans people aged 14–25 years (N = 859) and asked which "social activities" they used to support themselves, with "peers/friends" being the most popular response (83.3%), followed by "emotional partners" (54.1%) (Strauss et al., 2017, p. 67). Aside from this finding, this report is also punctuated with participant quotes throughout, highlighting the key supportive role of friends. However, authors do not unpack these, nor present this evidence as a key finding. Further, their use of the category "peers/friends" throughout highlights a lack of distinction between these relationships, as common to many of these reports.

In the *LGBTQ Youth Report* from the United States, participants most commonly reported being "out" about their sexual orientation to LGBTQ friends (61%) followed by siblings (36%) (Kahn et al., 2018, p. 18). Something similar was found regarding gender identity, with 47% being fully out to LGBTQ friends, followed by siblings (28%), parents (21%), and non-LGBTQ friends (20%) (2018, p. 18). Aside from these reported findings, the report does not discuss young people's friendship support, nor digital peer support, except for one undiscussed participant quote: "My fear keeps me from seeing a counselor about things like my anxiety and depression. I don't know how they might react [to my LGBTQ identity], so I'd rather go online or talk to my other queer friends about it" (2018, p. 6). The report is addressing parents, schools, and health professionals, highlighting key health and social problems faced by LGBT young people, before issuing recommendations. Throughout, young people are reported as needing "our help" (the help of adults and professionals), effectively backgrounding their peer support practices. Like much research that situates LGBTQ+ young people as marginalised, at-risk, and needing support from adults, professionals, health institutions, and policymakers, peer support is not included in these discussions.

The *Supporting LGBT Lives* study investigated the mental health and wellbeing of LGBTQ+ people from Ireland, and while not exclusively about young people, its findings similarly highlight the supportive roles of friends (Mayock et al., 2008). Survey respondents (N = 1,100) were asked to nominate "activities engaged in to feel better/forget about one's problems", and the most popular response was to talk to friends (62.3%), followed by listening to music (47.5%), and talking to a partner (37%) (2008, p. 131). The report concluded: "Friends emerged as the most commonly cited source of support, friendships playing a critical role in terms of everyday companionship and during difficult or challenging periods" (2008, p. 132). In the report, friendship support is associated with resilience – particularly in relation to coming out and mental health support. However, no recommendation mentions friendship and its vital role, nor is there a discussion on how health services and educators can support these friendship support practices that are most favoured by participants.

Elsewhere, the UK *Queer Futures* report – engaging LGBT young people with experiences of self-harm and suicidal feelings –includes friendship support as a key finding (McDermott et al., 2016, p. 9). The authors state, "Help was sought most frequently from friends and on the internet. Just less than one third of participants had accessed their GP, and a fifth had sought help from NHS mental health services" (2016, p. 9). It was noted that "Participants had the most positive experiences when asking for help online, from friends or from LGBT youth groups" (2016, p. 9). Further to this, 99.5% of survey participants said they used the internet when they were self-harming or feeling suicidal, and this was "for a range of reasons including distraction, information, connecting with friends and community, to find out about their feelings and to get support" (2016, p. 9). Of these participants, only 6.5% indicated that the internet had been unhelpful in these situations (2016, p. 9). Friendship and digital peer support are commonly discussed throughout this report, and findings about the valuable role of "the internet" were particularly highlighted:

> The internet was the only place where the majority of participants (80.5%, n=575) responded that they "never" or only "some of the time" had to hide their sexual orientation/ gender identity. The only other place where participants were more likely to share their sexual orientation/ gender identity was with friends outside of school (52%, n=364). (2016, p. 38)

Many studies, including this one, highlight young people's reluctance to seek support from professional health services. This is important, yet a central focus on service provision that is key to most of these reports often sidesteps a valuable conversation about why it is that young people primarily seek support from friends and digital peers, and how formal support continues to fail many young people.

To a lesser extent, the *You Learn From Each Other* report from Australia, of which I was an author,[5] also acknowledges the role of friends and peers in its key findings, stating: "Empowerment and confidence for mental health help-seeking is often achieved through peer and friend-based discussion and information sharing, and this should be supported by health professionals and service providers where possible" (Byron et al., 2017, p. 7). These terms are somewhat vague, however, and like in most of the other studies quoted above, there was little further exploration of this, because this was not the focus of the study (and presumably this goes for most other reports mentioned). Evidently, there has been no precedent to unpack and further consider LGBTQ+ young people's friendship and peer-based interactions for mental health support, given that this work mostly argues for improved (not reformed) health policy and services. However, there is room – and certainly a need – to include more discussion of peer support in these spaces, and to recognise how this would be valuable to policymakers, educators, and health professionals. This includes consideration of how and why peer support works for young people and how adult professionals might support that, rather than simply seeing it as peripheral to how *we* can support LGBTQ+ young people's mental health and wellbeing.

These are key reports on LGBTIQ+ young people's mental health, but they are not the full extent of current knowledge. Significantly, these all cite friendship and digital media as key sources of support for young people, yet they offer a narrow account of these support practices – more often quantifying rather than qualifying this support. Without more qualitative research attention, we cannot consider the dimensions of peer and friend-based support for LGBTQ+ young people's mental health. Knowing how much LGBTQ+ young people rely on digital cultures of care, we must consider what this looks like, how it plays out, and what it offers that other forms of support do not (but possibly could).

Digital mental health support

To further consider some of the limitations of reported findings about LGBTQ+ young people's mental health support needs and practices, this section reviews data from the two Australian studies mentioned earlier: the *LGBTIQ Mental Health Help-seeking* study and *Scrolling Beyond Binaries*. These studies involve young people of various ages and identities, with varied mental health experiences, and diverse experiences of peer support. Many participants also indicated that they have supported LGBTQ+ peers through digital media interaction and sharing, particularly through private Facebook groups and Tumblr.

In terms of social support, Ceglarek and Ward (2016) found that "sexual minority youth" gained more mental health support online than their heterosexual peers for whom digital media participation was more likely to negatively impact their mental health. This reinforces research evidence that digital peer support has been significant for LGBTQ+ young people. As noted, many researchers have looked at LGBTQ+ young people's uses of social media to foster identity, community, and belonging (Hanckel et al., 2019; Jenzen, 2017), including attention to specific platforms such as Tumblr (Byron et al., 2019; Cavalcante, 2018; Cho, 2018), YouTube (Dame, 2013; Horak, 2014), Facebook (Duguay, 2014; Haimson et al., 2015), Instagram (Duguay et al., 2020), Twitter (Jackson et al., 2017), and Reddit (Darwin, 2017; Triggs et al., 2019). Reading across this literature generates a complex account of how everyday support, friendship, and cultures of care permeate these many sites. As Rob Cover has argued:

online communications technologies are understood as having the capacity for broad, fundamental shifts in how queer youth in particular relate to themselves and others, particularly in terms of the availability of information and resources and the potential for building new forms of community and culture. (2012, p. 12)

There is a long history of research on peer support among LGBTQ+ people (considered early adopters of digital technologies) and this stretches back to pre-digital communication strategies for activism, community work, and health support. This includes early community responses to the HIV/AIDS epidemic beginning in the 1980s, or before that, threats of pathologisation and incarceration for being queer. For many, the social burdens of being part of a marginalised group are tempered through a sense of solidarity and shared struggle (Piepzna-Samarasinha, 2018). This solidarity has been generative of identities, political strategies, and social policy reform (Weeks et al., 2001). Such solidarities are as intimate as they are political.

In the MHHS survey, respondents who had experienced poor mental health were asked, *How would you and/or your friends most commonly access information relating to mental health?* Among the 403 responses, the most common choice was "online by using a search engine or Wikipedia" (74%), followed by "friends" (56%), and then "online from a mental health service/ site" (51%). There are several ways we could read this data. Firstly, we might be concerned that young people are getting a lot of information from friends who are not likely to know about mental health and how to adequately counsel their friends undergoing difficulties. As already discussed (see Chapters 2 and 3), much worry exists in health promotion and communication research that young people are not good sources of information and that this may disrupt them from accessing professional health care or accurate knowledge.

Unfortunately, the response options offered for the above question limit the data collected. For example, there are two options relating to digital media and together they do not comprise all digital sources of support. In particular, there was no option to nominate "social media", which was the most common "other" response given. Within these "other" responses, many named particular platforms – mostly Tumblr, Facebook, and YouTube – and gave further details on why these were useful.

Elsewhere in the survey we asked: *What sorts of digital technologies, if any, could improve how you and your friends access mental health information?* Here, 35% of responses (excluding "I don't know" responses) mentioned social media in some form. Examples include:

Social media has helped me a lot, it has helped me to meet people who feel the same way as me. (17, non-binary/androgynous, straight)

Social media is nice because of the sense of community. (21, female, bisexual)

Social media and apps, these are subtle things people can access to support themselves. (21, agender, panromantic demisexual)

Within these responses, Facebook was the most frequently mentioned platform, followed by Tumblr, YouTube, Twitter, and Instagram. Participants commonly noted that social media is accessible and ubiquitous, and for many, this is where they had already sourced mental health information and support. As the third participant quoted above noted, these are subtle forms of support. This subtlety was commonly mentioned, seemingly referring to the option to read, watch, learn, and "like" social media content without actively engaging, and with no need for asking for, nor perhaps even searching for, this level of support. Unlike attending a health clinic, there is no need to "sign up" and commit to an interaction that aims to solve a problem. In terms of mental health and how many participants experienced this, this subtle support is important and holds space for the complexity of negotiating mental health, for which a cure or simple resolution is rarely understood as likely.

Further discussion of social media as a key site of support commonly featured throughout the broader dataset. Many expressed that LGBTQ+ young people are avid users of social media, and are sometimes more comfortable communicating online than in person or speaking on the phone:

Online, text based versions of phone lines like Life Line are essential, because not everyone is comfortable talking on the phone. (20, female, queer/bisexual/pan)

What would make it easier to talk to health / mental health professionals about issues relating to gender/ sexuality/ intersex status?

not talking to them in person or over the phone. (16, male, gay)

Many participants indicated that they had undertaken "personal research" around mental health. This was typically done online, and in preparation for dealing with health professionals:

I guess the truth is that before I even went to see a GP, I did most of my research and questioning about what I was going through online – so by the time I actually saw a GP I was fairly certain that I was experiencing depression, and later, anxiety. So it wasn't as if they had to diagnose me – but I still went to see them for validation and advice on what to do about it. (24, female, bisexual)

Mental health professionals who were interviewed in the MHHS study found that informal digital support was increasingly common among their young patients:

Psychiatrist: They less commonly seem to source their information initially from a formal kind of website which is set up by some sort of publicly accountable organisation.

Counsellor: They talk about Tumblr. Tumblr doesn't seem to have a very good name, but they do talk about that. They talk about Facebook. What else do they mention? They probably mention other things that just go completely over my head.

The psychiatrist above spoke of how young people continually educated him on gender identity terms. It should be noted that, as specialists in the care of LGBTQ+ children and young people, these professionals are likely to be more aware of digital cultures of support than other practitioners, just as they are more aware of the health needs of LGBTQ+ young people. Among mainstream health providers, failures or refusals to engage with young people's identities (including the use of correct names and pronouns) further underscores a need for spaces, interactions, and media in which diverse gender and sexual identities can exist without negative judgement, questioning, and common misunderstandings (though this also happens in social media platforms). Arguably, digital peer interactions contribute to feelings of community and belonging, and can offer safeties and respite that are less easily found "offline", including from counsellors, as the following focus group participant mentions:

> Sometimes it's not even the counselling that you want but it's the empathy and that knowing someone else can relate to you and that you're both fighting this together can make you feel so much better that you're not all alone, that's yeah … that's what I like to see. (17, genderfluid, pansexual)

Participants highlighted how mental health support through social media is further necessitated by a lack of support found elsewhere, such as in schools and families. Many participants in the MHHS study told stories about health professionals who tried to simplify or downplay their gender or sexual identities to make these more understandable or palatable for them. The frustration of this experience, and participants' ability to speak to these frustrations in common terms – e.g. having to educate health professionals and seeing this as an unfair and unnecessary burden – references common peer discussions of negotiating formal health care. This also references a shared knowledge and politics that one has the right to be frustrated and to expect more from formal health care.

In a focus group within the MHHS study, with young people from Western Sydney, Taylor (aged 16) and Lucien (aged 20) discuss the difficulties of involving everyday friends in supporting their mental health experiences.

Taylor: It's sort of like, I don't want to burden my friends with giving them an overbearing amount of … "I need help. Oh my God, my life sucks, ah".

Lucien: If you see them happy, you don't want to ruin the mood.

Taylor: Yeah.

Lucien: So you just cover it up. On the serious side of things, if it gets really, really bad so much that you don't feel safe, then you worry about what their reaction's going to be like. Like, "Oh my God, really?"

While acknowledging the value of friend-based support, the sense that "I don't want to burden my friends" suggests an important distinction between friends and peers in the context of mental health support. Taylor and Lucien discuss not wanting to "bring the mood down" or become *that* friend who is more negative, serious, and depressed than everyone else. As participants often indicated, friendships are precious and nourishing, and so introducing one's mental health struggles into that space may seem risky to the friendship, potentially disrupting the dynamic of a friendship or friendship group. It could mean that friends overreact, as Lucien worries about above, or that friends may start unnecessarily checking up on them, wanting to workshop their experiences in unhelpful ways. Friendship, for many, was a site of comfort and support that need not be involved in the negotiation of difficult experiences, including depression and anxiety.

Mental health on Tumblr

This section adds to discussion of *Tumblr care* initiated in Chapter 2, with the current discussion focussing on LGBTQ+ young people's use of Tumblr for mental health negotiation and support. As noted in Chapter 2, Tumblr is commonly considered a queer platform. As well as a queer counterpublic (Byron et al., 2019; Renninger, 2015), it has been described by researchers as a "huge queer ecosystem" (Cho, 2015), a "queer affective public" (Vivienne, 2017), a "queer utopia" and "queer vortex" (Cavalcante, 2018), a "community of care" for trans people (Hawkins & Haimson, 2018), a "queer archive" (Engelberg & Needham, 2019), and a "trans technology" (Haimson et al., 2020).

Importantly, negotiations of mental health are often entangled with negotiations of gender and sexuality for LGBTQ+ young people, as expressed by participants of the MHHS project:

> It's not like formal mental health support but I often message a Tumblr group about non-binary issues. (17, genderfluid, pansexual)

> Tumblr is a great mental health resource. It pretty much educated me on the majority of what I know about gender, sexuality, mental health and identity. Maybe health professionals could tap into that? (18, male, queer/bisexual)

Tumblr is not the only source of support for most LGBTQ+ young people, and indeed not all LGBTQ+ young people use Tumblr, but it was framed as an important site for many participants across the two studies. This importance needs recognition among mental health researchers and health professionals. While volumes of literature express concern about young people accessing unreliable and inaccurate health information online, as discussed, there is also evidence that young people typically source health information (and support) from multiple sites (Gray et al., 2005; Fergie et al., 2015). This was certainly the case for many participants, including an MHHS survey participant who states:

> Learning about things from trusted organisations and non-triggering accounts from individuals with lived experiences has helped me understand what I'm going through and how to deal with it and this has helped me to have a better quality of life. (16, agender, grey-asexual/sensual)

Finding spaces where other LGBTQ+ people share their experiences of mental health alongside their negotiations of gender and sexual identities, assists young people with developing a clearer sense of their identities and mental health status – or perhaps greater comfort in living with uncertainties (by witnessing other people doing the same). Experiential knowledge shared on Tumblr includes strategies for negotiating unsupportive spaces that can include families, health professionals, and schools. Survey participants in the SBB study indicated that the combination of gender diversity and mental health issues meant that there was a small and specific support community available through Tumblr – a community that would be difficult to find elsewhere. Through social media networks that encourage and normalise the sharing of personal experiences and feelings, young people not only produce shared responses to common experiences of discrimination and non-acceptance but also open spaces for dialogue and a range of expressions and identities, particularly accommodating intersectional experiences (Fink & Miller, 2014) (e.g. queer people of colour, or queer and disabled people), where peers share experiences and mobilise strategies for self-determination and increased wellbeing. A discourse of neurodiversity has also been supported and furthered on Tumblr (Anselmo, 2018). Much of this interaction promotes mental health visibility – a concept that could usefully inform public health strategies seeking to improve young people's mental health and well-being, particularly since the issue of mental health stigma is already well recognised in formal mental health discourse.

SBB data indicates that Tumblr users are more trans, more likely to have a non-binary gender, and less likely to be male. Across both studies, participants indicated that Tumblr was their primary resource for understanding mental health alongside negotiating gender and sexual identities:

> My friends and I usually find a lot of information on tumblr because it can be like a big support group at times and you can talk to people

going through the same things as you ... I often see mental health info and handy sites and organisations on my dash[board] ... . It's really useful because it's part of something that I'm doing anyway. You don't have to go out of your way searching for info. (17, female, lesbian)

Noted here is the way that information on Tumblr simply presents itself to users, somewhat organically, rather than being a site where one is likely to seek such resources (going "out of your way"), or where support is directly delivered, as though from doctor to patient, expert to amateur. This tells us something about expertise and how it operates on sites like Tumblr. Tumblr being "like a big support group" offers peer support in a manner that is subtle, appreciated, and knowingly accepted as coming from a good place, despite little sense of who is sharing such content. It seems that the authenticity of care is read into the material or comments shared, not the qualifications or identity of who produces or shares this material. This challenges existing hierarchies of expertise, as discussed in Chapter 3.

In an SBB interview, Carter, a 26-year-old queer-identifying trans man, based in rural Western Australia, acknowledges that Tumblr is better than turning to one's friends for mental health support:

And when you're really mentally under the weather you don't want people to be concerned about you, or I don't want people to be concerned about me and I think that's quite common, especially people you know because you don't want to be a burden. And it's effort if they're concerned about you and you have to be, you have to try and reassure them or whatever, whereas on Tumblr because you don't know each other, it's more like, "Oh yeah, I feel like that too and this is what I do. It might work for you". And "I'm here if you want to chat".

As with Taylor and Lucien's discussion presented earlier, Carter is concerned about burdening his friends. The option to sidestep one's friends is available through the use of Tumblr, and this is safer on account of it not disrupting established and important friendship intimacies. As a space for shared struggle and social connections, one MHHS participant describes Tumblr as lifesaving, saying, "Tumblr is filled with amazing supports, I definitely wouldn't be here without my followers and the people I follow" (17, female, bisexual/demisexual).

As Baym argues, social media interactions enable the "separation of presence from communication", and this offers us "volume control" to regulate our social environment and manage our encounters" (2015, pp. 3–4). In other words, the ability to put distance between yourself and others you communicate with affords more subtle and careful interaction and the ability to move away or pause from interactions, including difficult disclosures. For example, in Alex's story of coming out as trans on Facebook, told in Chapter 1, she timed this with an overseas holiday in order to have more emotional distance from this disclosure, should that be necessary. Many digital media spaces afford the option to safely leave interactions should they become hostile, unfriendly, or triggering. In terms of mental health, the separation of presence from communication seems to align with common strategies of self-care, where distancing and volume control offer safety. Creating distance from friends is part of this, as per the concerns mentioned by Lucien, Taylor, and Carter, among others, where the use of Tumblr can offer multiple safe spaces.

Mental health support on Tumblr is typically oriented to sharing one's experiences on Tumblr (for the benefit of self and others), rather than offering advice or engaging in more direct discussion. For SBB interviewee Casey, aged 20, agender, bisexual, and based in rural Victoria, mental health advice was not sought nor taken on Tumblr:

> A lot of times if I'm looking up anything for mental health, it's to see if anyone else has the same problems, and so I don't think I'm alone in that. I don't really take any advice.

This speaks to the more subtle aspects of Tumblr support, as mentioned earlier, as well as the volume control that Baym (2015) discusses. Carter similarly states:

> Tumblr [is used] quite heavily for mental health. Not advice, but like people with mental illness saying, "This is what works for me". And then getting ideas from other people.

Casey also notes that mental health is a common topic because "people take it very seriously on Tumblr". This tells us something important about the culture of the platform and why it is known as supportive. Along with the anonymity that Tumblr offers, this respect for people giving accounts of their mental health experiences makes it a safer space for mental health support than most other social media platforms. Further emphasising how Tumblr mental health discussion is not about advice seeking or young people "peer educating" each other but accounts of using Tumblr to broadcast one's feelings and experiences without needing or expecting advice. Carter likens Tumblr to "shouting into the void", and notes that the ease of Tumblr use for mutual support is the distance offered by its text-based and platform-based communication:

> it's like shouting into the void and the void answers back and you don't know each other, so it becomes a lot easier. And also because it's via text, you're not actually talking, it makes it easier to be like for instance, you know, "I want to die today and it makes me scared", and for other people to be like, "I feel like that too sometimes." And have, yes, that peer support.

Of all interview participants, Carter perhaps had the most to say about Tumblr and its value for mental health support. At one point he compares interactions with his psychiatrist to peer support found on Tumblr:

> So my psych is regularly saying, "You're doing really well. Look where you were before and look where you are now". And putting things in perspective, but social media is, yes, it's the peer support that I don't get elsewhere, and it's great to be like, for her to tell me, "You're not alone, I have this other client who had similar experiences". It's another thing to actually talk to another person with those experiences, even if it's just via text communication.

Here, the need for informal care sourced through people with lived experience is not something that rules out or competes with formal health care. Rather, it is complementary, and in some ways, it is more reassuring than a psychiatrist's evaluation. Mental health support through digital media can be both synchronous and asynchronous, depending upon the platforms, communities, or individuals involved. But outside private chat with friends, this is likely to be asynchronous. This is less demanding, to authors and audiences alike, as a response is not expected nor required, yet it is often welcome within the space of interaction that is opened by sharing one's experiences or feelings. In spaces like Tumblr, there is no demand to respond at all, and responses can be as simple as a heart, or perhaps a reblog. Though many posts of difficult disclosure are responded to with brief notes of acceptance and resonance, such as "same" or "I feel this".

Beyond "help-seeking"

The focus of this chapter, on LGBTQ+ young people's mental health negotiations, further elaborates the difficult distinctions between peers and friends in young people's digital support practices. This discussion offers insight for health researchers and health professionals alike, encouraging more careful consideration of how to "help" young people, including consideration of how young people are already helping themselves and each other through digital peer support practices.

In negotiating mental health, LGBTQ+ young people's support networks commonly extended beyond their immediate and everyday friendships, as per discussions of Tumblr in this chapter. This was contextualised, by some participants, as a form of protecting friends or preserving friendship dynamics. For some, a distancing of mental health support from their everyday friendships, speaks to mental health stigma that many LGBTQ+ young people must negotiate. However, there was also a sense that this ensured that support was found among peers who are often more competent than one's friends in engaging with the complexities of negotiating mental health alongside gender and sexualities.

Often, young people are not *attending* media sites and platforms with clear agendas of needing support from these spaces. Yet health research discussions have tended to frame young people's "online" and social media practices as transactional or instrumental in focus – much like visiting a clinic. But we engage social media platforms without a strict agenda – firstly, because they offer and provide a range of things, and secondly, because these are everyday social spaces. This unclear orientation of social media use troubles a digital health research that focuses on "online health information seeking", as discussed throughout this book. Data in this chapter also trouble dominant health research frames of "help-seeking" as well as broader discussions of "information seeking". The concept of *digital cultures of care*, offered throughout this book, opens space for us to consider more complex digital practices of giving as well as receiving care, but also building and fostering spaces of care. In such spaces, support is often indirect and offered to anyone who may need it. As a concept, "help-seeking" often suggests a vulnerable and disempowered young subject in need of help, and such a frame (much like risk frameworks) forfeits our attention to LGBTQ+ young people's survival skills and practices, including their digital competencies in finding, fostering, and building peer support networks. The term "information seeking" is also increasingly redundant for the way it distinguishes information from support, and how it overlooks much information that is embedded in support practices.

While parents, health professionals, and educators certainly have a role to play in supporting LGBTQ+ young people, their emphasis within the community research reports discussed in this chapter, highlights a limited engagement with young people's lived experiences of negotiating mental health. As is evident, there is common awareness and discussion of the roles friends and peers play (particularly online peers) in assisting one's mental health, gender, and sexuality negotiations, and that these relationships are typically more beneficial to young people than their relationships with family members, health professionals, educators, and sometimes their friends. Notably, these findings do not commonly present as "key findings" but are peripherally mentioned alongside a discussion centring on health service provision and policy. But further exploration of these supportive relationships could usefully inform mental health policy and service provision by what these tell us about the support that sustains many young people.

This chapter also broadens the concept of "personal communities" that was discussed in Chapter 2 (Pahl & Spencer, 2004). Pahl and Spencer usefully blur hard lines between friendship and family practices and consider the suffusion of these intimacies. However, their discussion does not accommodate care and support that is administered by invested yet anonymous peers, where there are no strong bonds or any recognised social connection. Invested peers seemingly perform friendship beyond its usual parameters, expanding friendship's practice and its relational possibilities.

When our research discussions focus on health, and these discussions operate at the level of policy and service provision, this is usually guided by pre-existing discourse that limits the field of enquiry, as per Butler's discussion of reiterative practices (1993), or John Law's discussion of research methods as "inscription devices" (2004). In this case, existing knowledge of LGBTQ+ young people's mental health does not centrally engage with friend/peer-based support, and therefore these findings do not read as findings. These findings are beyond the discursive norms of this research discussion. They are notable and of interest, but they are not seen to offer a solution to an outlined problem whose solution has already been identified as improvements to formal health care. Further, within this attention to "vulnerable young people who need our help", there is no space for engaging with young people's expertise in defining, finding, and providing support needed among friends and peers. This, of course, reflects a denial of young people's expertise (see Chapter 3), whether this regards their health and wellbeing, their digital competencies, or their digital practices of support.

As data in this chapter reveals, Tumblr and similar sites offer subtle forms of support that also recognise a diversity of experiences and that nobody is an expert. Content shared by many people on Tumblr is oriented to support provision, referencing the care and safety of the site that users seek to preserve and foster. Such content is not directly given but shared for anyone who may need it, further suggesting a recognised mode of subtlety and indirect care. In this context, it would seem improper to give direct advice, since the adviser would not know the full context of the situation. It would also be improper to give advice where this is not explicitly requested. Knowing such "rules" constitutes familiarity with these spaces and their social customs, and this can be considered in the context of Tumblr users' expertise. It also indicates Tumblr users' recognition and respect for the expertise of those sharing their lived experiences, and the value of keeping space open for all such knowledge and expertise to be shared and passed around.

While the health reports discussed are punctuated by quotes and case studies of young people who frequently cite the pivotal role of friends and digital media, and these are often presented in large quotes or within text box illustrations, these are largely "an aside". They speak to resilience, and "give voice" to young people, but they do not mobilise such voices. Sealed in text boxes or speech bubbles, these do not contaminate the key findings and recommendations that these reports offer. A more generous reading is that researchers would assume that their readers cannot action anything with (qualitative) findings such as these, but that they should be included anyway. But returning to my cynicism, maybe these are emotional devices used to get the attention of policymakers, advocacy groups, researchers, and other concerned parties. The statements about young people's peers and friends might also be read as common sense, as something we already know, but something that operates beyond formal health care strategies. Except this is not the case, as evident in the ways young people simultaneously manage formal and informal systems of support, and how informal care practices quite directly speak to the inadequacies of formal health care.

It is problematic to consistently find that young people – particularly trans and gender diverse young people – are getting a lot of valuable support from their friends and digital networks, yet still retain an unwavering belief that only formal health services, as they currently exist, can properly support young people's mental health. The provision of formal health care is certainly important, but it must be built for the needs of patients and publics rather than expecting all users to adjust to institutionalised forms of care in order to be seen and helped. Though it is simplistic to distinguish between care cultures (as everyday practice) and structures (as health institutions), since these are not mutually exclusive and each contributes to the reality of the other. The same can be said of peer support and social media platforms, where one does not simply house or challenge the other, but these are mutual constructions. Notably, Tumblr was not specifically designed to be a site for mental health peer support, nor for LGBTQ+ politics and interaction, yet its affordances – including user anonymity, its openness, and the ability to listen without active engagement, made this happen. And despite this lack of intent, Tumblr use has sharpened our present cultural awareness of LGBTQ+ experiences of mental health and supported complex understandings of how these intersect with negotiations of gender and sexual identities, along with intersections of race, ethnicity, class, disability, chronic illness, and more. Tumblr use for mental health support also signifies young people's awareness of the limitations of friendship in relation to their mental health.

Young people's accounts of Tumblr use in this chapter offer a sense of the vitality of this space.[6] As adults working with and for young people, we do not need to (and likely cannot) understand all the content, networks, and discourse involved in Tumblr practice. But we do need to listen to young people when they say that this is a vital space that has offered more support for mental health than they have encountered elsewhere, including from families, schools, and formal health care settings. Common experiences of finding support through a range of sources speaks to many young people's competencies in navigating systems of support that are formal and informal, friend-based, digitally networked, and more. It also shows these negotiations as complex, as per some participant's strategies for shielding and protecting their everyday friendships from their mental health-related difficulties.

Unlike most health strategies, policies, and interventions, different dimensions of health are not isolated and treated in separate spheres among Tumblr users. On Tumblr, there is space (and precedence) to speak across a range of intersecting experiences at once – of gender dysphoria, anxiety, and autism, for example – with less tendency to prioritise one factor over another, or to see one factor as causing another. Presumably, one appeal of Tumblr use for personal struggles is the cultural competence in handling complexity, informed by a more intersectional understanding of well-being and social experience. Arguably, Tumblr cultures have generated new literacies of mental health and well-being, and these accommodate gender and sexual diversities in ways that most other platforms (and most health professionals) cannot. Though this is not to say that Tumblr offers all LGBTQ+ young people everything they need in terms of mental health support.

Notes

1 See Introduction for more details about each of these projects.
2 This is not to suggest that all LGBTQ+ young people have ample support, as they do not. These support practices can also be read as evidence that LGBTQ+ young people are in greater need of social support than many of their peers.
3 In Australia, a general practitioner initiates a patient's mental health plan, and this is necessary so that up to ten counsellor visits per year can be subsidised through Medicare.
4 Usenet (an abbreviation of user network) began in 1979 as a distributed discussion system in which users could read and post to newsgroups, generating threaded discussion in a format that would later be associated with online forums.
5 This reports on findings from the *Mental Health Help-Seeking* study discussed here.
6 Data presented in this chapter constitute LGBTQ+ young people speaking to their use of Tumblr, but do not offer a detailed review of Tumblr content. I am aware that this could limit the reader's feel for Tumblr, particularly if you are not a user, but Tumblr research literature is cited throughout this chapter.

References

Anselmo, D. W. (2018). Gender and queer fan labor on Tumblr. *Feminist Media Histories, 4*(1), 84–114.

Baym, N. (2015). *Personal connections in the digital age* (2nd ed.). Cambridge: Polity Press.

Baym, N., & boyd, d. (2012). Socially mediated publicness: An introduction. *Journal of Broadcasting and Electronic Media, 56*(3), 320–329.

Bryan, A. (2017). Queer youth and mental health: What do educators need to know? *Irish Educational Studies, 36*(1), 73–89.

Butler, J. (1993). *Bodies that matter: On the discursive limits of sex.* New York, NY: Routledge.

Byron, P., Rasmussen, S., Wright Toussaint, D., Lobo, R., Robinson, K. H., & Paradise, B. (2017). *"You learn from each other": LGBTIQ Young People's Mental Health Help-seeking and the RAD Australia Online Directory.* Sydney: Western Sydney University & Young and Well Cooperative Research Centre. Retrieved from http://researchdirect.westernsydney.edu.au/islandora/object/uws:38815.

Byron, P., Robards, B., Hanckel, B., Vivienne, S., & Churchill, B. (2019). "Hey, I'm having these experiences": Tumblr use and young people's queer (dis)connections. *International Journal of Communication, 13,* 2239–2259.

Cavalcante, A. (2016). "I did it all online:" Transgender identity and the management of everyday life. *Critical Studies in Media Communication, 33*(1), 109–122.

Cavalcante, A. (2018). Tumbling into queer utopias and vortexes: Experiences of LGBTQ social media users on Tumblr. *Journal of Homosexuality*, 66(12), 715–1735.

Ceglarek, P. J. D., & Ward, L. M. (2016). A tool for help or harm? How associations between social networking use, social support, and mental health differ for sexual minority and heterosexual youth. *Computers in Human Behavior*, 65, 201–209.

Cho, A. (2015). Queer reverb: Tumblr, affect, time. In K. Hillis, S. Paasonen & M. Petit (Eds.), *Networked affect* (pp. 43–58). Cambridge, MA: MIT Press.

Cho, A. (2018). Default publicness: Queer youth of color, social media, and being outed by the machine. *New Media and Society*, 20(9), 3183–3200.

Clare, S. D. (2017). "Finally, she's accepted herself!" coming out in neoliberal times. *Social Text*, 35(2), 17–38.

Cover, R. (2012). *Queer youth suicide, culture and identity: Unliveable lives?* Farnham: Ashgate.

Cover, R. (2013). Queer youth resilience: Critiquing the discourse of hope and hopelessness in LGBT suicide representation. *M/C Journal*, 16(5).

Craig, S. L., & McInroy, L. (2014). You can form a part of yourself online: The influence of new media on identity development and coming out for LGBTQ youth. *Journal of Gay and Lesbian Mental Health*, 18(1), 95–109.

Dame, A. (2013). "I'm your hero? Like me?": The role of "expert" in the trans male vlog. *Journal of Language and Sexuality*, 2(1), 40–69.

Dame-Griff, A. (2019). Herding the "performing elephants": using computational methods to study usenet. *Internet Histories*, 3(3–4), 223–244.

Darwin, H. (2017). Doing gender beyond the binary: A virtual ethnography. *Symbolic Interaction*, 40(3), 317–334.

Deuze, M. (2012). *Media life.* Cambridge: Polity Press.

Duguay, S. (2014). "He has a way gayer Facebook than I do": Investigating sexual identity disclosure and context collapse on a social networking site. *New Media & Society*, 18(6), 891–907.

Duguay, S., Burgess, J., & Suzor, N. (2020). Queer women's experiences of patchwork platform governance on Tinder, Instagram, and Vine. *Convergence*, 26(2), 237–252.

Engelberg, J., & Needham, G. (2019). Purging the queer archive: Tumblr's counterhegemonic pornographies. *Porn Studies*, 6(3), 350–354

Eysenbach, G. (2008). Credibility of health information and digital media: New perspectives and implications for youth. In M. J. Metzger & A. J. Flanagin (Eds.), *Digital media, youth, and credibility, the John D. and Catherine T. MacArthur foundation series on digital media and learning* (pp. 123–154). Cambridge: MIT Press.

Fergie, G., Hilton, S., & Hunt, K. (2015). Young adults' experiences of seeking online information about diabetes and mental health in the age of social media. *Health Expectations*, 19(6), 1324–1335.

Fergie, G., Hunt, K., & Hilton, S. (2013). What young people want from health-related online resources: A focus group study. *Journal of Youth Studies*, 16(5), 579–596.

Fink, M., & Miller, Q. (2014). Trans media moments: Tumblr, 2011–2013. *Television and New Media*, 15(7), 611–626.

Fox, N., & Ward, K. (2006). Health identities: From expert patient to resisting consumer. *Health*, 10(4), 461–479.

Gowen, L. K. (2013). Online mental health information seeking in young adults with mental health challenges. *Journal of Technology in Human Services*, *31*(2), 97–111.

Gray, N. J., Klein, J. D., Noyce, P. R., Sesselberg, T. S., & Cantrill, J. A. (2005). Health information-seeking behaviour in adolescence: The place of the internet. *Social Science and Medicine*, *60*(7), 1467–1478.

Haimson, O. L., Brubaker, J. R., Dombrowski, L., & Hayes, G. R. (2015). *Disclosure, stress, and support during gender transition on Facebook*. Paper presented at the Proceedings of the 18th ACM Conference on Computer Supported Cooperative Work & Social Computing, Vancouver, BC, Canada. Retrieved from https://dl .acm.org/citation.cfm?id=2675152.

Haimson, O. L., Dame-Griff, A., Capello, E., & Richter, Z. (2020). Tumblr was a trans technology: The meaning, importance, history, and future of trans technologies. *Feminist Media Studies*, 1–17.

Haimson, O. L., & Hoffmann, A. L. (2016). Constructing and enforcing "authentic" identity online: Facebook, real names, and non-normative identities. *First Monday*, *21*(6).

Hanckel, B., & Morris, A. (2014). Finding community and contesting heteronormativity: Queer young people's engagement in an Australian online community. *Journal of Youth Studies*, *17*(7), 872–886.

Hanckel, B., Vivienne, S., Byron, P., Robards, B., & Churchill, B. (2019). "That's not necessarily for them": LGBTIQ+ young people, social media platform affordances and identity curation. *Media, Culture and Society*, *41*(8), 1261–1278

Hawkins, B., & Haimson, O. (2018). *Building an online community of care: Tumblr use by transgender individuals*. Paper presented at the Proceedings of the 4th Conference on Gender & IT, Heilbronn, Germany.

Hillier, L., Jones, T., Monagle, M., Overton, N., Gahan, L., Blackman, J., & Mitchell, A. (2010). *Writing themselves in 3: The third national study on the sexual health and wellbeing of same sex attracted and gender questioning young people*. Melbourne: Australian Research Centre in Sex, Health and Society, La Trobe University.

Hillier, L., Mitchell, K. J., & Ybarra, M. L. (2012). The internet as a safety net: Findings from a series of online focus groups with LGB and non-LGB young people in the United States. *Journal of LGBT Youth*, *9*(3), 225–246.

Horak, L. (2014). Trans on YouTube: Intimacy, visibility, temporality. *TSQ: Transgender Studies Quarterly*, *1*(4), 572–585.

Jackson, S. J., Bailey, M., & Foucault Welles, B. (2017). #GirlsLikeUs: Trans advocacy and community building online. *New Media and Society*, *20*(5), 1868–1888.

Jenzen, O. (2017). Trans youth and social media: Moving between counterpublics and the wider web. *Gender, Place and Culture*, *24*(11), 1626–1641.

Kahn, E., Johnson, A., Lee, M., & Miranda, L. (2018). *LGBTQ youth report*. Washington, DC: Human Rights Campaign Foundation. Retrieved from https:// www.hrc.org/resources/2018-lgbtq-youth-report.

Law, J. (2004). *After method: Mess in social science research*. London & New York, NY: Routledge.

Lovelock, M. (2019). "My coming out story": Lesbian, gay and bisexual youth identities on YouTube. *International Journal of Cultural Studies*, *22*(1), 70–85.

Lytle, M. C., Silenzio, V. M. B., Homan, C. M., Schneider, P., & Caine, E. D. (2018). Suicidal and help-seeking behaviors among youth in an online lesbian, gay, bisexual, transgender, queer, and questioning social network. *Journal of Homosexuality, 65*(13), 1916–1933.

Mayock, P., Bryan, A., Carr, N., & Kitching, K. (2008). *Supporting LGBT lives: A study of mental health and well-being.* Dublin: National Office for Suicide Prevention.

McDermott, E. (2015). Asking for help online: Lesbian, gay, bisexual and trans youth, self-harm and articulating the "failed" self. *Health, 19*(6), 561–577.

McDermott, E., Hughes, E., & Rawlings, V. (2016). *Queer Futures.* Lancaster, UK: Department of Health Policy Research Programme.

McNair, R. P., & Bush, R. (2016). Mental health help seeking patterns and associations among Australian same sex attracted women, trans and gender diverse people: A survey-based study. *BMC Psychiatry, 16*(1), 209.

McNeil, J., Bailey, L., Ellis, S., Morton, J., & Regan, M. (2012). Trans mental health study 2012. Edinburgh: Scottish Transgender Alliance. Retrieved from http://www.scottishtrans.org/wp-content/uploads/2013/03/trans_mh_study.pdf.

Pahl, R., & Spencer, L. (2004). Personal communities: Not simply families of "fate" or "choice". *Current Sociology, 52*(2), 199–221.

Piepzna-Samarasinha, L. L. (2018). *Care work: Dreaming disability justice.* Vancouver: Arsenal Pulp Press.

Raun, T. (2015). Video blogging as a vehicle of transformation: Exploring the intersection between trans identity and information technology. *International Journal of Cultural Studies, 18*(3), 365–378.

Renninger, B. J. (2015). "Where I can be myself … where I can speak my mind": Networked counterpublics in a polymedia environment. *New Media and Society, 17*(9), 1513–1529.

Robinson, K., Bansel, P., Denson, N., Ovenden, G., & Davies, C. (2014). *Growing up queer: Issues facing young Australians who are gender variant and sexuality diverse.* Melbourne: Young and Well Cooperative Research Centre. Retrieved from http://www.twenty10.org.au/growing-queer-issues-facing-young-australians-gender-variant-sexually-diverse-2013-young-well-crc-research/.

Saewyc, E., Frohard-Dourlent, H., Ferguson, M., & Veale, J. (2018). *Being safe, being me: Results of the Canadian trans youth health survey. Vancouver, BC: Stigma and Resilience Among Vulnerable Youth Centre, 2015.* Vancouver, BC: Stigma and Resilience Among Vulnerable Youth Centre, School of Nursing, University of British Columbia.

Scannell, P. (2014). *Television and the meaning of "live": An enquiry into the human situation.* Cambridge: Polity Press.

Shifman, L. (2014). *Memes in digital culture.* Cambridge, MA: MIT press.

Sillence, E., Hardy, C., & Briggs, P. (2013). *Why don't we trust health websites that help us help each other?: An analysis of online peer-to-peer healthcare.* Paper presented at the Proceedings of the 5th Annual ACM Web Science Conference, Paris, France. Retrieved from https://dl.acm.org/citation.cfm?id=2464488.

Smith, E., Jones, T., Ward, R., Dixon, J., Mitchell, A., & Hillier, L. (2014). *From blues to rainbows: The mental health and well-being of gender diverse and transgender young people in Australia.* Melbourne: The Australian Research Centre in Sex, Health and Society.

Strauss, P., Cook, A., Winter, S., Watson, V., Wright Toussaint, D., & Lin, A. (2017). *Trans pathways: The mental health experiences and care pathways of trans young people. Summary of results.* Perth, Australia: Telethon Kids Institute.

Retrieved from https://www.telethonkids.org.au/our-research/brain-and-behav iour/mental-health-and-youth/youth-mental-health/trans-pathways/.

Triggs, A. H., Møller, K., & Neumayer, C. (2019). Context collapse and anonymity among queer Reddit users. *New Media and Society*, 1461444819890353.

Vivienne, S. (2017). "I will not hate myself because you cannot accept me": Problematizing empowerment and gender-diverse selfies. *Popular Communication*, *15*(2), 126–140.

Wargo, J. M. (2017). #donttagyourhate: Reading Collecting and curating as Genres of Participation in LGBT Youth Activism on Tumblr. *Digital Culture and Education*, *9*(1), 14–31.

Weeks, J., Heaphy, B., & Donovan, C. (2001). *Same sex intimacies: Families of choice and other life experiments*. London: Routledge.

6 Friends with dating apps

This chapter adds to the book's discussion of friendship and its central role in digital cultures of care, this time in relation to young people's use of dating/hook-up apps.[1] It elaborates on previous discussion of young people's friendship support for sex and sexual relationships in Chapter 4, where I argued that close friendships can be considered as sexually intimate on account of friendship disclosures and shared intimate knowledge of friends' sexual experiences, preferences, and histories. A similar argument is made in relation to dating/hook-up app use, as per the support, feedback, and insight received through friend-based discussions of their use. These data were collected ten years after the data used in Chapter 4, so this also tracks some key changes in the way digital cultures further imbricate friendship and sexual intimacies. This chapter has two main focus points – how dating/hook-up app use typically involves friendship support, and how young people are making and extending friendships through their use of dating/hook-up apps. This extension can include making new friendships, as well as broadening the intimate practices of existing friendships. I consider what this tells us about the intimacies of app use, as well as young people's ongoing commitment to, and orientations toward, friendship.

Data from this chapter is taken from workshops and interviews with young people (18–35 years) in Sydney and regional New South Wales. Participants range from LGBTQ+ to straight, and their self-nominated identity details will be included alongside statements presented in this chapter. These data are taken from the *Safety, Risk and Wellbeing on Digital Dating Apps* study based at Swinburne University, and collected between 2018 and 2019.[2] These data demonstrate that dating/hook-up app use is an everyday practice for many young people and that these media increasingly intersect and overlap with broader social media such as Instagram and Snapchat. The bleed between social media and dating app cultures seems to be increasing, as will be discussed. This suggests a decreased level of stigma for digital dating, where young people are openly using apps and commonly sharing access to their other social media profiles and networks within their dating/hook-up app profiles. Further to the discussion of friendship support throughout this book, this chapter's discussion of dating/hook-up app use also considers how friends help each other negotiate the techno-cultural aspects of these platforms. For some young people, dating/hook-up apps are uncomfortable spaces for the ways they might challenge expectations of sex and dating. For others, app use is fun, and friends are integrated into this site of play.

In our workshops and interviews, participants were asked to map their use of dating/hook-up apps over the years, and to discuss which apps they like/dislike, the app features they like/dislike, and their experiences of engaging with people through apps. Across these discussions, friends were frequently mentioned as part of participants' app negotiations. This might be in relation to direct support, such as guiding each other's app use, or through more indirect emotional support, as part of ongoing discussions of sex and dating. Friends sometimes used apps together, in seriousness and fun. In relation to the support available among friendships, this mainly took place in the following ways:

- friends introducing each other to apps and encouraging their use;
- sharing screenshots of profiles and conversation with friends for discussion;
- sharing information with friends about an organised date or hook-up, sometimes sharing location details and asking them to be on standby in case they wanted an excuse to leave;
- friend-based comparison of app use, including advice for improving one's experiences; and
- using apps with friends in social/domestic settings (often playfully).

Beyond this, friendship featured more indirectly, such as in assessing the app profiles of other users and reviewing their friendship networks when there is access to other social media profiles, such as an embedded link to their Instagram. Many participants discussed the value (and safety) of having mutual friends with an app-based stranger. Indirect or unexpected engagements with friends discussed by participants include:

- the perceived safety of having mutual friends;
- encountering existing friends on dating apps, and sometimes messaging them;
- developing a sense of an app ecology through learning about a range of apps used by friends;
- allowing non-app-using friends to browse/use one's apps;
- developing a sense of one's personal app-use styles and preferences through witnessing friends' practices;
- concern about engaging with users who seem like they could be friendless (based on their profile); and
- becoming friends with people met on apps.

From these themes, it is obvious that friendships not only support app nego-tiations but can also be found through app use. Some participants actively sought friendship in their use of dating/hook-up apps and reported vary-ing levels of success. As per the shifting infrastructures of many popular apps (e.g. Tinder and Grindr) where users often include links to other social media profiles such as Instagram, many app users can review a potential date/hook-up's friendship networks. Personal information offered through social media profiles reveals more about who that person is – beyond how they represent themselves, more can be understood about them based on who they know. As such, intimacies can be generated more quickly than in earlier versions of apps and online dating, where a user's details were con-fined to a single profile and gave little indication of their social networks.

Friendship intimacies can involve sharing devices, with the passing of phones back and forth being an intimate practice that requires a level of trust. Sometimes friends will scroll on each other's behalf. If not sharing physical space, friends can share screenshots of app profiles, pics, and chats, for feedback or humour. When app use intersects with friendship practices, there is potential for the app user to develop a greater sense of their personal style and strategies of app use, through friendship comparison. This can be generative of app literacies and shared understandings and expertise around app use, including knowledge of specific app cultures and the kinds of prac-tices or users to avoid. This level of expertise was obvious in our research discussions – particularly our workshops, where participants frequently shared their strategies and communicative preferences with each other.

Approaching dating/hook-up apps as friend spaces

Research on dating/hook-up app use is often quite narrow, and aside from sex and dating practices that emerge from app use, little is known about other forms of intimacy found or practised on these sites. An instrumental approach to app use is commonly taken, with users asked what they seek from apps and whether they find this – sometimes through a "uses and grati-fications" approach (e.g. Van De Weile and Tong, 2014). Such questions support this narrow understanding of app use, as do any questions about media platforms that imagine a simple trajectory of use in terms of *seek-ing and finding* a particular outcome. In many research accounts, dating/hook-up apps are only understood as facilitating sexual and romantic con-nections. Researchers who are literate in queer uses of digital media tend to be more open to the manifold uses and orientations of media platforms and cultures, including dating/hook-up apps. As suggested in Chapter 1, friend-ship research can have queering effects in the way it challenges institution-alised and normative approaches to intimate and social relationships – the same can be said of queer approaches to digital media use.

Research literature has engaged with friendships on dating/hook-up apps, but mostly only as an outcome of app use. Typically, this varies between populations studied, with research focusing on LGBTQ+ app users being more inclined to see friendship as overlapping with sexual, dating, and romantic relationships. This is informed by decades of queer research that has considered friendships as part of sexual intimacies, as discussed in Chapter 1 and references to gay culture being founded on friendship (Foucault, 2000), historical research on love between women (Faderman, 1981), and empirical research on "families of choice" (Weeks et al., 2001; Weston, 1991). Together, these examples highlight a queer history in which friendship, romance, and sex overlap. Recent scholarship on polyamory has continued this work (Klesse, 2014), including its digital media representations and communities (Tiidenberg, 2014). This work further supports Pahl and Spencer's (2004) theory of "personal communities" which increasingly involve suffusion of family and friendship roles and relationships. As will be noted in my data analysis, many queer participants were open to making friends on apps, and some used apps while in open relationships, including with their partners. These practices trouble research that frames app use as a site for single people to privately communicate.

Many dating/hook-up apps give users the option to indicate friendship seeking (not just dates or hook-ups), and this seems to be more common in apps for gay/queer men (Chan, 2016; Fitzpatrick et al., 2015). As such, friendship seeking is part of the infrastructure of popular apps such as Grindr and Scruff but is less built into apps like Tinder. Colin Fitzpatrick et al. (2015) found that Grindr users who say they are looking for romance and friendship are more likely to have profiles with public face pics. Tinder, however, as the current most popular dating app used among young people in Australia, does not allow users to indicate that they are seeking friendship, but this could be added to one's profile text. That this feature does not exist in the app infrastructure tells us something about Tinder, its design, and its user base.

Scraping data from 25,365 Grindr profiles across North America, Fitzpatrick et al. (2015) mapped user goals (what profiles indicate they are looking for) and found that the most common goal was friendship (43.4%), followed by chat (36.75%) and dates (31.74%). However, they propose that "friends" and other goal categories can also be used as euphemisms. They are reluctant to accept that Grindr users most commonly seek friendship, given what is known about the app from previous research. This includes research from Christian Licoppe et al., who argue that "[t]he typical Grindr contact does not involve participants as friends but as hunters and 'preys'" (2016, p. 2547). They argue that Grindr-based chats "are unfit for Grindr users looking for casual sexual hook-ups, who forcefully deny being 'friends' … and want to avoid any relational build-up" (2016, p. 2555). As such, they argue that conversation that leans toward friendship (i.e. friendly chat) poses a risk to finding sex.

For heterosexuals, finding and practising friendship is more commonly associated with popular social media platforms such as Facebook and

Instagram. Increasingly, however, dating/hook-up apps used by straight people overlap with these other platforms, with users increasingly linking their "socials" (mostly Instagram) to their dating app profiles. In some ways, this moves dating/hook-ups more into the field of social media, inviting unknown app users into one's social media where they can further consider their interest and compatibility.

Where there has been attention to friendship within communication studies research on dating/hook-up apps, these often deploy uses and gratifications theory, as noted, where study participants are asked to address their individual (needs-based) goals of app use, rather than engaging with app use as more complex and multi-directional (Lutz and Ranzini, 2017; Ranzini and Lutz, 2017; Van De Wiele and Tong, 2014). While suggesting that friendships are a desirable outcome of dating/hook-up apps for many users, these studies tell us nothing about the practices of friendships on apps, just that they can be sought and found. Typically, most research on friendship and dating apps relates to Grindr use among gay men, though Lutz and Ranzini (2017) engaged with Tinder (adopting a framework used by Grindr researchers). They discussed "friendship seeking" as one of many motives for using Tinder (other motives identified were seeking hook-ups, partners, travel, self-validation, and entertainment) (2017). Using a different approach, Yeo and Fung argue that the temporality of Grindr/Jack'd use among gay men in Hong Kong was incongruent with the tempo of forming friendships or romance (2018). Their participants note that the speed and directness of app-based interaction are more attuned to finding quick sex (2018). Once again, friendship as a potential outcome of app use is pitted against sex as an outcome, as though these are mutually exclusive connections.

Goal-oriented studies of dating/hook-up apps commonly present an individualised account of users engaging with apps privately, isolated from other social networks and friendships. But as data in this chapter demonstrates, app use is often embedded in friendships and their everyday intimacies. As such, there is more to apps than being "tools" for sex or dating. We might also consider them as friendship-mediated platforms, as will be discussed.

In Tinder research featuring straight people, Green et al. (2018) argued that when Tinder indicates mutual Facebook connections, this can prevent sexual health discussion within apps due to fears that this communication may be relayed to mutual friends (2018). Other research has found that some people use Tinder to expand their dating practices beyond friendship networks (Newett et al., 2017). But beyond many brief mentions of friends surrounding young people's app use, and beyond brief discussions of platform connections (it was formerly a prerequisite to sign up to Tinder via one's Facebook profile), little has been reported about the role of friendships in and around the use of Tinder. In Pond and Farvid's (2017) research on bisexual young women's use of Tinder, however, some participants reported telling their friends about where they would be going for a date or bringing friends to the date, if they were worried about safety.

It is more common among researchers of LGBTQ+ app users to not simply focus on the relational goals and outcomes of app use, and to be open to broader forms of intimacy and communication. For example, researchers have considered how app use relates to diversifying traditional forms of intimacy (Race, 2015; Stempfhuber & Liegl, 2016), negotiating masculinity (Bonner-Thompson, 2017; Rodriguez et al., 2016) and the embodied aspects of digital space (Roth, 2014), experiences of racism and racialised desire (Carlson, 2020; Raj, 2011), queer cosmopolitanism (Ong, 2017), learning how to be gay (Castañeda, 2015; Jaspal, 2016), negotiating femmephobia (Miller & Behm-Morawitz, 2016), practising self-pornography (Phillips, 2015; Tziallis, 2015), and developing a sense of queer community (Masden & Edwards, 2015). While connected to the relational aspects of dating/hook-up app use, this research is more attentive to app-use processes rather than outcomes, predominantly adopting a techno-cultural construction approach to digital media (van Dijck, 2013).

Dating/hook-up app research from China has paid greater attention to how social and sexual media are enmeshed, reflecting the ambiguity of many apps that are popular among Chinese young people. From their survey of dating app users in mainland China, Solis and Wong (2019) found that the fear of being seen on these sites by friends (a "risk of exposure") reduced users' likelihood of meeting for casual sex, but not for dating. Like other Chinese app research, it was also noted that many sites (such as Momo, in this case) are marketed as social networks, rather than specifically for sex and dating. According to Solis and Wong, while developers claim that their apps are "aimed to allow users to broaden their social networks by connecting with strangers and making new friends" (2019, p. 205), they are culturally understood as apps for sex and dating. Tingting Lui also notes Momo's insistence to market itself as a friendship app to move away from its reputation as an app for casual sex (2016). This hybridity, whether felt as such by users, offers greater safety in the use of apps like Momo, given the plausible deniability offered, if one is seen to be using the app.

Elsewhere, Lik Sam Chan discusses Momo's reputation of being "a powerful tool for hooking up" (2019) – a public impression fuelled by mass media discussion, which most of Chan's participants, who used Momo in mainland China, were aware of. Chan's participants also indicated the role of friends in supporting and discussing their app use – with many initially learning about Momo from friends (2019). Aside from using Momo to look for sex or relationships, the third most common reason given by Chan's participants was to make friends. For one participant, Momo afforded a more private space to make friends and discuss personal details, without other networks seeing this, such as family members who could witness WeChat interactions (2019, p. 7). Meanwhile, other research on Chinese social media and digital dating/hook-up platforms have noted that the "people nearby" services available on WeChat also support practices of dating and hooking up, since these features are commonly associated with Momo and Tinder (Xue et al., 2016). Minhui Xue et al. refer to these as "find-and-flirt" services – part of a range of platforms that can be used for friendship and hooking up. On WeChat, for example, users are invited to "request friendship" from people nearby, which can, of course, include sexual friends.

While the above research refers to app cultures that differ to many (but not all) participants in our study, this research demonstrates attention to socio-sexual cultures of digital media use, and young people's expertise in navigating digital spaces that (like non-digital spaces) host a range of intimacies. This work demonstrates young people's competencies in navigating public privacies, and the potential visibility of sexual identities, desires, and practice. This work also highlights how app use also involves negotiations of pleasure and ethics (Byron & Albury, 2018).

In Chapter 3, I made a case for young people's social media use to be considered and understood as expertise. I argued that health promoters and researchers could learn from this expertise, in which young people knowingly spoke of Facebook and its potential for sexual health promotion. As with social media platforms like Facebook, researchers commonly discuss the potential of health promotion interventions within dating/hook-up apps. The focus is also predominantly on sexual health, as discussed in our report from this project (Albury et al., 2019). Apps are likely seen as a more suitable site for sexual health promotion as opposed to other social media, due to an expectation that people are using these platforms to organise sex. As with some social media interventions, app-based interventions are not simply focusing on the delivery of static health information, with apps also being used for research recruitment (Landovitz et al., 2013), community outreach (Brennan et al., 2018; Mowlabocus et al., 2016), and gathering health surveillance data (Baral et al., 2018).

Much of this health research sees apps as "venues" for intervention (as with social media platforms, discussed in Chapter 3), or perhaps more so, as "tools" for intervention. A discussion similar to that of Chapter 3 could be had about health researchers' and promoters' *use of apps* as opposed to young people's everyday *use of apps*, in which a discourse of "tools" (i.e. imagining that app users are taking an instrumental approach to apps, and using these to simply find dates and hook-ups), carries from *formal readings* of these spaces, into formal practices of health promotion and research. Again, professional uses of these spaces seem to align with professional misunderstandings or simplifications of these spaces, guided by an instrumental approach to digital media. This also suggests a technological determinist understanding of media – where the apps are understood as responsible for the social and sexual practices involved in their use, including STI transmissions (Enomoto et al., 2017). This chapter's focus on young people's accounts of dating/hook-up app use, including their broader discussions of safety and risk, can usefully expand current health promotion and research approaches.

The following section explores three key themes of friendship that emerged in these data. Firstly, practices of making friends, which was sometimes intentional, but more often accidental. Secondly, the practice of identifying mutual friends and how most participants preferred to have these social connections with potential dates. And thirdly, the support that friendships offer to young people's app use.

Making friends on dating/hook-up apps

While some participants sought friendships on dating/hook-up apps, more often these accidentally formed. LGBTQ+ participants more commonly spoke of making friends through app use, though a small minority of heterosexual participants indicated that they had done so. For many LGBTQ+ participants, distinctions between sexual/romantic connections and friendships were not necessarily clear cut. This references more fluid cultures of sex and friendship, as discussed in Chapter 1.

In workshop discussions, many participants noted that Tinder and other dating apps were more ambiguous than they had initially expected in terms of the types of connections they supported. Lauren, for example, a White Sydney workshop participant who is lesbian (age unknown), felt that friendship on Tinder was becoming more common: "I feel like there's a new wave of people on Tinder to find friends as well".

Some of the ambiguity of dating/hook-up app connections, and the blurred distinctions between sexual and friendship communication, relates to how social media have infiltrated app infrastructures and their cultures of use. Friending and following one's Tinder matches on Facebook, Snapchat, or Instagram was common for many participants. Many linked their "socials" (most commonly Instagram) to their dating app profiles, and increasingly expected this of others. For some, moving an app-initiated chat to social media such as Instagram or Facebook Messenger was rapid, often depending on the type of interaction they were seeking from that person and how much they wanted to know about each other. On one level, this could be voyeuristic, but on another level, this usually meant becoming more intimate and sometimes friend-like through the insight this generated. When participants more specifically used apps to arrange sex, adding someone to social media was less common. This speaks to Licoppe et al.'s findings that friendly interactions (such as chat) could disrupt sex from happening (2016). Yet many participants still connected with hook-ups on social media to get a quick sense of that person and verify that they were who they presented themselves to be.

Many gay/queer male participants indicated that they saw apps like Grindr as sex apps, so felt these were unlikely to offer new friendships. Some discussed their failed attempts at finding friends there. Interview participant

Wei, who is gay, aged 29 and Chinese, spoke of his attempt to use a gay dating site some years ago (he thinks it was Gaydar) to find a friend to explore the London gay scene with. Following a night out with a guy, Wei decided to sleep over but told his "friend" that he did not want sex. Despite this, the man tried to initiate sex on several occasions. Elsewhere in the interview, Wei told a story about a Grindr date with a White man in Hong Kong who sexually grabbed him in an elevator, "without consent", after which he "felt very disrespected". Wei described the event as likely relating to racial hierarchies among gay men in Hong Kong, wondering if the date "felt he was entitled". Wei communicated his feelings to the man afterwards, via Grindr, but this was shrugged off – "Maybe the person thought I was too uptight about it, maybe the person thought I was short of humour … . There was no apology". From experiences such as these, Wei is dubious about the possibility of making friends on gay apps, just as he is cautious about engaging with "older, middle age White males". While he may not have been seeking friendship from the White man in Hong Kong, both these experiences speak to a lack of respect for boundaries, and a lack of care that suggests, for Wei, that apps do not foster practices of friendship, but are more associated with disrespect, sexual harassment, and existing racial hierarchies.

Seeking friendship on apps was also dependent on where a user was based and whether that was an ongoing or temporary situation. For example, several participants were temporarily studying in Australia, and their app use centred on casual sex, casual friendship, or both. "Casual friendship" (my term, not theirs) refers to an openness to meeting up, hanging out, and seeing what happens. Among permanent residents of Australia, the roles and expectations around app connections seemed to be identified more quickly, with more initial emphasis on figuring out what a connection would become (or not). More openness tended to be a key aspect of app-found friendships, where users felt less urgency to determine what an interaction would become. This openness was also seen in participant stories of travelling abroad and feeling more adventurous with their app use, and more open to loosely defined connections.

As with Wei's experiences above, many participants indicated that cisgender male app users had not always respected their requests or boundaries, and this too influences the affective experiences of dating/hook-up apps, and a common sense that these are not friend-like spaces (despite many friendships forming there). While some gay men reported making friends on Grindr and similar apps, they too did not see this as common. For example, Robert, a White gay man aged 30, says, "I found a good few decent friendships, and relationships, even if the initial intention was to hook-up". He then notes that this is "definitely the exception to the rule". Gabriel, a gay Filipino man aged 31, had also made friends on apps, and when asked how friendship works on apps, he said it was "challenging". He recalls a time when he attempted to use Grindr for friendship while he was in a monogamous relationship but found that many users seemed not to read his profile and kept requesting sex.

Stephen, a bisexual trans man, aged 27, stated in a workshop that he used Scruff because it seemed to offer more room for diverse connections. He said, "I've made new friends and found people to hook up with". Also in that workshop was Max, aged 23, non-binary transmasculine and queer, who mentioned that Tinder had been good for them in terms of meeting other trans people for friendship in their regional city. Along with some queer cisgender women, trans participants expressed more openness toward friendship and often had more experiences of making friends on apps. For example, Alex who is non-binary, lesbian, Aboriginal/European, and aged 26, spoke of their preference for apps where it was more acceptable to meet to "go out for coffee, go to the movies, go down the beach, cuddle", rather than apps more focused on hooking up or seeking a long-term relationship.

Among apps commonly used by straight participants, Bumble offered more (on an infrastructural level) in terms of seeking friendship. This is in the form of Bumble BFF, a section of the app where you can swipe for potential friends, rather than potential dates/hook-ups. On their website, Bumble justifies the need for Bumble BFF as follows:

> Whether you're new to a city or looking to expand your social circle, Bumble BFF is a simplified way to create meaningful friendships ... . As our lives evolve, so does our need for authentic friendships. We created Bumble BFF to make it easy to build a supportive community around you – no matter where or who you are. (https://bumble.com/bff)

This marketing blurb might be mistaken for sociological theories of friendship discussed in Chapter 1, particularly its reference to a shifting social world (i.e. late modernity) that makes friendships more important than ever. Indeed, the suggestion is that the conditions of modern life call for stronger, supportive, "authentic" friendships. Our research participants were mostly unconvinced that Bumble BFF was useful for finding friends, and noted the context collapse of moving a single profile (including its content and photos) between dating, friendship, and business profiles.[3] However, the (obviously market-tested) existence of Bumble BFF speaks to how sexual and social networks overlap and co-mingle, digitally and otherwise. While we might consider this in terms of "context collapse" (Marwick & boyd, 2011), this might better be understood as an inevitable bleed, going by participants' accounts of app use. Indeed, these are leaky spaces (Chun, 2016), and social media users, according to Wendy Chun, are becoming somewhat habituated by the instability and flux of these leaky media (2016).

Other apps have incorporated friendship in different ways, such as Tinder Social – a no longer active section of Tinder where you used to be able to arrange group dates with friends. In one workshop, Ellie, aged 20, who is straight, Indigenous, and regional-based, spoke of using Tinder Social and being disappointed that it is no longer available:

> I liked when they have their big group things because you comfortably go on dates with your friends as well. I didn't like when they got rid of that … . You used to be able to join a group of two or three other people in the queue and then you'd match with other groups of people and you'd go on group dates and stuff … . It was a lot more comfortable.

Even participants whose app use was more sex-focused, or for non-serious dating, sometimes ended up making friends, as was the case for Jackie, aged 23, who is African-American, bisexual, and based in Sydney for her studies:

> So one dude who I met when I first got here, we were talking the entire time. We still text every now and again now, and he was a good friend. But yeah, we won't be together. But I don't know, maybe conversation-wise, so I have somebody on this time zone who I can talk to.

Miles, aged 26, a White gay/queer man from Sydney stated, "the single biggest thing that annoys me on things like Grindr is when people [say] they're looking for friends and the moment they see I'm in a relationship, they're not interested. Well, hang on". In the same workshop, Charles, who is 34, gay/queer, and White, suggests that friendship is a liminal zone of Grindr chat which will lead nowhere. He states, "Grindr seems to have that very long continuum that you can have a good conversation with them and it sort of moves into a friendship and then stops". This suggests that friendship, or too much friend-like interaction, was often a dead end and would ensure the conversation fades out, as described by Licoppe et al. (2016).

Interview participant Ruby, who was aged 29, and is bisexual, White and Sydney-based, discussed using Bumble with her male partner to find women to date together. She noted that they were also open to making friends:

> it's fun for us. It's another thing we do as a couple together that lots of other couples don't do … . When we're using them, we're not always using them just to meet someone to date or have sex with. We are quite open to going out and meeting someone just to have a beer and having a laugh with and making a new friend. There is an element to it that it's a different way of meeting people in a context that's quite protected, particularly because we don't talk to lots of our friends about our dual dating stuff. It's a different way of meeting people in an open way.

This offers another example of the openness of app use that is more generative of friendship, or more creative forms of intimacy beyond casual sex and dating. Ruby notes that she has made several friends on Bumble, including meeting women to go on group motorcycle rides with. She has found that making friends is an enjoyable aspect of Bumble use, particularly as she can be more open about her relationship with new friends found on Bumble, since most of their friends did not know about their open relationship and "dual dating".

The safety of mutual friends

Many participants indicated that an awareness of having mutual friends with a prospective date made them feel safer and more trusting of that person. This knowledge was typically only available through access to that person's social media – either via a link on their profile, or sharing this information once chatting. This feeling of safety highlights the level of trust that many young people place in friendship networks. Sharing mutual friends offered not only a sense of safety but a sense that they would have something in common. If any mutual friends were close friends, participants were likely to ask them about this person. Doing so generated a better sense of whether it was worth meeting or exploring the connection further.

In a regional workshop featuring mostly straight women, participants discussed their preference for meeting men in public rather than at someone's house. In this discussion, Rachel, aged 20, straight, and White, says, "Unless he had mutual friends and stuff and I kind of knew of him or whatever, it'd be fine". In other words, the safety implied in having mutual friends meant that typical safety precautions, like meeting in a public place, might be relaxed. This may not involve asking mutual friends to vouch for a person, since knowing that they have several mutual friends was assurance enough for some participants. Having mutual friends suggested not only that this person was authentic and already connected through social/friendship networks but that this person would likely be compatible on some level, even as friends. A similar logic – of the safety of meeting people who had mutual friends – sometimes guided other safety practices, such as telling a friend about a date/hook-up and sharing one's location. Many straight female participants in a Sydney workshop discussed sharing locations or details of dates with friends for safety reasons, and within this discussion, Eve, aged 23, straight, and White, agreed with this: "Yeah, if it's off a dating app and you don't, like if you don't have a mutual friend, like all that kind of jazz, definitely".

In the regional workshop for LGBTQ+ women, Chelsea, aged 19, bisexual, and White, mentioned that she has messaged friends of friends on Instagram whom she found attractive. She stated, "Yeah, basically mutual friends or people that I've found on Instagram in the area kind of thing. I probably sound like a stalker but yeah". This highlights how social media is also sometimes used like a dating app, but with the added assurance that these are people in one's social networks.

Having mutual friends was also discussed as a fun aspect of dating app connections, where initial conversations could involve figuring out how each other knows the mutual friends, as discussed by Amy, aged 29, queer, and White, in a Sydney workshop:

> I remember matching with a girl – we had specific mutual friends, so she was like, yes, you must [be] really involved with this or this, at uni, and I was like, yeah, I am, and you must be involved with this, because of our – so we figured out our connection, based off the very unique subset of friends that we had that were matching. So that was fun.

Doing some research to check for mutuals (on Facebook, if you have their full name) was also discussed in the following regional workshop with straight and bisexual women:

> *Megan:* I think for me, if I can find out their last name then I'm going to look them up on Facebook because everyone has or has had a Facebook account and given the nature of [regional city], we're going to have mutual friends. And if we don't have mutual friends … . This happened the other night. I messaged Rachel because she was one of my five mutual friends and Rachel was like, "oh yeah, he's fine". Then I messaged another one of my good friends from uni and she was like, "don't go there, he's weird, he will message you 500 times", and then, yeah.
> *Rachel:* Oh …
> *Megan:* You had an old experience with him.

This example shows how some participants would check with several mutual friends about a prospective date. In this case, Rachel's assurance was seen as less reliable than another mutual friend who had had a more recent interaction with this guy.

Friendship support for app use

Participants discussed friendship support throughout their use of dating/hook-up apps, including guidance on which apps to use and why, assessing the profiles of other app users, and workshopping app-based interactions. From discussing their experiences of apps with friends, users and their friends extended their knowledge of what app use can offer but also furthered their intimate knowledge of each other through mutual disclosures and discussion of sexual and dating practices. Some participants sought help from friends in creating their app profiles, and others reported helping their friends. In a regional workshop for users of Grindr and similar apps, Dan, aged 24, gay, and White, stated:

> Well, I guess we always help our friends to make – well, I do help friends make their profiles because they're generally – it is a sweeping

generalisation but I have to help my straight friends a lot more with their profiles than gay friends.

This comment led to further discussion and recurring jokes throughout that workshop about straight men's inability to take selfies or to know what a good photo looks like. Help with profile building was commonly discussed in other workshops too, including our Sydney workshop with straight men. Here, participants reported sharing their profile with friends for further suggestions (though they did not admit to having terrible selfie skills). The men in this group said that advice-seeking was irregular and that advice offered among other friends was not detailed, but mostly just involved a quick look, according to Henry, aged 24 and White:

> Yeah. I think maybe early on, just a casual sharing with friends – guy and girl friends, just more of a, "what does your profile look like? This is what mine looks like". Not so much instructive.

Straight male participants of a regional workshop expressed even more reluctance to consult friends about their app profiles, especially other straight male friends. As suggested by Noah, aged 19 and Australian/Japanese, men were not the intended audience, so they were unlikely to offer any valuable advice. He states:

> some of my mates didn't really want to show me because it was more like the way they wanted to be portrayed to the girls. If I saw it, they probably would be like, think that I would laugh at it kind of thing, if you get me?

In this discussion, Duncan, aged 19 and Australian/Eastern European adds, "well, you don't want to be embarrassed about it or anything in front of the boys". Others agreed, and some participants indicated that they had asked female friends for feedback on their profiles. Meanwhile, Kai, aged 21, who is agender, lesbian, and White, and also participated in this workshop, discussed how they commonly gave advice to friends about their profiles. When asked what this entailed, they said:

> Usually just how to do their bio; what photos look good, what ones I shouldn't put up. If I see them on Tinder and I swipe through their photos and I see one that I personally wouldn't like if I was into them, I would tell them.

Kai also mentioned that a female friend of theirs who recently developed an interest in other women asked them to help with her app use. Of this, Kai states: "Yeah, because she had just come out as bi and she was like, 'I need your help. I don't know what the red flags are, I don't know what to look for'".

Elsewhere, in a regional workshop with LGBTQ+ women, Kat, aged 34, bisexual, and White, discussed signing up to dating apps on the advice of her friend. She thought this friend was a good source of recommendation on account of her having had success with meeting women through apps. Kat states:

> For me it was kind of like I had the one gay female friend and I was just sort of starting out in the meeting women through dating apps kind of thing. She had used a couple and she'd met some women through these apps and so then I was like, well, had to do it, what advice? I'd keep asking her questions even though she – she lives overseas but yeah, it's good when you're just starting out to have somebody to ask those questions.

This story illustrates how dating app use is often integrated into friendship intimacies – from the point of joining the app (and knowing which app/s to join), to the availability of advice while using apps. No doubt Kat and her friend had other things to discuss too, about their lives, now that they lived in separate countries. Whether Kat's app use was constituted as a particular "project" of that friendship is hard to know, but Kat elsewhere discussed her lack of non-heterosexual friends, suggesting that this friend offered particular insight that she could not get from other friends.

In a Sydney workshop of straight women, most participants indicated that they showed their profiles to friends for feedback and advice. Here are some examples from these discussions:

> Gabriella (22, Maltese): Yeah, I definitely workshop bios with friends and stuff like that, just like, would you swipe on this?

> Eve (23, White): Definitely, multiple times, I've had like mates of mine essentially like create my Tinder account. So they'll pick my photos they think I should use, write my bio, what I'm like …

> Brej (20, White, Italian, Jewish): Yeah, the first time I went on Tinder I asked my friend, I was like "what pictures do I choose?" Like I have a million pictures and … she just picked them out and I was like okay, this makes sense, I understand that.

These examples, along with others, indicate that straight women in our study were much more inclined than straight men to share, discuss, and workshop their dating app profiles. They were also more likely to share screenshots of interactions with friends for feedback and advice. There was less concern (than among straight men) about whether feedback would come from their intended audience. As such, straight women were more confident that other straight women were literate in app profile building and how to decode messages, chats, and other aspects of app-based interaction. Similarly, in our reference groups with app users for this project, we found that many young women (straight and queer) spoke with a deep knowledge of app cultures – a knowledge that was no doubt constituted through friendship.

It was evident that friendship talk generated greater expertise in the digital cultures of certain apps, or of dating app cultures more broadly. One example of this can be seen in a regional workshop with straight and bisexual women, where participants initiated a discussion of *fuckboys* and *softboys*. This transformed the workshop into a peer learning environment, where participants shared their knowledge of these dating app figures, highlighting the red flags to watch out for. This knowledge was likely drawn from experiences, as well as a cultural literacy of such figures. This discussion was also a learning moment for the research team, many of us unfamiliar with the intricate details of the fuckboy and softboy,[4] and how they were part of app culture for many young women. This is an example of peer learning and a lateral sharing of expertise, as discussed in Chapter 3. This expertise is generated through media practice and the peer and friend-based sharing and learning that happens alongside app use, generating cultures of knowledge that far surpass researchers' understandings of dating apps.

A similar example of learning how to identify and characterise certain behaviours of men on dating apps was discussed in an interview with Abby, aged 30, mostly hetero, and White, who lived in a regional city and mostly used Bumble. In describing a difficult dating experience to friends, these friends identified and named the behaviour of the man involved:

> I was talking to some friends about it and one of the girls said "yeah, that's love bombing" ... I was like, "what on earth is love bombing?" I looked it up and it's an actual thing, it's happening through online dating. It's scary and it's dangerous, I think.

She described love bombing as when someone's interactions are "hard and fast and passionate to quickly get a need met", therefore advancing things quickly, showering the other person in compliments, but eventually it "blows up and crashes very quickly". For Abby, this term and its existence helped her understand why dating a particular man had been difficult for her. It offered assurance that she was not misreading or misinterpreting something, but that these were recognised patterns of behaviour that have been recorded and discussed. For Abby, her awareness of love bombing emerged through friendship support.

Among their friends, many participants (mostly women) supported each other by sharing details of their dates, where they were going, and who they would be with. Some discussed sharing their GPS location with friends or having friends on standby should they need to opt out. These strategies highlight the *feelings of unsafety* that apps have generated for many users, predominantly users who meet up with straight, cisgender men. Workshop discussions among predominantly straight women suggest that that the role of friendship support expanded well beyond "keeping watch" or being on standby, but included workshopping app-based interactions prior to meeting up. This was particularly the case if the participant had some doubts, based on their interactions so far. In a Sydney workshop with straight women, Brej (20) said that while she did not usually seek such advice herself, sometimes "people just don't really know what to say, so it's fine to ask for advice. Like not to seem too pushy or like if you want to be sort of suggestive". These practices demonstrate how app use is integrated into friendship support for many users, where – typically through digital chatting where screenshots of "private interactions" can be shared – friends become intimately involved in one another's app-based interactions.

Sometimes sharing screenshots was less for advice and more for keeping friends up to date. This integration of friendship into app negotiations was a common point of discussion in the Sydney workshop with straight women. When asked if sharing screenshots of profiles and chats was common, most participants replied with "Absolutely". Further to this, it was said:

Jess: It's a talking point.
Brej: Like is he cute? I can't tell because he looks different in every picture.
Katie: Yeah, like I'm meeting up with him, like what are your thoughts on him?
Brej: But shit yeah, we'll talk.

For some, friendship support around app use was less detailed and involved and could be about which apps to use and why, or comparing experiences of an app that friends also use. As noted by regional workshop participant Beth, aged 19, bisexual, and White, advice was rarely technical, but more about the cultures of particular apps:

I feel like a lot of the advice I see is not how the app works because we all use phones every day and we kind of get it, it's more of the cultural thing. So "what's not okay to put as my photos? What should I do for my bio? What do you think of this person? If they ask me about this, what should I say?" That kind of thing.

Some participants also discussed sharing amusing profiles they see on apps with their friends, further extending app encounters into friendship chat. For example, Eve, aged 23, straight, and White, states:

I did used to have like a Facebook Messenger group that was dedicated to sending a few of my really good mates really bad pick-up lines from Tinder that guys would send me. So I'd just like screenshot them and send them off. So that was rather entertaining, there were probably like a good 20 that I would send in a session. But yeah, besides that just – and again they were still close friends so it was like a group of like 4 people.

Similarly, interview participant Abby (30) also "confessed" to collecting screenshots of certain Bumble profiles, saving these, and showing them to friends when they would meet up.

> I have a confession. I sort of take the piss out of this app, as well, and I keep a folder in my phone of screenshots, called the boys of Bumble. It's gotten to the point where I categorise them and my friends and I will go out for drinks and go through and have a good laugh.

These examples suggest that dating app interactions and encounters offer fun content to share with friends – sometimes through a shared dismay about app profiles, or sometimes to amuse friends who do not use apps. Screen grabbing and redistributing content that "takes the piss" out of apps, is a friend-based activity – as is much of the fun associated with using dating/hook-up apps. Another example of this is participant practices of handing their phones and apps to friends to play with, as discussed by George and Bart in a Sydney workshop with straight men:

George: A few of my friends who are generally the ones that have been in relationships have wanted to swipe on my behalf. They'll be on my app, it's not for them, but they just want to have a go at the gamification kind of experience, I guess.
Bart: Sometimes it gives you that feeling of, "I've got good taste. You need my help, you need my good judgement", I think. Yeah, some people like going into that role.
George: Then they go a bit wild, yeah.

Sometimes friends used apps within the same space, including social settings, but also in domestic spaces, among housemates. Swiping with friends seemed to be common practice for many participants. This was often constituted as fun and playful app use that seemed to centre the friendship intimacies more so than the potential intimacies found through the apps. Often friends who did not use apps wanted to "play" with them or watch participants swipe and get involved in decision-making processes.

In one example of swiping with friends, Amber, aged 22, bisexual, and White, mentioned playing with apps with her housemates when bored at home:

> When you're bored with your housemates. I have had so many times where all five of us are just sitting in the lounge room on our Tinders. Yeah. It'd be like, oh, look at this guy, look at this guy.

Beyond swiping with friends in social interactions, the domestic space of this scenario tells us something about friendships as also playing out in everyday sites like shared lounge rooms, suggesting a sense of kinship. In such a scene, lines of intimacy can be traced in many directions, between app users, between housemates, and from these housemates to the apps of many screens. If all five housemates are on Tinder, then they are likely swiping on some of the same profiles and may be encountering people known to their housemates, given the social networks they share, the geolocative aspects of apps like Tinder, and the familiarity they are likely to have with each other's sexual intimacies, tastes, and practices. Suggesting a form of queer kinship, this example takes us back to Pahl and Spencer's concept of "personal communities" and family-like-friends (2004). There is also something to be said for overlapping spaces here, in which friends sharing the domestic home space are also sharing digital spaces (even if they do not directly encounter each other or interact there).

Dating app play, which could be about relieving boredom, can also arise through chatting about dating app encounters and so needing to show these to friends. Playing with dating apps could also involve letting others swipe and message on your behalf, and vice versa. Straight men in a Sydney workshop, for example, spoke of daring friends to use each other's apps, including messaging people and pretending to be them. Bart aged 21, and Italian/Jewish Australian, told a story about handing his phone to a friend to chat with a random, finding that his match was quite receptive to the silliness of his friend's messages: "I was like, okay, maybe the silly works".

Participants had friends who did not use dating apps but always wanted to play with them or talk about them. Holding a phone between them, this "show and tell" engagement with "personal" dating apps can open up new spaces for discussing sexual and dating intimacies – learning of a friend's experiences and frustrations, and effectively learning about their tastes and orientations. In these encounters, the phone can become a portal into these intimacies, but also a mediator of the friendship intimacies that play out in these interactions.

Depending on a particular app, there was inconsistency around the types of connections people expected. This was typically based on users' past experiences of particular apps or the experiences of friends who introduced them to a particular app. Even Tinder offered quite different experiences among participants. For example, Sydney interview participant Sam, aged 23, non-binary, pansexual, and White, indicated having had no bad experiences on Tinder, yet recognised that this set them apart from a lot of their friends, who discuss their bad experiences. For Sam, they put this down to being more selective than many of their friends, as well as having a detailed bio that indicated what they were looking for. Of the people they had met on Tinder, Sam said: "they tend to be positive experiences; where we date or become friends or develop a relationship. I think that's because I set high standards in my profile". This demonstrates how one's app use, and one's sense of the kind of app user you are, are generated through friendship talk and comparison.

Friends with apps

From this research, it is evident that young people's friendships intersect with their experiences of dating/hook-up app use across many dimensions of use. Some participants discussed making friends through apps, both intentionally and accidentally, and matching with someone who had mutual friends would indicate greater safety, and sometimes an acceleration of the meet-up process. Elsewhere, friends supported each other, in a variety of ways, in their use of dating/hook-up apps. Many compared their experiences of app use with friends' experiences, and friends sometimes encouraged each other to use apps. App support among friends could enhance feelings of safety or could help assess certain experiences, profiles, and interactions.

While Chapter 4 centred on how friendships – particularly "close friendships" – inform and support sex, relationships, and sexual health, this chapter considers how friendship intimacies inform and support digital dating practices. Together, these chapters highlight how friendship and sexual intimacies are not mutually exclusive for many young people, and that friendship intimacies can accommodate sex or its potential. This is supported by the lack of social norms that young people's (and many other people's) friendships have. As with Chapter 4, data from this chapter demonstrates that friendships can foster intimate knowledge of our friends' sex and dating practices. This extends the possibilities of friendship support through friends' abilities to offer and receive personalised counsel and feedback, if and when desired.

Dating/hook-up apps are everyday media for many young people, and the fact that many comfortably link their social media profiles to their app profiles, suggests that stigma around app use is decreasing. As noted, studies of dating/hook-up apps often take an instrumental approach, where data collected speaks to user intentions or motivations. This ensures a limited account of their use, as well as neglected attention to the everyday and often playful context of app use. As found in our research survey data, that accompanied the data discussed here, boredom was the number one "reason for use" of apps among participants (Albury et al., 2019).

This chapter has considered many intersections between friendship and app-based negotiations of sex and dating. While platforms designed and marketed as sex and dating technologies are not commonly associated with friend-making, many participants in our research indicated that they had made friendships through these platforms. Sometimes this was intentional, but largely this was an unintended consequence of app use. This speaks to the porousness of these media, as well as their proximity and overlap to social media platforms such as Instagram. As everyday media, these increasingly connect to Instagram and other social media. With conversations commonly moving from apps to Facebook Messenger or WhatsApp, app-found connections can swiftly move into friendship modes.

For participants, engaging with friends around app use ranged from serious to fun, where apps were not simply a topic of discussion, but also social devices and play objects passed between friends. This draws our attention to the non-human aspects of these intimate media. This includes the touch and hold of our phones, but also the design and infrastructures of apps and the affective practices of messaging, swiping, and moving our fingertips across the faces and bodies of others (David & Cambre, 2016; Roth, 2014). Many researchers have already said much about the intimacies of these apps and the phones we use them on, but there has been less discussion on how these fold into and extend friendship intimacies.

The phone as an intimate device (in the hands of its user), that is also a portal to intimacy, is noticeable in research encounters where participants are asked to use their phones. Toward the end of each interview in this study, we invited participants to open an app on their phone if they were comfortable doing so (everyone was). Without showing us, we asked them to talk us through some profiles – how they read them, whether or not they were interested in those people, etc. Having only just met each participant roughly 45 minutes prior, the shift in intimacy was felt when participants looked away from us and spoke through their phones, discussing attractions, curiosity, disgust, disinterest, and more. These feelings, and the language given to them, came easy for most participants, demonstrating a comfort in reading profiles, and doing so with others present. But typically, this would be with friends, sometimes partners. As such, this activity and its shift in intimacy suggest a research encounter that momentarily fell into a rhythm of friendship. Similar research intimacies, where participants are browsing or scrolling their phones or social media feeds have been discussed, particularly by Kristian Møller in his media go-along method (Jørgensen, 2016) and in the scrollback method devised by Brady Robards and Sian Lincoln (2017).

Close friends could be heavily involved in one's dating app interactions, though this was particularly the case for women and non-binary participants and for some queer/gay and/or trans men. Friends consoled each other, learned more about each other and had someone to fall back on when things went wrong, to help decode messages and profiles, to be on standby, or to laugh with. Sharing stories and screenshots of potential and experienced dates and hook-ups produces insight not only into the potential intimacies that can be found through meeting people on apps but also into the intimate lives of our friends. Through such practices, friendship intimacies are practised and seemingly extended, demonstrating how apps not designed for friendship, effectively draw in friendship's practice, intimacy, and support.

This chapter addresses the need "for more research which focuses on friendship, 'non-conventional' forms of sexual/love relationships, and the interconnections between the two" (Roseneil & Budgeon, 2004, 139). Unlike most research on dating apps, this chapter has centred friendships – not simply as potential outcomes of app use, but as existing intimacies that surround and inform app use.

While researching dating/hook-up apps over the years, I have also used them. This has elaborated my knowledge of apps, as have conversations with my friends who also use apps. We have sometimes used apps together, comparing grids and conversations, sharing details of chats had, pictures received, or dates forthcoming. Research findings with young app users tell a similar story – that app use is socially embedded, and is a feature of every-day friendship intimacies, whether through boredom, play, or deeper-level disclosure and support. Sometimes my friends ask about my research find-ings, and sometimes I invite friends into this research space,[5] but mostly we engaged in mutual storytelling. These friend-based interactions (like any) are multi-focal, where we simultaneously share personal experiences, reference knowledge of each other's sex and dating histories, acknowledge and discuss the cultures of these apps, and introduce other stories we have witnessed or heard about, through friendship or other sources. We nav-igate space together, in ways that many people commonly do – through friendship.

In the study discussed throughout this chapter, the diversity of our research participants allowed us to consider and compare a range of plat-forms whose uses intersect with a range of identities, intimacies, and expec-tations that permeate dating/hook-up app cultures. What we did not attract, unfortunately, were many straight, cisgender men to take part in the study. Engaging with cisgender heterosexual men in digital intimacies scholarship can be difficult when participation relies on an arms-length invitation to enrol. For this study we invited participants to discuss app use *safeties and risks*, so it seems likely that this framework did not resonate with many such men who have less concern for safety in digital spaces (as with most spaces they occupy). Tellingly, the "cis straight guy" commonly emerged in this research through grievances about app environments, often dis-cussed as a figure to avoid or approach with caution. It was commonly noted among straight participants that on swipe-based apps such as Tinder, straight women right-swiped carefully and sparingly, whereas straight men swiped right much more frequently. For some straight male participants, these spaces were associated with a lack of "success" that was supported by watching straight female friends use Tinder, seemingly dismissing most men. Straight male participants also indicated that they were far less likely to chat about their dating app use among friends, though some reported asking for feedback on their profiles. But overall, their friend-based involve-ment in app use was minor.

Throughout this study, many participants highlight a certain openness and flexibility of app use. Sometimes surprising connections were made (including friendships). The flexibility of dating/hook-up apps was met with more acceptance among LGBTQ+ participants, once again referenc-ing broader expectations and fewer restricted models of sex and dating practices. This more relaxed approach may also be due to a greater sense of friendship support that accompanied app use, as well as sex, dating, and relationships in general. Along with those friendships came knowledge (produced through friendships) that one's frustrations and disappointments with dating/hook-up apps were common. But so too were the excitements and pleasures of app use. Not everyone spoke about friendship support, however, and it must be remembered that this is more common and available to some young people than others. Yet, knowing the value of this support (as illustrated throughout this chapter) offers something useful for health promoters and educators to reflect upon when engaging with straight men.

Finally, the openness and flexibility of dating/hook-up apps discussed above, and their reduced distance from everyday social media platforms, underscores the queer affordances of dating app use. By this, I am not simply referring to their use among queer people, but to how these can be (and indeed are) creatively used to forge a variety of intimacies, rather than simply adhering to, or mirroring, traditional forms of private courtship and/or casual sex encounters. As per other examples of digital cultures of care through this book, this knowledge of dating app intimacies becomes available to us through qualitative research that centres young people's expertise.

Notes

1 I use the term "dating/hook-up apps" throughout this chapter, though as I argue, these apps have broader uses and orientations. However, this is a recognised term in digital media research. As is often the case with many terms that congeal around digital media genres ("social media" for example), it simplifies practice. Yet digital media users commonly understand practices as more complex than the frames we apply to them.

2 This study was led by Kath Albury at Swinburne University of Technology, with a team comprised of Anthony McCosker, Kane Race, Tinonee Pym, and myself. See Introduction chapter for details of study partners and participants. This chapter would not exist without ongoing conversations with this research team.

3 Another extension offered is Bumble Bizz, to expand one's professional networks.

4 A fuckboy is generally understood as someone only interested in sex with little regard for his partner. A softboy is generally understood as a fuckboy who presents a more sensitive and emotional side but is still as manipulative and focused on sex.

5 I trialled a survey for Scruff users on my friends in 2018. The study never eventuated, but I have written about this process, which I intend to discuss in a forthcoming journal article.

References

Albury, K., Byron, P., McCosker, A., Pym, T., Walshe, J., Race, K., ... Dietzel, C. (2019). *Safety, risk and wellbeing on dating apps: Final report*. Melbourne: Swinburne University of Technology. Retrieved from https://apo.org.au/node/268156.

Baral, S., Turner, M. R., Lyons, E. C., Howell, S., Honermann, B., Garner, A., ... Millett, G. (2018). Population size estimation of gay and bisexual men and other men who have sex with men using social media-based platforms. *JMIR Public Health and Surveillance*, 4(1), e15.

Bonner-Thompson, C. (2017). "The meat market": Production and regulation of masculinities on the Grindr grid in Newcastle-upon-Tyne, UK. *Gender, Place and Culture*, 24(11), 1611–1625.

Brennan, D. J., Souleymanov, R., Lachowsky, N., Betancourt, G., Pugh, D., & McEwen, O. (2018). Providing online-based sexual health outreach to gay, bisexual, and queer men in Ontario, Canada: Qualitative interviews with multisectoral frontline service providers and managers. *AIDS Patient Care and STDs*, 32(7), 282–287.

Byron, P., & Albury, K. (2018). "There are literally no rules when it comes to these things": Ethical practice and the use of dating/hook-up apps. In A. S. Dobson, B. Robards & N. Carah (Eds.), *Digital intimate publics and social media* (pp. 213–229). London: Palgrave Macmillan.

Carlson, B. (2020). Love and hate at the Cultural Interface: Indigenous Australians and dating apps. *Journal of Sociology, 56*(2), 133–150.].

Castañeda, J. G. M. (2015). Grindring the self: Young Filipino gay men's exploration of sexual identity through a geo-social networking application. *Philippine Journal of Psychology, 48*(1), 29–58.

Chan, L. S. (2016). How sociocultural context matters in self-presentation: A comparison of U.S. and Chinese profiles on Jack'd, a mobile dating app for men who have sex with men. *International Journal of Communication, 10*, 6040–6059.

Chan, L. S. (2019). Multiple uses and anti-purposefulness on Momo, a Chinese dating/social app. *Information, Communication and Society*, 1–16. [online ahead of print].

Chun, W. H. K. (2016). *Updating to remain the same: Habitual new media*. Cambridge, MA: MIT Press.

David, G., & Cambre, C. (2016). Screened intimacies: Tinder and the swipe logic. *Social Media + Society*, 2(2).

Enomoto, C., Noor, S., & Widner, B. (2017). Is social media to blame for the sharp rise in STDs? *Social Sciences*, 6(78).

Faderman, L. (1981). *Surpassing the love of men: Romantic friendship and love between women from the renaissance to the present*. New York, NY: Morrow.

Fitzpatrick, C., Birnholtz, J., & Brubaker, J. R. (2015). *Social and personal disclosure in a location-based real time dating app*. Paper presented at the 48th Hawaii International Conference on System Sciences (HICSS), Kauai, HI.

Foucault, M. (2000). Friendship as a way of life (J. Johnston, Trans.). In P. Rabinow (Ed.), *Ethics, subjectivity and truth: Essential works of Foucault 1954–1984* (pp. 135–140). London: Penguin Books.

Green, S. M., Turner, D., & Logan, R. G. (2018). Exploring the effect of sharing common Facebook friends on the sexual risk behaviors of tinder users. *Cyberpsychology, Behavior, and Social Networking*, 21(7), 457–462.

Jaspal, R. (2016). Gay men's construction and management of identity on Grindr. *Sexuality and Culture*, 21(1), 187–204.

Jørgensen, K. M. (2016). The media go-along: Researching mobilities with media at hand. *MedieKultur*, 60(60), 32–49.

Klesse, C. (2014). Polyamory: Intimate practice, identity or sexual orientation? *Sexualities*, *17*(1–2), 81–99.

Landovitz, R. J., Tseng, C.-H., Weissman, M., Haymer, M., Mendenhall, B., Rogers, K., … Shoptaw, S. (2013). Epidemiology, sexual risk behavior, and HIV prevention practices of men who have sex with men using GRINDR in Los Angeles, California. *Journal of Urban Health*, *90*(4), 729–739.

Licoppe, C., Rivière, C. A., & Morel, J. (2016). Grindr casual hook-ups as interactional achievements. *New Media and Society*, *18*(11), 2540–2558.

Liu, T. (2016). Neoliberal ethos, state censorship and sexual culture: A Chinese dating/hook-up app. *Continuum*, *30*(5), 557–566.

Lutz, C., & Ranzini, G. (2017). Where dating meets data: Investigating social and institutional privacy concerns on Tinder. *Social Media + Society*, *3*(1).

Marwick, A., & boyd, d. (2011). I tweet honestly, I tweet passionately: Twitter users, context collapse, and the imagined audience. *New Media and Society*, *13*(1), 114–133.

Masden, C., & Edwards, W. K. (2015). *Understanding the role of community in online dating*. Paper presented at the International ACM Conference on Human Factors in Computing System. Seattle, WA. Retrieved from https://dl.acm.org/doi/10.1145/2702123.2702417.

Miller, B., & Behm-Morawitz, E. (2016). "Masculine guys only": The effects of femmephobic mobile dating application profiles on partner selection for men who have sex with men. *Computers in Human Behavior*, *62*, 176–185.

Mowlabocus, S., Haslop, C., & Dasgupta, R. K. (2016). From scene to screen: The challenges and opportunities of commercial digital platforms for HIV community outreach. *Social Media + Society*, *2*(4).

Newett, L., Churchill, B., & Robards, B. (2017). Forming connections in the digital era: Tinder, a new tool in young Australian intimate life. *Journal of Sociology*, *54*(3), 346–361.

Ong, J. C. (2017). Queer cosmopolitanism in the disaster zone: "My Grindr became the United Nations". *International Communication Gazette*, *79*(6–7), 656–673.

Pahl, R., & Spencer, L. (2004). Personal communities: Not simply families of "fate" or "choice". *Current Sociology*, *52*(2), 199–221.

Phillips, C. (2015). Self-pornographic representations with Grindr. *Journal of Visual and Media Anthropology*, *1*(1), 65–79.

Pond, T., & Farvid, P. (2017). "I do like girls, I promise": Young bisexual women's experiences of using Tinder. *Psychology of Sexualities Review*, *8*(2), 6–24.

Race, K. (2015). Speculative pragmatism and intimate arrangements: Online hook-up devices in gay life. *Culture, Health and Sexuality*, *17*(4), 496–511.

Raj, S. (2011). Grindring bodies: Racial and affective economies of online queer desire. *Critical Race and Whiteness Studies*, *7*, 55–67.

Ranzini, G., & Lutz, C. (2017). Love at first swipe? Explaining Tinder self-presentation and motives. *Mobile Media and Communication*, *5*(1), 80–101.

Robards, B., & Lincoln, S. (2017). Uncovering longitudinal life narratives: Scrolling back on Facebook. *Qualitative Research*, *17*(6), 715–730.

Rodriguez, N. S., Huemmer, J., & Blumell, L. (2016). Mobile masculinities: An investigation of networked masculinities in gay dating apps. *Masculinities and Social Change*, *5*(3), 241–267.

Roseneil, S., & Budgeon, S. (2004). Cultures of intimacy and care beyond "the family": Personal life and social change in the early 21st century. *Current Sociology, 52*(2), 135–159.

Roth, Y. (2014). Locating the "Scruff guy": Theorizing body and space in gay geosocial media. *International Journal of Communication, 8*, 2113–2133.

Solis, R. J. C., & Wong, K. Y. J. (2019). To meet or not to meet? Measuring motivations and risks as predictors of outcomes in the use of mobile dating applications in China. *Chinese Journal of Communication, 12*(2), 204–223.

Stempfhuber, M., & Liegl, M. (2016). Intimacy mobilized: Hook-up practices in the location-based social network Grindr. *Osterreichische Zeitschrift fur Soziologie, 41*(1), 51–70.

Tiidenberg, K. (2014). There's no limit to your love – scripting the polyamorous self. *Journal für Psychologie, 22*(1), 1–27.

Tziallas, E. (2015). Gamified eroticism: Gay male "social networking" applications and self-pornography. *Sexuality and Culture, 19*(4), 759–775.

Van De Wiele, C., & Tong, S. T. (2014). *Breaking boundaries: The uses & gratifications of Grindr*. Paper presented at the 2014 ACM International Joint Conference on Pervasive and Ubiquitous Computing. Seattle, WA.

Van Dijck, J. (2013). *The culture of connectivity: A critical history of social media*. Oxford & New York, NY: Oxford University Press.

Weeks, J., Heaphy, B., & Donovan, C. (2001). *Same sex intimacies: Families of choice and other life experiments*. London: Routledge.

Weston, K. (1991). *Families we choose: Lesbians, gays, kinship*. New York, NY: Columbia University Press.

Xue, M., Yang, L., Ross, K. W., & Qian, H. (2016). Characterizing user behaviors in location-based find-and-flirt services: Anonymity and demographics. *Peer-to-Peer Networking and Applications, 10*(2), 357–367.

Yeo, T. E. D., & Fung, T. H. (2018). "Mr right now": Temporality of relationship formation on gay mobile dating apps. *Mobile Media and Communication, 6*(1), 3–18.

Conclusion
Everyday care

Presented here, throughout this book, is a partial and targeted account of young people's friendship and digital peer support practices. I have focused on digital media practices that foster and support young people's health and wellbeing, and I have offered ways to better understand and engage with these – as researchers, health promoters, supporters, and friends. I have argued for greater recognition of young people's expertise.

At the heart of this book is a need for greater attention to care practices within everyday digital and social media interaction. While my focus has been on young people, this argument can be extended to broader populations. While some older people are not seen to be as fluent in peer support and digital friendship practices as many young people, they can certainly learn from them.

This book attends to the ways we find and give care among close friends, distant friends, and people we know nothing about. Focussing on *informal care* within everyday digital interactions, I have considered how this operates and who is involved, moving between a range of sites and practices that include young people's negotiations of sexual health, mental health, sexual relationships, and app-based connections. Common to these scenes are friendship and peer support that contour young people's intimacies and inform their use of digital platforms, devices, and space. I do not argue that digital media have made us more caring, nor that care practices guide the features of digital media platforms, but I draw attention to the entangled relationship between informal care and digital media use, taking a *social shaping* approach (Baym, 2015). This book recognises that digital cultures of care are significant and defining, as young people have pointed out for quite some time now.

Throughout, I propose a need for social and health policy to recognise changing media landscapes and how these relate to shifting cultures of support available to, and practised by, young people. This responds to research that fails to consider young people's digital media expertise. Such research typically considers young people's media practices from above – distanced from the affective details of their everyday lives. For most young people, digital media is significant, affective, and centres friendship intimacies. Considering their concurrent use of multiple media devices, apps, platforms, and interfaces, and how their friendship intimacies are woven through these, we must recognise young people's media use as complex and beyond the scope of our full understanding. As such, we must invite them to lead digital health policy and research discussions.

Social media, safety, and being online

Social media are not always safe and supportive spaces. I have not included much discussion of the negative experiences of young people's digital practices simply because these are highlighted (and often exaggerated) in countless other literature. The recognition of social and digital media as sites of care for many young people is central to this book's discussion because it is missing from much literature that considers digital media from a health perspective.

Young people are embedded in cultures of care, where care is not always sought (young people are not simply *going online* to seek help) but is available through everyday networked interactions. Since my doctoral research on young people's sexual health, I am increasingly bothered by accounts of young people *going online* to find health information. Almost as tiring are references to health promoters and professionals *going online* to share health information with young people (see Chapter 3). The logic (though it is slowly shifting) is that young people congregate and socialise in online spaces, so messages can be placed on social media platforms to reach them. Young people are indeed socialising and finding information through social media, but they are rarely *entering* or *attending* these "sites" with such intentions. Depending on a platform or app and what it offers, young people are often unlikely to seek specific connections or interactions in social media, and certainly not in the ways they would if entering a health clinic. Yet this comparative spatial language – i.e. platform as venue – persists in health promotion literature.

As data throughout this book attests, we do not always have a clear idea of the support and care we need until we receive it. As such, this book challenges a sense of young people and digital "help-seeking" that is direct and instrumental. Instead, there is a need to focus on how information sharing, support, and care practices (giving, receiving, and circulating care) are more dynamic and specific and therefore generative of new spaces, practices, and relationships of care. While research on young people's social media often presents these media as tools for administrating friendships, they are much more than this. They are also sites that generate intimacy, sharing, entertainment, fun, and a sense of affiliation with (and difference from) others.

This includes learning from others, accessing intimate disclosures and experiential knowledge, and participating in collective moments of reaction, response, and feeling.

Returning to everyday practice

By taking a ground-up approach to the analysis of digital media use, this book focuses on how care is framed and presented by research participants. This has the effect of opening discussion, seeing diversity, and maintaining a dynamic sense of digital media and their potential. Certeau argues, "It is in any case impossible to reduce the functioning of a society to a dominant type of procedures" (1988, p. 48). As such, we must sit with, and think through, complexity (Ang, 2011). In foregrounding everyday practice, Certeau argues that this is not always at odds with institutional strategies, and we can consider public health as an example of this. Foucault argues similarly in relation to biopower (1978). Public health goals for disease control, for example, largely align with our own will to maintain a healthy life. Yet these forces for health operate on different axes – what Foucault describes as bio-politics and anatomo-politics (1978, p. 139). The former relates to the social body, whereas the latter relates to the bodied subject. This connection and overlap between a health population and "the health subject" can be observed in the ways formal and informal health care overlap and conspire to produce cultural understandings of health and wellbeing that always exceed formal knowledge (Lyotard, 1991).

As Foucault also outlined, public health expertise has developed from its governing and administrative systems through which health subjects are tested, treated, watched, and recorded to generate "medicine" – an expertise for the maintenance of life and wellness (1994). If sectors of the population are less inclined to enter those governing and life-supporting systems, whether due to prohibitive costs, distrust, or discrimination faced in those settings, health systems are compromised. Such systems not only fail many people but produce incomplete health knowledge since they only collect data from those who are more comfortable in those spaces. The circularity of public health knowledge (produced through formal care that generates population health data) cannot *know* about health practices it does not see. Often such "invisible" practices are brought to the attention of policymakers by activists or advocacy groups, as per the LGBTQ+ youth reports discussed in Chapter 5. But these too are guided by policy discourse, more so than everyday practice and what this tells us about young people's lives, and their tactics for wellbeing. Further, young people in Australia do not have much lobbying power in national health policy settings, unlike many other "health populations".

To develop better academic understandings of young people's digital cultures of care, it is necessary to foreground their expertise as informal care practitioners and to listen to how young people currently support each other. This is also important when engaging with other groups who also have limited ability to influence policy-making.

Formal care

In health and academic discussions, a discourse of care is typically oriented toward vocational and governing aspects of health care delivery, or to domestic family settings. *Healthcare*, like childcare, is a term that connotes out-of-home care. It is something we pay for, something we expect to work, and something we sometimes demand of governments. Politicians sometimes promise new hospitals, more hospital beds, and more clinical and nursing staff to appeal to our needs for accessible and life-saving healthcare. Meanwhile, in domestic settings, home-based care (for children, mostly), is normalised to the point that we less commonly refer to this as *care*, since it is just what families do. Elsewhere, "carers" are appointed family members or friends who support someone with a disability or chronic illness and are, in turn, supported by welfare systems that recognise their care *work*. This care, while embedded in interpersonal everyday life, is formalised through its state recognition of care roles (as is parenting and its state regulation), suggesting that care must be governed if it is to be formally recognised. Elsewhere, there is an abundant dispensation of care, between friends, peers, and strangers, but we have a limited understanding of this.

In domestic settings, the term "caregiver" did not emerge from care practice itself, but from governing schemes and discourse – a public recognition of caregiving that is necessary for welfare administration and medical support, and for determining who has decision-making responsibilities on behalf of someone else. This language and understanding of caregiving likely influence our understanding of care in broader social interactions – where care can suggest power, kinship, and gender relations. Home-based childcare entangles with broader understandings of care through its gendered associations, as per the gender disparities in care professions. We can trace these lines into our own friendship practices. For example, what does it mean for of us to "mother" a friend? Care is undoubtedly gendered, and more easily associated with some people than others. This example of the family as our first encounter with care highlights a hierarchy through which care is typically organised – by someone responsible for your life. The *knowledge* of care may also relate to our inability to recognise and understand the vital significance of care among strangers – a situation without assigned roles or governance, and with less congealed forms of intimacy and responsibility.

I am not suggesting that we need to formalise informal care, nor build systems that administrate or regulate this. However, I do think we need to recognise informal care and what it offers and creates among those involved. Informal care practices not only highlight the shortcomings of formal care systems but also challenge our dominant frameworks for understanding what it means to care.

It is problematic to think that support is only orchestrated by state manoeuvres and institutions. More state-support for care practices can be useful, of course, but perhaps the immeasurable expansion of caregiving through digital cultures relates, in part, to current issues of state-governance (such as declining welfare support) that predicate a greater need for peer and friendship support. Perhaps young people's greater awareness of political corruption, expanding wealth disparities, a global climate catastrophe, and lack of invitation to public discussions about their future, enhance their need for care; to sustain living and hope. This is not the focus of this book, but it is a backdrop worth considering.

This book offers a detour from dominant discourses of "healthcare" and "caregiving", focussing instead on where care is found, sought, and arranged digitally and informally, beyond family and healthcare settings. Yet, I recognise that the distinction between formal and informal care is not always clear cut. Some participants spoke of feeling close to health professionals, suggesting that support found in formal spaces can offer authentic forms of care. As one young person said of their GP, "it's like they really care" (MHHS study). Such examples trouble a clear distinction between professional and personal care, and many LGBTQ+ youth services also mediate this distinction by facilitating young people's access to "queer friendly" health services where practitioners may indeed "really care".

Digital support tactically operates away from traditional notions and hierarchies of care, which is not to say it reacts against formal systems of care. Informal care is dispersed, often involving audiences of many, not just a single "patient". It is also often reciprocal – where a carer can also be cared for, and where there need not be defined roles in a traditional sense, as is true of friendship. What often matters most in digital cultures of care, is experience. Having and sharing lived experience offers a significant form of care that is less easily found in one's everyday physical surroundings. Multiple narratives of experience and practices of listening and bearing witness also matter. Sometimes care is simply about feeling seen and heard, and not giving/seeking advice or counsel.

Digital cultures of care

Throughout this book, my use of data foregrounds young people's expertise. Seeing young people as experts – that is, recognising that they navigate their lives with competence and know-how – I foreground the language and frameworks used by participants. As a concept, digital cultures of care is productive; accommodating practice, feeling, and a host of relationships – among friends, peers, and intimate strangers. In digital cultures, care is everyday practice that operates within and across platform structures and the networks and interactions they foster. It can also be traced through the ways friends and peers assist each other in negotiating a range of media platforms, networks, and interactions.

Arguably, social media interactions are more oriented to *caring about* rather than *caring for* others (Bowlby, 2011; Silk, 1998), with the latter presumed to be more "in person". But these dimensions of care are not contained to separate spheres and practices, and the affordances of social media platforms foster multiple spaces and dimensions of care, including new ways to care for and about others, and new modes of feeling seen, heard, and cared for. Social media do not cause us to care, but they offer more ways to practice and feel care – among friends and strangers alike. Digital cultures of care are often subtle, and like Andre Cavalcante, in his research of digital care and support among trans people, I am interested in "thinking through quieter, less heroic, and less politically charged forms of media use" (2016, p. 111).

Digital care constitutes many actions beyond support, such as sharing information, giving feedback, listening, learning from and with others, amplifying the needs and feelings of others, validating people's feelings, and more. This can be done through "likes", responses, (semi-)public discussion, gif-sharing, private messaging, reblogging, retweeting, re-posting, tagging, uprating, and more. Each of these gestures not only involves humans but platforms and their affordances. Tracing these lines of care through digital and social media, we can locate care through countless platforms, channels, interactions, and relationships. We obviously care for our friends, as commonly seen through our digital interactions, but we also care about (and for) people we do not know. We are affected by the stories of strangers.

I arrived at *digital cultures of care* because of its utility to incorporate close and everyday friendships and their digital practices, as well as the intimacy that lies beyond friendships and can be found and felt among strangers. From my research that considers how young people's health practices intersect with or differ from health settings and policy, I have found that many young people do not have sustained relationships with health professionals, and that health-related care is often more horizontally practised. In part, this relates to the inaccessibility and prohibitive costs of formal healthcare. It can also relate to how formal health discourse does not resonate as particularly supportive or caring for many young people.

Care as labour has not been explored in this book, as commonly considered through the concepts of emotional labour (Hochschild, 2012) and affective labour (Papacharissi, 2015). This is because the labour of care is not discussed by research participants within. There is little indication that caring is difficult, burdensome, and time consuming for the young people participating in this research, although this may be true of other scenes of digital care. An exception in these data might be where LGBTQ+ young people discuss not wanting to burden their friends with their mental health issues. Yet we do not know if those friends would actually feel burdened by this. Typically, care practices are considered as somewhat innate, and something one willingly engages in, especially (but not only) with friends.

Friends and peers

This book has considered spaces of care across friendship and peer relations. As discussed in Chapters 1 and 2, traditional understanding of "friends" and "peers" can limit how we understand and approach young people's digital cultures of care. Friendship plays a defining role in the health and wellbeing of young people, and friendship's practice is now more visible than ever, thanks to digital and social media (Baym, 2015). Friends and friendship relations often tell us who we are – e.g. "they know me better than I know myself". Many sociologists have sought to define friendship, outlining its key functions and practices, but my research approach retains the openness of friendship, neither containing nor defining it but recognising it as a relational practice with great diversity and creative potential.

In much health research, young people's peers represent risk. Evident from existing research is how health policy and research practices, methods, and presuppositions have guided certain frameworks for "thinking about youth" – particularly enacting a reality in which young people are risk subjects who lack the experience and knowledge to practice and negotiate healthy lifestyles. This overlooks young people's skilful practices in building and managing friendships and social networks that offer support where it is otherwise unavailable.

Much sociology of friendship tends to re-centre the family as a primary experience through which to understand what friendship is and is not. Doing so re-situates our families as the primary social relations through which we measure and understand other intimacies. There have been important feminist and queer critiques of this approach, as discussed in Chapter 1 (Roseneil, 2004; Roseneil & Budgeon, 2004). Even in sociology, the discussion of friendship has been limited due to a belief that this relationship holds less social and economic significance. As such, friendship's practice has been less defined, constrained, or mapped onto social practices and institutions that govern and contour our lives. Yet this is part of friendship's power and everyday influence. As a non-institutionalised relationship (Foucault, 2000; Roach, 2012), friendships are practised in manifold ways, creatively, and often without needing to adopt sanctioned and normalised approaches to intimacy and care. Friendship itself can be considered as a social relationship with a queer agenda – it is well placed to disrupt hetero-familial norms and has already done so.

To arrive at an understanding of what we mean by "peers" it seems useful to look at how that term is discursively arranged in existing research, as I offer in Chapter 2, through attention to peer influence, peer education, and peer support. Through my research experiences, "peer" is not a word young people commonly use to explain their relationships, networks, or social interactions, but is more formally ascribed, with a particular force. In health research discussions, "peer" does not suggest intimacy, but more so, risk.

This book has not engaged with algorithms, yet these are also shaped by peer influence. As Jill Walker Rettberg notes, "Google sees links as a kind of peer endorsement" (2014, pp. 71–72) – that is, your top search results will typically be sites with a higher volume of inbound traffic. This suggests an indirect form of support, in which all users of Google Search can be considered peers, whose search practices invariably influence our own digital practices and exposures to information and support networks. If "on the internet" we are all peers, then we are all, in some ways, moved toward *friendship's practice*. As I have argued, digital practices of seeking, finding, and providing support reference friendship dynamics, including practices of mutual care, listening, and responsiveness. These practices may also generate new and important friendships, or expand personal networks, but friendship's attainment is not usually the goal of these everyday friendship practices.

Friends, sex, dating, intimacy

As explored throughout this book, friendship practices commonly influence one's romantic and sexual relationships, as well as a sense of what we can expect or want from these. Friendship is a key space of intimacy through which young people find support and advice regarding their sexual practices. In friend communications, stories of sexual intimacy can be shared to process feelings and reservations, and friendship intimacies support our negotiations of sex and relationships. Within this, institutional parameters of sexual health can be circumvented or tactically incorporated into the ways young people relate to each other – sexually, romantically, ethically, and as friends. Formal sexual health information and support cannot know and understand the specific details of a young person's sexual intimacies and relationships, unlike their close friends. Workshopping friends' sexual intimacies can also expand the friendship intimacies involved, galvanising circuits of mutual support.

That young people's sexual and friendship relations can overlap is significant for current sexual health promotion efforts that typically focus on engaging with the individualised young person, implying that sex is private. As demonstrated in Chapters 4 and 6, young people's friends often hold intimate knowledge of their sexual experiences and histories (though this appears to be less common among straight, cisgender men). Common studies of young people's friendships rarely delve into friendship cultures to consider how negotiations of sex and sexual health are embedded in everyday scenes of friendship. Further to this, research on young people's uses of dating/hook-up apps rarely considers how these spaces are not only negotiated with friends, but can directly involve friends, as discussed in Chapter 6. With this recognition comes the opportunity to engage with young people as embedded in cultures of care, particularly through everyday friendship support.

The Tumblr *affect*

In Chapters 2 and 5, I discussed Tumblr as a site of care, drawing upon qualitative data with young people. These data were captured before Tumblr's content changes of December 2018, after which "not safe for work" content would no longer be supported. This followed a decade-long history of experiencing Tumblr as an open and seemingly unregulated platform, and hence its appeal for sharing and viewing material that was queer, sex-positive, pornographic, and more. The backlash against Tumblr following these changes, particularly among LGBTQ+ users, sex workers, and producers of "adult content" included many people "calling out" this platform for not caring about its users (Byron, 2019). As Tarleton Gillespie has highlighted, social media users are often dubious that platform regulators have their best interests in mind (2018). The Tumblr fallout largely centred on a disconnect between Tumblr practices of care, and a Tumblr public relations discourse of care and community that was felt to be insincere (Byron, 2019). The feeling that platforms do not care was also noted by research participants in Chapter 2 – e.g. "there is poor moderation of spaces and abusive accounts by Facebook, Twitter, etc. Over and over again, both companies have demonstrated they do not give a damn about more marginalised users" (SBB study). Understandings of platforms as money-driven corporations that just happen to house friendships, community, and peer support practices, can suggest to users that it is up to us to practice, ensure, and regulate care within platform cultures.

Tumblr practices cannot be isolated from broader negotiations of identities and communities – for LGBTQ+ users and many others. Finding support from random strangers – whose knowledge of you is entirely based on what you anonymously share on Tumblr (or Reddit or any other sites) – opens opportunities to disclose, express, and share your feelings and experiences in ways that would be risky among friends and other social contacts. As such, Tumblr attracts and houses volumes of experience-based knowledge of gender dysphoria, transitioning, asexuality, pansexuality, kink/BDSM, and much more. It has also been associated with pro-ana (anorexia) discourse (Park et al., 2017) and other health communities determined as risky on account of a presumed peer influence, such as discussions of self-harm and suicide (Cavazos-Rehg et al., 2017). The default anonymity of Tumblr protects users across many levels, for what it opens in the way of discussing taboo or stigmatised feelings, practices, and identities, but also for the protection it offers when engaging with strangers.

Often, Tumblr mental health posts do not ask for direct help or guidance, and Tumblr care is largely indirect. Further, Tumblr reblogging allows users to circulate content without knowing who it reaches or expecting dialogue to follow. As such, Tumblr is easy, offering a less normative approach to communicative exchange, with no expectation of dialogue. Given that this is not a dedicated friend-space, those who read posts about mental health experiences and difficulties are less compelled to offer written and detailed support. Or perhaps some people are compelled to respond for other reasons, such as acknowledging and echoing the sentiments expressed, perhaps by saying "that happened to me too" (Byron & Hunt, 2017). As care practices more oriented to sharing feelings and space, this offers a different dynamic to care practices on Facebook, Instagram, and other common platforms.

While I state that Tumblr is not a friend-space, there is a connection between Tumblr peer support and friendship. As noted throughout this book, social media offer many spaces for *practising friendship* and are not simply sites for hosting friendships. As argued, peer support can constitute friendship as a practice, even with unknown people. This blurring of peers and friends is also evident through the support that is offered, including supporting others to develop self-sovereignty. As Tom Roach argues, "To encourage a friend to develop self-sovereignty in a form he [*sic*] finds most suitable is neither to impose one's will nor to influence that development through eloquent, convincing instructions" (2012, pp. 28–29). In other words, friendship does not instruct us to be who we are, but it *supports* us to be who we are. This references the self-invention (as opposed to self-discovery) that Foucault discussed in relation to friendship's creative potential (2000).

Mental health care

A lack of knowledge or definition of friendship and friendship support has been noted throughout this book. Often, friendship appears in research findings about digital "help-seeking" yet it is not often presented as a key finding. This suggests that friendship is an unremarkable everyday fact, and so is peripheral to questions of health and wellbeing. However, there is common evidence that LGBTQ+ young people feel most supported – in terms of mental health, but also regarding their gender/sexual identities – by friends and digital peer networks. Given repeated findings and statistics of LGBTQ+ young people's poor mental health, we should look further into support practices that LGBTQ+ young people have indicated to be useful, supportive, and life-affirming.

Discussion of LGBTQ+ young people's digital media practices often suggests that they are compelled to find support online due to a lack of support and community "in real life". But these spaces are not distinct, and digital cultures of communication are indeed part of real life (Deuze, 2012). Approaches that centre LGBTQ+ young people's "help-seeking", rather than considering their support networks, continue to overlook meaningful practices and networks of support. For many LGBTQ+ participants dealing with mental health problems, friendships offer fun and respite from life's pressures. Some young people facing mental health problems practised *friendship care* through not disclosing mental health issues to friends, and hence not "burdening" them. A common alternative strategy is to engage with peers through digital media, where the sharing of difficult information, or engaging with other people's experiences, was not burdensome, but often informative, and embedded in digital cultures of sharing and mutual support.

Another commonly cited value in finding mental health support through digital media was not having to directly ask for or provide help but indirectly contributing to broader discussions, in subtle yet informative ways, that generate self-knowledge, community, and a shared sense of care and camaraderie. As one participant described, telling mental health stories on Tumblr was "speaking into the void". These practices ensure that close friendships are less affected by one's mental health issues and that those friendship dynamics – and their health-giving benefits – are sustained. Yet these peer-based interactions also invoke friendship practices, given the reciprocity, informality, and trust involved.

Digital health promotion

Social media facilitate knowledge practices and information sharing that is more lateral and also entwined with the affective dimensions of particular platforms and their networks. Therefore, introducing static health information into these spaces is unlikely to engage young people. Nor will such content circulate through young people's friendship networks. For health information to circulate through social media, it must, firstly, be welcome, and secondly, it needs to resonate with users. Accordingly, health promotion must be more fluent in, and open to, the dynamic flows and intensities of platformed communication to gain traction in digital media spaces. Since many young people have greater social media expertise than many health professionals – produced through everyday digital media cultures – it is important to centre their expertise and allow this to guide social media interventions. Yet the reluctance and institutional barriers of health promoters sharing the space of expertise continues (Albury, 2019; Mowlabocus et al., 2016).

While young people appreciate and seek out "accurate" and "credible" health information, this does not cover the entirety of young people's knowledge needs or practices. It is often through intimate relations and friendships that young people come to learn about sex, health, sexual health, gender diversity, mental health, and more. Therefore, prioritising formal sexual health knowledge in ways that exclude other ways of knowing these things fails to address how young people's intimacies and friendships operate as sites of knowledge production and exchange. It also fails to consider the digital cultures of care. As experts of their social media cultures, young people need to be part of health conversations that seek to engage them through digital and social media.

Some final words

The care aspects of intimate relationships often work to expand our understandings of wellbeing in productive ways. In doing so, this can support a public health agenda. There is no need for formal health initiatives to compete with informal peer and friendship support (as peer education initiatives suggest). Young people are not *against* the practices and principles of formal health care, but often those things do not work for them. They may be inaccessible, or they may be inadequate. Given a strong tendency for health professionals to diminish or overlook young people's skills and expertise, and a preference to see them as vulnerable and unknowing, this may be another reason that formal health care and resources, along with digital media interventions and outreach, do not resonate with many young people.

Social media platforms do not tell us how to be and have friends, but they offer infrastructure that supports friendship and/or its practices. As such, these have become, and continue to be, important sites. These sites are not primarily used for explicit forms of peer and friendship support, but they offer this in consistent, subtle, and indirect ways. Sometimes, support is practised more directly, but more often we feel and demonstrate care as we scroll, like, comment, or message the people with us – as we hold them close, in our hand, throughout our everyday life.

Young people are not all digitally active in the same way but navigate and produce a vast range of digital connections, networks, identities, affects, hierarchies, and experiences of wellness. Without a better understanding of young people's everyday friendships and digital peer networks, and the support and care they foster, health initiatives will continue to have limited connection to young people's concerns and experiences of wellbeing. That these networks and practices will differ among young people, between platform cultures, and depending on the health issue, is indeed a challenge for health professionals and others who seek to support young people's wellbeing. In closing, you should probably ask young people what you must do to better support their health and wellbeing, and this can be done without diminishing or disregarding their digital cultures of care.

References

Albury, K. (2019). "Recognition of competition" versus Will to App: Rethinking digital engagement in Australian youth sexual health promotion policy and practice. *Media International Australia*, 171(1), 38–50.

Ang, I. (2011). Navigating complexity: From cultural critique to cultural intelligence. *Continuum: Journal of Media and Cultural Studies*, 25(6), 779–794.

Baym, N. (2015). *Personal connections in the digital age* (2nd ed.). Cambridge: Polity Press.

Bowlby, S. (2011). Friendship, co-presence and care: Neglected spaces. *Social and Cultural Geography*, 12(6), 605–622.

Byron, P. (2019). "How could you write your name below that?" the queer life and death of Tumblr. *Porn Studies*, 6(3), 336–349.

Byron, P., & Hunt, J. (2017). "That happened to me too": Young people's informal knowledge of diverse genders and sexualities. *Sex Education*, 71(3), 319–332.

Cavalcante, A. (2016). "I did it all online:" Transgender identity and the management of everyday life. *Critical Studies in Media Communication*, 33(1), 109–122.

Cavazos-Rehg, P. A., Krauss, M. J., Sowles, S. J., Connolly, S., Rosas, C., Bharadwaj, M., … Bierut, L. J. (2017). An analysis of depression, self-harm, and suicidal ideation content on Tumblr. *Crisis*, 38(1), 44–52.

Certeau de, M. (1988). *The practice of everyday life* (S. Rendall, Trans.). Berkeley, CA: University of California Press.

Deuze, M. (2012). *Media Life*. Cambridge: Polity.

Foucault, M. (1978). *The history of sexuality volume 1: An introduction*. London & New York, NY: Penguin.

Foucault, M. (1994). *The birth of the clinic: An archaeology of medical perception*. New York, NY: Vintage Books.

Foucault, M. (2000). Friendship as a way of life. (J. Johnston, Trans.). In P. Rabinow (Ed.), *Ethics, subjectivity and truth: Essential works of Foucault 1954–1984* (pp. 135–140). London: Penguin Books.

Gillespie, T. (2018). *Custodians of the internet: Platforms, content moderation, and the hidden decisions that shape social media*. New Haven & London: Yale University Press.

Hochschild, A. R. (2012). *The managed heart: Commercialization of human feeling*. Berkley, CA: University of California Press.

Lyotard, J.-F. (1991). *The postmodern condition: A report on knowledge*. Manchester: Manchester University Press.

Mowlabocus, S., Haslop, C., & Dasgupta, R. K. (2016). From scene to screen: The challenges and opportunities of commercial digital platforms for HIV community outreach. *Social Media + Society*, 2(4).

Papacharissi, Z. (2015). *Affective publics: Sentiment, technology, and politics*. New York, NY: Oxford University Press.

Park, M., Sun, Y., & McLaughlin, M. L. (2017). Social media propagation of content promoting risky health behavior. *Cyberpsychology, Behavior and Social Networking*, 20(5), 278–285.

Rettberg, J. W. (2014). *Blogging*. Cambridge, UK: Polity Press.

Roach, T. (2012). *Friendship as a way of life: Foucault, AIDS, and the politics of shared estrangement*. New York, NY: SUNY Press.

Roseneil, S. (2004). Why we should care about friends: An argument for queering the care imaginary in social policy. *Social Policy and Society*, 3(04), 409–419.

Roseneil, S., & Budgeon, S. (2004). Cultures of intimacy and care beyond "the family": Personal life and social change in the early 21st century. *Current Sociology*, 52(2), 135–159.

Silk, J. (1998). Caring at a distance. *Philosophy and Geography*, 1(2), 165–182.

Index

adult concerns/anxieties 3, 11, 52–53, 84, 90, 119–120
adults 4, 10, 55, 125, 138
advice 57, 61, 64, 107, 111, 120, 134, 137, 157–158, 160; *see also* friendship, friendship support; peers, peer support
affect 2, 8, 12, 39, 42–43, 65–66, 164, 175, 178–179
algorithms 120, 177
anonymity 66, 68, 120, 122–123
anonymous care/support 50, 62, 66, 68, 118–119, 134, 136, 178
Ardern, Jacinda 5–6
Aristotle 23–25, 42
assets-based approach 2, 69, 82

Berlant, Lauren 8, 100, 112–114
biopower 172
blogging 36, 44; *see also* Tumblr
Broad City 31
Bumble 153–155, 159, 161

care: as a concept 12–16; gendered aspects 6, 15; as a public discourse 5–6
Certeau, Michel de 1, 8–9, 29, 76–78, 87–88, 172
Circle, The 7
coming out 35, 67, 78, 122, 133–134
community 37–38, 66–69, 122–123, 129–133
counterpublics 66–68

dating apps 144–166; stigma 144, 163
David and Jonathan 31
digital cultures of care 1, 3, 6, 11–12, 15, 118–119, 136, 172–181
digital health interventions 14, 75–76, 78, 80–81, 86–90, 105, 181

digital intimacies 6–8, 15, 112–113
disclosures 35–37, 44, 60, 64, 68, 110, 133–135
discourse analysis 4, 96

everyday practice 1, 3, 8–10, 29, 70, 77–78, 87, 89–91, 172
expertise 14, 61–62, 68–71, 75–91, 133, 146, 150, 159, 170, 172, 174, 180–181

Facebook 33–40, 64–65, 83–85, 89, 122, 148, 156
Facebook groups 63–65, 127
Facebook Messenger 40, 160
families of choice/queer kinship 27–28, 162
family (and kinship) 24–29, 34–35, 39, 112, 162, 173–174, 176
feminism/feminist approaches 23, 43, 112–113
Foucault and friendship 25–26, 42–43, 114, 176, 179
Friends (sitcom) 32
friendship: close friends 37–40, 50, 59, 85, 98–99, 106–108, 114–115, 164, 180; friending 25, 33, 37–39, 151; friendship difficulties 30, 40–41, 43, 83; friendship in popular culture 30–32; friendship support 35–38, 40, 43–44, 96–98, 107, 114–115, 156–163, 166, 177, 181
friends with benefits 101, 105, 108

gay male friendships 23, 57, 152
Goffman, Erving 38

harassment/abuse 65, 152
healthcare (formal) 9–10, 13–14, 50, 60–61, 119–121, 135, 137–138, 175, 181

health communication (as a discipline)
56, 78–79, 87–88
health information seeking 52–53, 56,
69, 78–80, 132, 136, 171
health policy 10–11, 60, 70, 75, 112,
127, 136–137, 172, 176
health promotion 49–50, 55,
69, 75, 77–78, 86–90, 171,
180–181; *see also* sexual health
promotion
help-seeking 119–120, 135–137, 171,
178–180
heteronormativity 8, 25, 101, 114
heterosexuality/heterosexuals 15, 32,
104, 112, 147–148, 153, 155–162,
165–166
HIV/AIDS 15, 23, 27, 128

Indigenous knowledge/approaches
12–13
informal care 1, 13–14, 65, 68–69, 135,
170, 172, 174
information and support 56, 61–62, 69,
91, 119–121, 129, 177
Instagram 34, 148, 151, 155
intimacy 7, 59, 68, 100, 110, 112–114,
146, 161–166; *see also* digital
intimacies; sexual intimacy
intimate publics 8, 98, 113, 122

knowledge (theories of) 76, 86–89

latent ties 33–34, 58–59, 62
Lewis, C.S. 27, 30
LGBTQ+young people 4, 34–36,
40–42, 61–68, 118–139, 147–149,
151–161, 178–179
listening 38, 60, 66, 98, 174
lived experience 10, 50, 61, 64,
67–68, 90, 106, 119, 132–133,
135–137
Lyotard, Jean-François 76, 88

mental health 36, 60–62, 64–65,
118–139, 178–180; stigma 36, 60,
132, 135
Momo 149–150

networked publics 89

online/offline 2–3, 56, 119–120, 171
online forums 60–65, 79–80, 103, 115,
120–122

peers: invested peers 50, 62, 64–65, 68,
70, 136; peer education 49, 53–57,
59, 67–70, 98, 134; peer influence
49–54, 59, 69–71, 81, 177–178; peer
pressure 51, 58; peer support 9–10,
49–53, 56–71, 118–139, 170–171,
177, 179–181
personal communities 26–27, 136,
147, 162
phones 119–120, 129, 146,
160–162, 164
play 38–39, 145, 161–165
privacy 35–36, 39, 84–85, 90, 112–113
public health 9–10, 54, 77, 80–82,
87–90, 113–114, 119, 172

queer friendship 23, 27–28, 31,
42–43, 176
queer theory/approaches 8, 23, 25, 32,
98, 112–113, 146–147

race 10, 13, 43, 138
risk focus/approach 2, 10–12, 49–54,
60, 69, 81–83, 87–88, 120, 176

safe sex 99–102, 105, 111, 114
safe spaces 39, 64, 67–68, 102, 109,
119–120, 122, 134, 171
safety 99–103, 102–103, 109, 111–114,
122, 130–134, 155–156, 163,
165, 171
school 40–41, 51, 55, 59, 124
self-care 15, 134
sex 54, 97–105, 108–115
sexual health 51–54, 56–57, 60, 84–87,
90–91, 96–98, 104–106, 110–114,
177, 180; stigma 76, 84–85, 89
sexual health promotion 76–77, 80–83,
89, 97–99, 101, 103–106, 111, 113–
114, 150; *see also* health promotion
sexual intimacy 97–115, 177
sexual pleasure 97–103, 106–107,
110–114
Snapchat 38–39, 66
sociology of friendship 28–29, 32, 42,
99, 112
Spice Girls 30–31
storytelling 107, 113, 115, 165

Tinder 147–148, 151, 153–154,
157–158, 160–162, 165; Tinder
Social 153–154
Trump, Melania 5

Tumblr 50, 63, 65–68, 70–71, 118–119, 131–135, 137–139, 178–179
Twitter 5–6, 40, 65

vulnerability 10, 51, 70, 119–120, 136–137

weak ties 33, 37
WeChat 49–50
women's friendship 23, 26, 31, 43

young people, consulting/involving 10, 50, 52, 55, 58, 87, 90–91

Printed in the United States
By Bookmasters